DOCTOR STRANGE VOL. 2: THE LAST DAYS OF MAGIC. Contains material originally published in magazine form as DOCTOR STRANGE #6-10 and DOCTOR STRANGE: LAST DAYS OF MAGIC #1. First printing 2017. ISBN# 978-0-7851-9933-5. Published by MARVEL WORLDWIDE, INC., a subsidiary of MARVEL ENTERTAINMENT, LLC. OFFICE OF PUBLICATION: 135 West 50th Street, New York, NY 10020. Copyright © 2017 MARVEL No similarity between any of the names, characters, persons, and/or institutions in this magazine with those of any living or dead person or institution is intended, and any such similarity which may exist is purely coincidental. **Printed in the U.S.A.** DAN BUCKLEY, President, Marvel Entertainment; JOE QUESADA, Chief Creative Officer; TOM BREVOORT, SVP of Publishing; DAVID BOGART, SVP of Business Affairs & Operations, Publishing & Partnership; C.B. CEBULSKI, VP of Brand Management & Development, Asia; DAVID GABRIEL, SVP of Sales & Marketing, Publishing; JEFF YOUNGQUIST, VP of Production & Special Projects; DAN CARR, Executive Director of Publishing Technology; ALEX MORALES, Director of Publishing Operations; SUSAN CRESPI, Production Manager; STAN LEE, Chairman Emeritus. For information regarding advertising in Marvel Comics or on Marvel.com, please contact Vit DeBellis, Integrated Sales Manager, at vdebellis@marvel.com. For Marvel subscription inquiries, please call 888-511-5480. **Manufactured between 5/5/2017 and 6/6/2017 by LSC COMMUNICATIONS INC., SALEM, VA, USA.**

10 9 8 7 6 5 4 3 2 1

DOCTOR STRANGE

The Last Days of Magic

Jason Aaron
WRITER

Chris Bachalo
PENCILER/COLORIST

TIM TOWNSEND, AL VEY, MARK IRWIN, JOHN LIVESAY, WAYNE FAUCHER, VICTOR OLAZABA & JAIME MENDOZA
INKERS

CHRIS BACHALO, JAVA TARTAGLIA & ANTONIO FABELA
WITH RAIN BEREDO
COLORISTS

"A Day Without Magic"

MIKE DEODATO JR., JORGE FORNÉS, KEV WALKER & KEVIN NOWLAN
ARTISTS

RAIN BEREDO & KEVIN NOWLAN
COLORISTS

CHRIS BACHALO & TIM TOWNSEND
COVER ART

The Last Days of Magic #1

Zelma Stanton Framing Sequence
JASON AARON
WRITER

LEONARDO ROMERO
ARTIST

JORDIE BELLAIRE
COLORIST

Doctor Voodoo
GERRY DUGGAN
WRITER

DANILO BEYRUTH
ARTIST

DAN BROWN
COLORIST

The Wu
JAMES ROBINSON
WRITER

MIKE PERKINS
ARTIST

ANDY TROY
COLORIST

MIKE PERKINS & ANDY TROY
COVER ART

VC'S CORY PETIT
LETTERER

CHARLES BEACHAM
ASSISTANT EDITOR

DARREN SHAN
ASSOCIATE EDITOR

NICK LOWE & EMILY SHAW
EDITORS

DOCTOR STRANGE CREATED BY STAN LEE & STEVE DITKO

COLLECTION EDITOR: JENNIFER GRÜNWALD
ASSISTANT EDITOR: CAITLIN O'CONNELL
ASSOCIATE MANAGING EDITOR: KATERI WOODY
EDITOR, SPECIAL PROJECTS: MARK D. BEAZLEY
VP PRODUCTION & SPECIAL PROJECTS: JEFF YOUNGQUIST
SVP PRINT, SALES & MARKETING: DAVID GABRIEL
BOOK DESIGNER: JAY BOWEN

EDITOR IN CHIEF: AXEL ALONSO
CHIEF CREATIVE OFFICER: JOE QUESADA
PRESIDENT: DAN BUCKLEY
EXECUTIVE PRODUCER: ALAN FINE

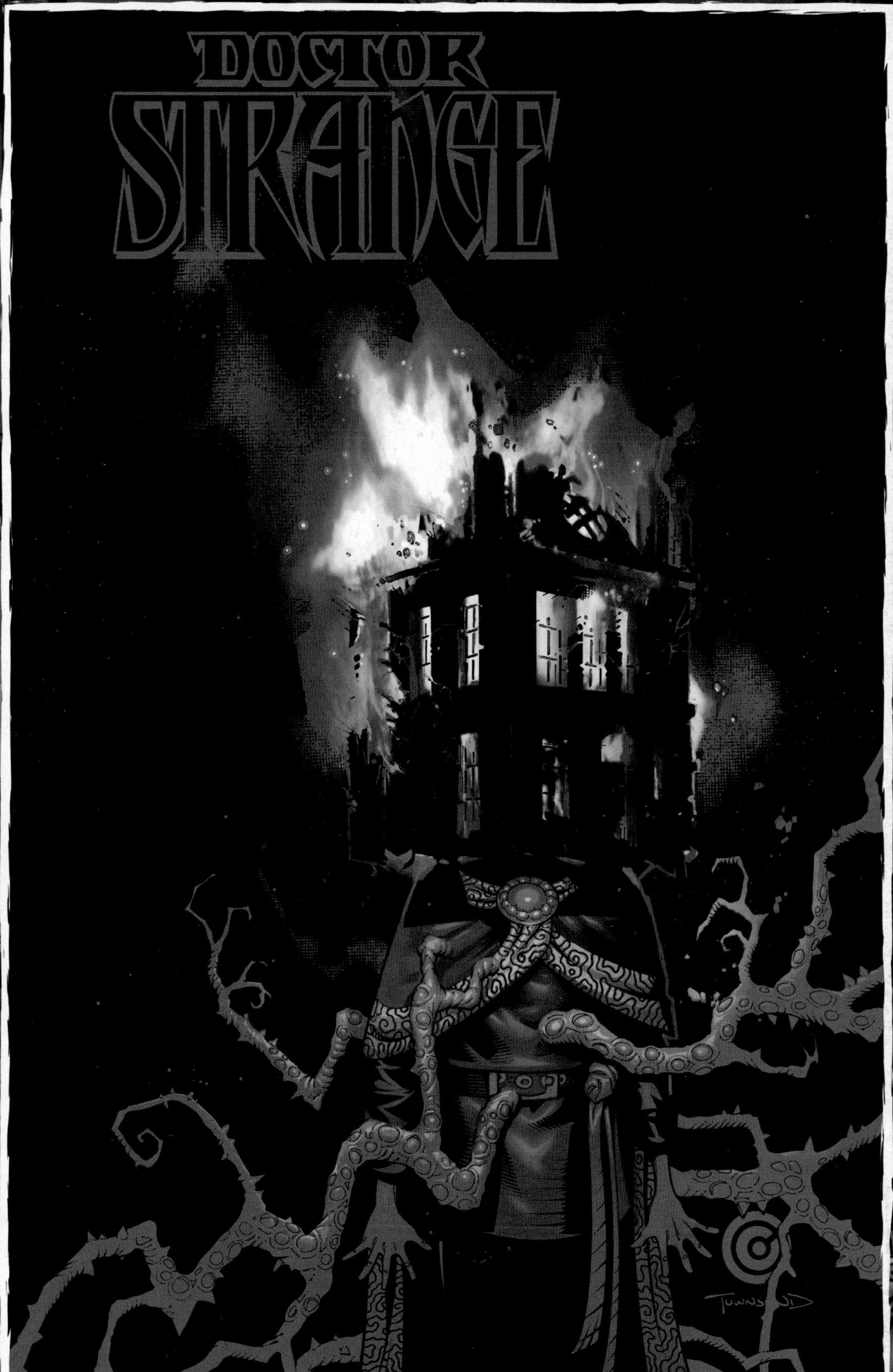
DOCTOR
STRANGE

DOCTOR STRANGE — THE LAST DAYS OF MAGIC
CHAPTER ONE

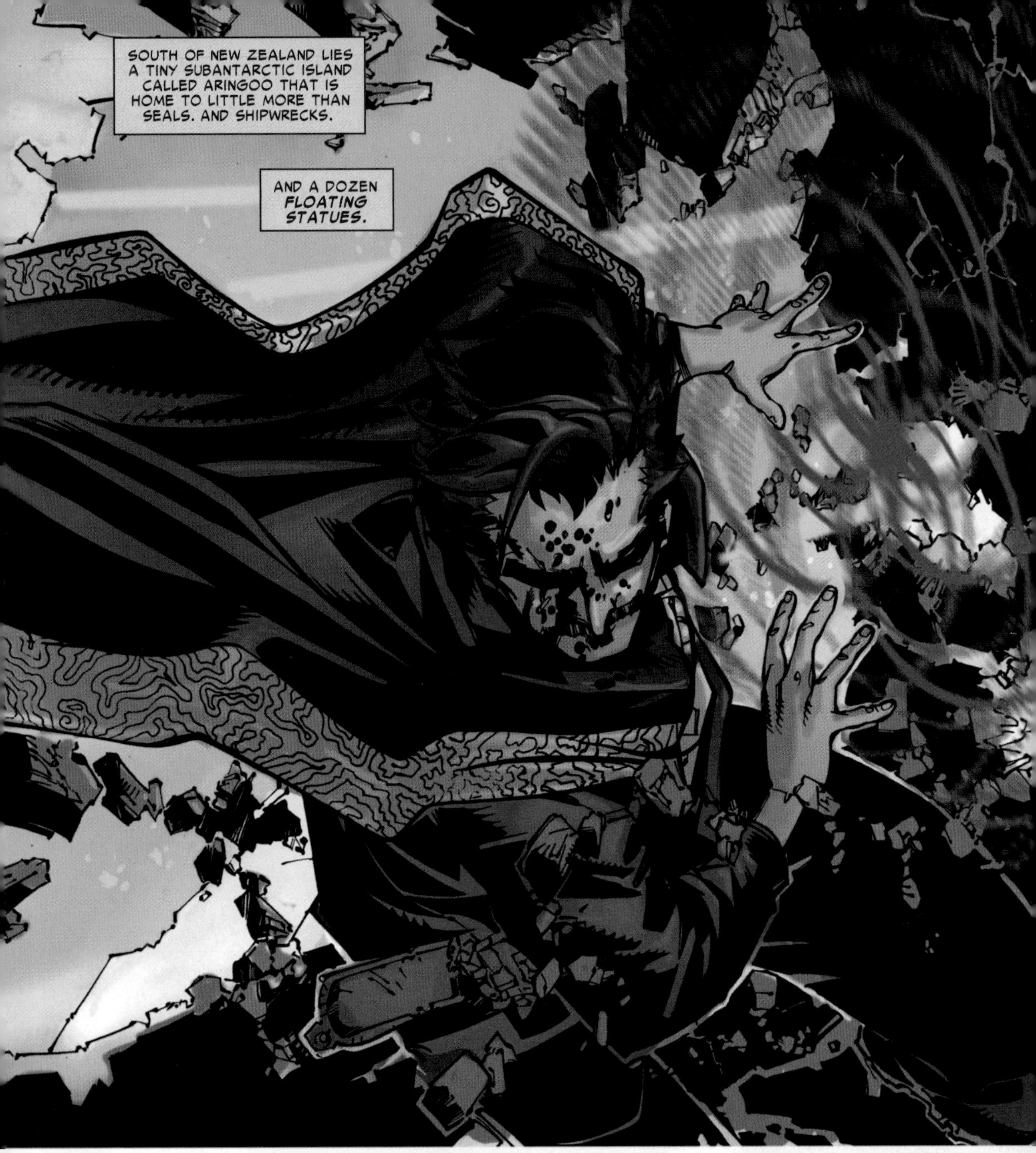
SOUTH OF NEW ZEALAND LIES A TINY SUBANTARCTIC ISLAND CALLED ARINGOO THAT IS HOME TO LITTLE MORE THAN SEALS. AND SHIPWRECKS.
AND A DOZEN *FLOATING STATUES.*

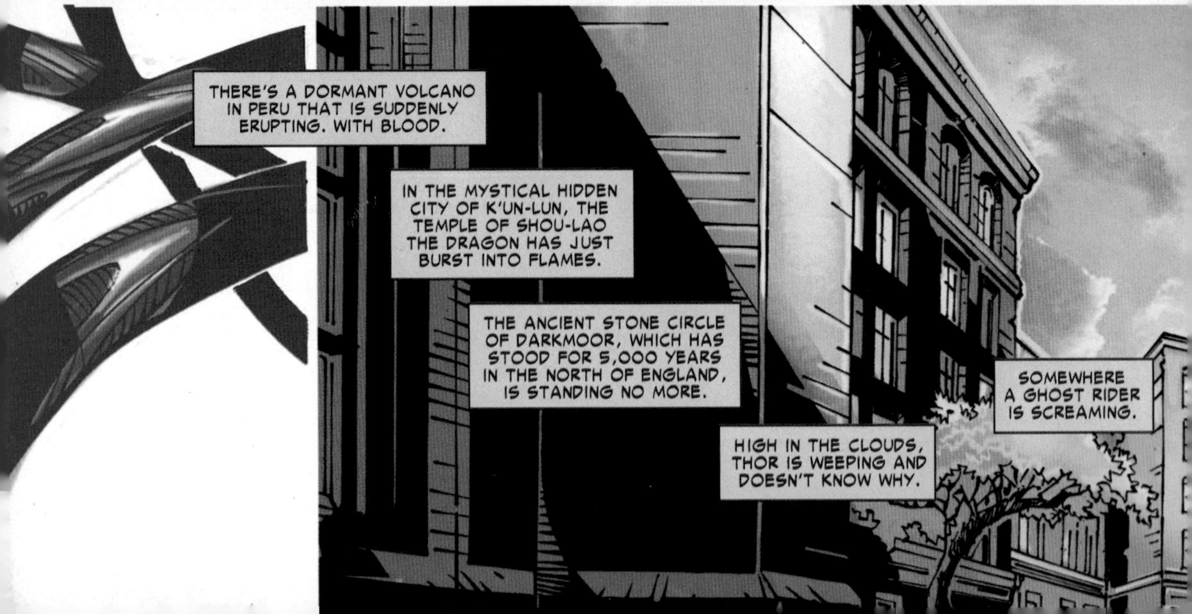
THERE'S A DORMANT VOLCANO IN PERU THAT IS SUDDENLY ERUPTING. WITH BLOOD.
IN THE MYSTICAL HIDDEN CITY OF K'UN-LUN, THE TEMPLE OF SHOU-LAO THE DRAGON HAS JUST BURST INTO FLAMES.
THE ANCIENT STONE CIRCLE OF DARKMOOR, WHICH HAS STOOD FOR 5,000 YEARS IN THE NORTH OF ENGLAND, IS STANDING NO MORE.
HIGH IN THE CLOUDS, THOR IS WEEPING AND DOESN'T KNOW WHY.
SOMEWHERE A GHOST RIDER IS SCREAMING.

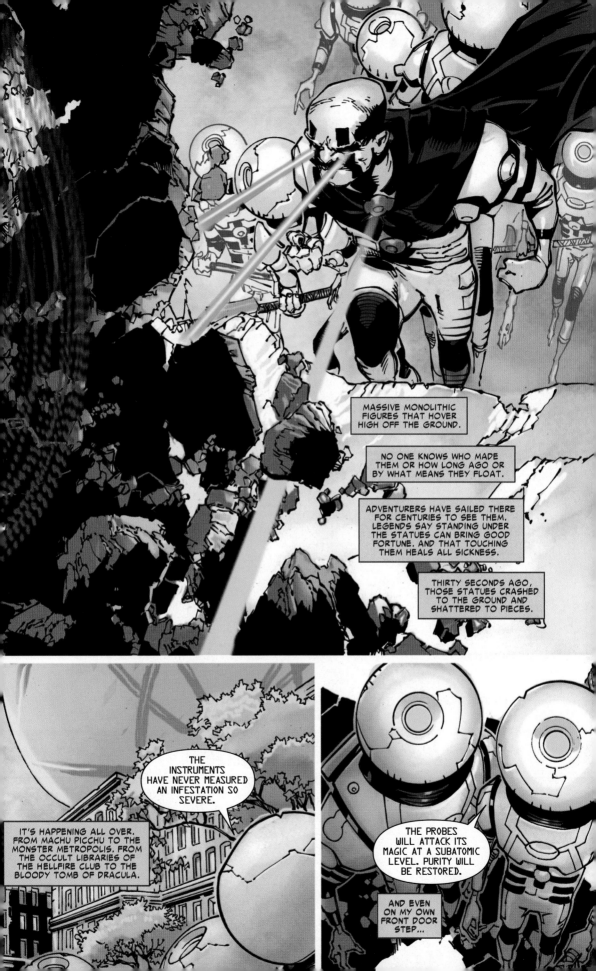

MASSIVE MONOLITHIC FIGURES THAT HOVER HIGH OFF THE GROUND.

NO ONE KNOWS WHO MADE THEM OR HOW LONG AGO OR BY WHAT MEANS THEY FLOAT.

ADVENTURERS HAVE SAILED THERE FOR CENTURIES TO SEE THEM. LEGENDS SAY STANDING UNDER THE STATUES CAN BRING GOOD FORTUNE. AND THAT TOUCHING THEM HEALS ALL SICKNESS.

THIRTY SECONDS AGO, THOSE STATUES CRASHED TO THE GROUND AND SHATTERED TO PIECES.

THE INSTRUMENTS HAVE NEVER MEASURED AN INFESTATION SO SEVERE.

IT'S HAPPENING ALL OVER. FROM MACHU PICCHU TO THE MONSTER METROPOLIS. FROM THE OCCULT LIBRARIES OF THE HELLFIRE CLUB TO THE BLOODY TOMB OF DRACULA.

THE PROBES WILL ATTACK ITS MAGIC AT A SUBATOMIC LEVEL. PURITY WILL BE RESTORED.

AND EVEN ON MY OWN FRONT DOOR STEP...

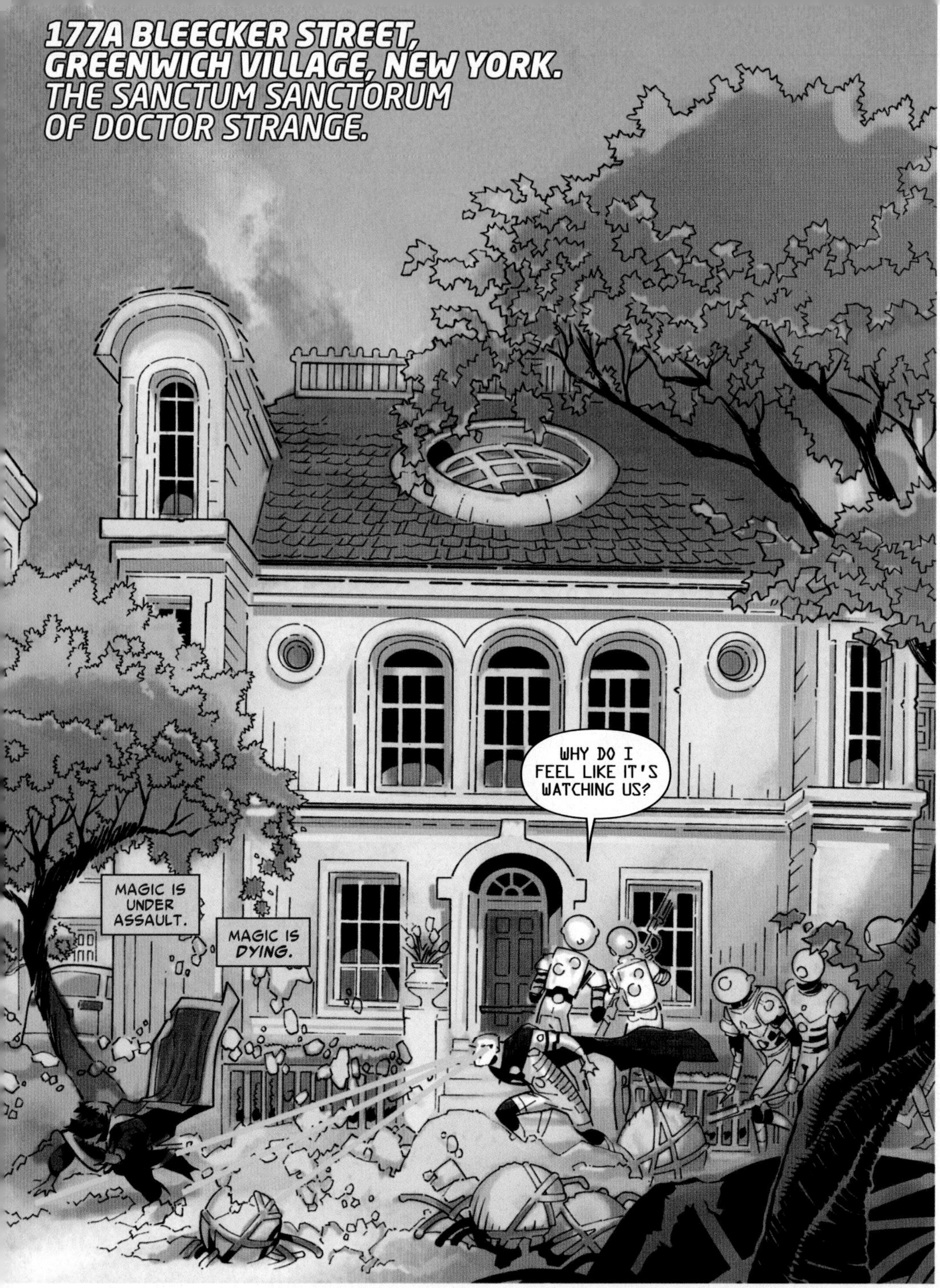
177A BLEECKER STREET,
GREENWICH VILLAGE, NEW YORK.
THE SANCTUM SANCTORUM
OF DOCTOR STRANGE.
WHY DO I FEEL LIKE IT'S WATCHING US?
MAGIC IS UNDER ASSAULT.
MAGIC IS DYING.

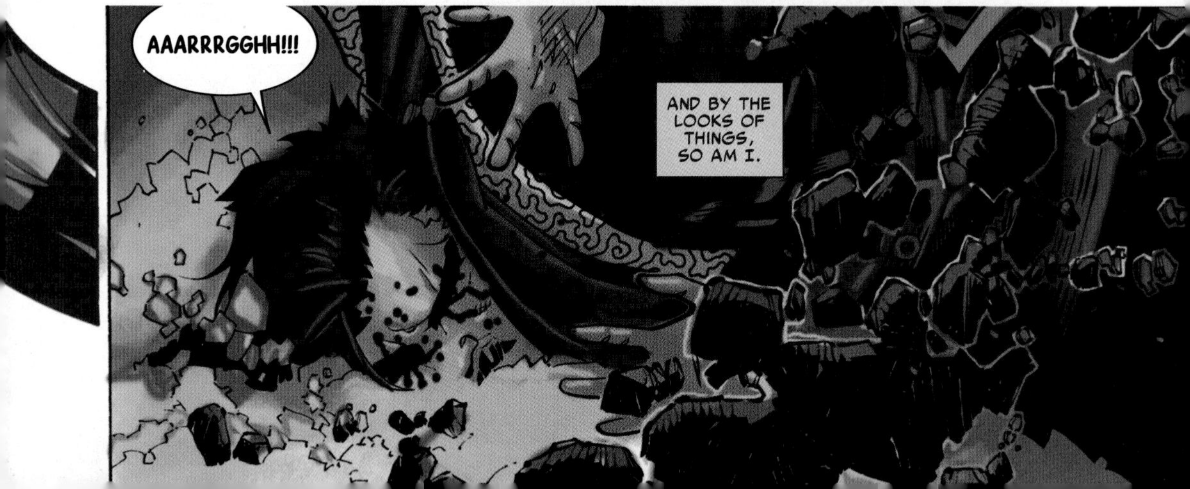
AAARRRGGHH!!!
AND BY THE LOOKS OF THINGS, SO AM I.

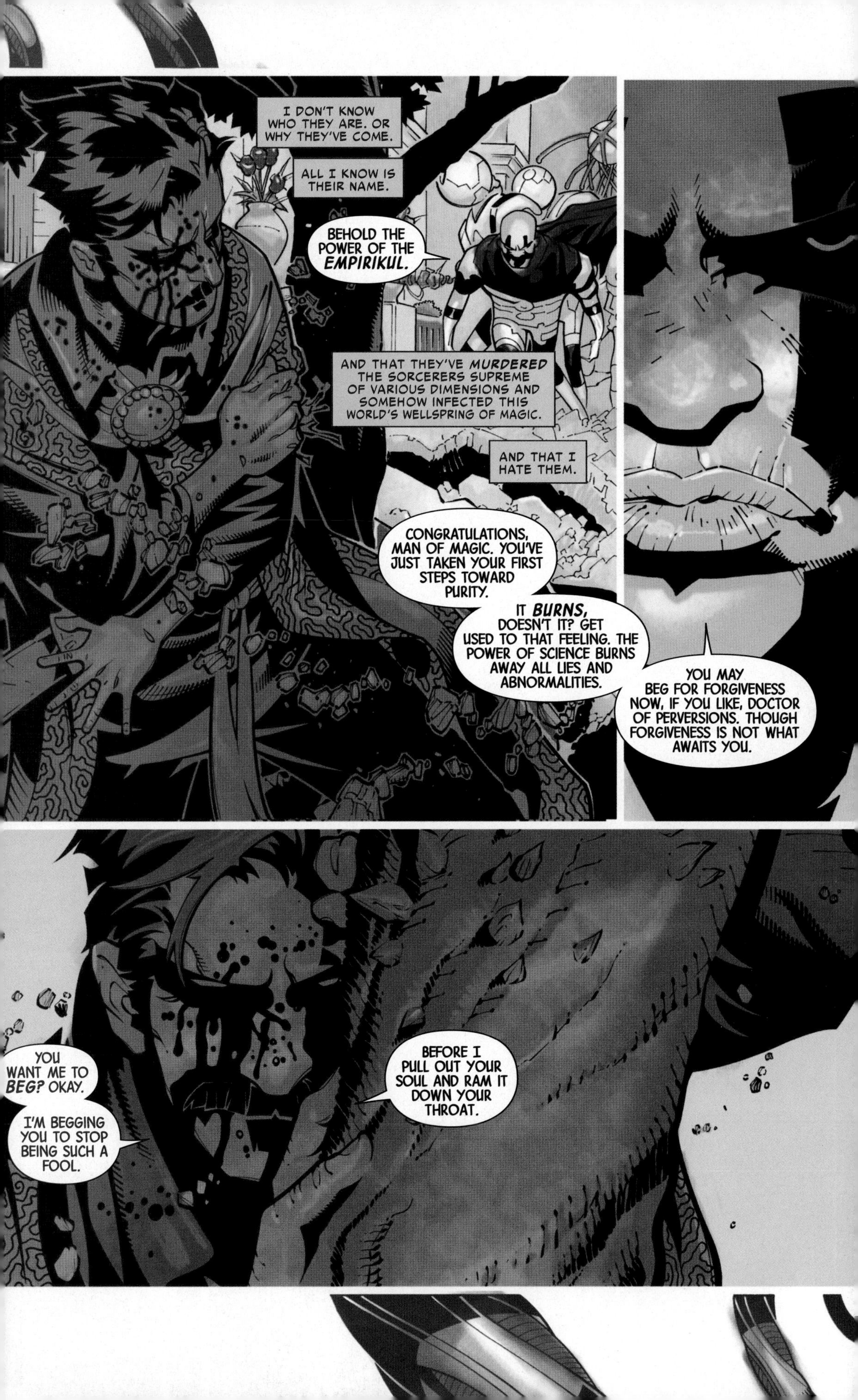

I DON'T KNOW WHO THEY ARE. OR WHY THEY'VE COME.
ALL I KNOW IS THEIR NAME.
BEHOLD THE POWER OF THE EMPIRIKUL.
AND THAT THEY'VE MURDERED THE SORCERERS SUPREME OF VARIOUS DIMENSIONS AND SOMEHOW INFECTED THIS WORLD'S WELLSPRING OF MAGIC.
AND THAT I HATE THEM.
CONGRATULATIONS, MAN OF MAGIC. YOU'VE JUST TAKEN YOUR FIRST STEPS TOWARD PURITY.
IT BURNS, DOESN'T IT? GET USED TO THAT FEELING. THE POWER OF SCIENCE BURNS AWAY ALL LIES AND ABNORMALITIES.
YOU MAY BEG FOR FORGIVENESS NOW, IF YOU LIKE, DOCTOR OF PERVERSIONS. THOUGH FORGIVENESS IS NOT WHAT AWAITS YOU.
YOU WANT ME TO BEG? OKAY.
I'M BEGGING YOU TO STOP BEING SUCH A FOOL.
BEFORE I PULL OUT YOUR SOUL AND RAM IT DOWN YOUR THROAT.

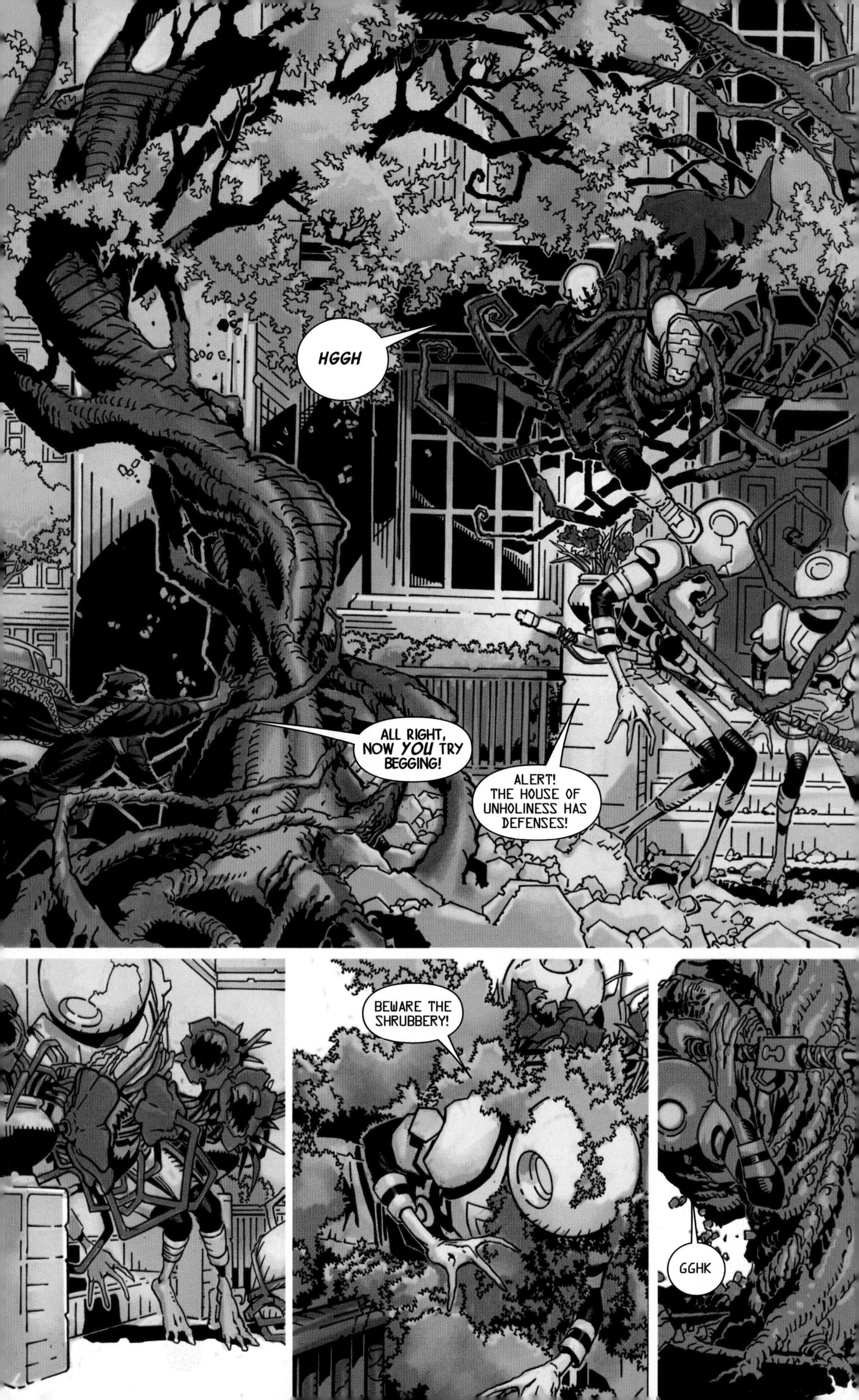
HGGH
ALL RIGHT, NOW YOU TRY BEGGING!
ALERT! THE HOUSE OF UNHOLINESS HAS DEFENSES!
BEWARE THE SHRUBBERY!
GGHK

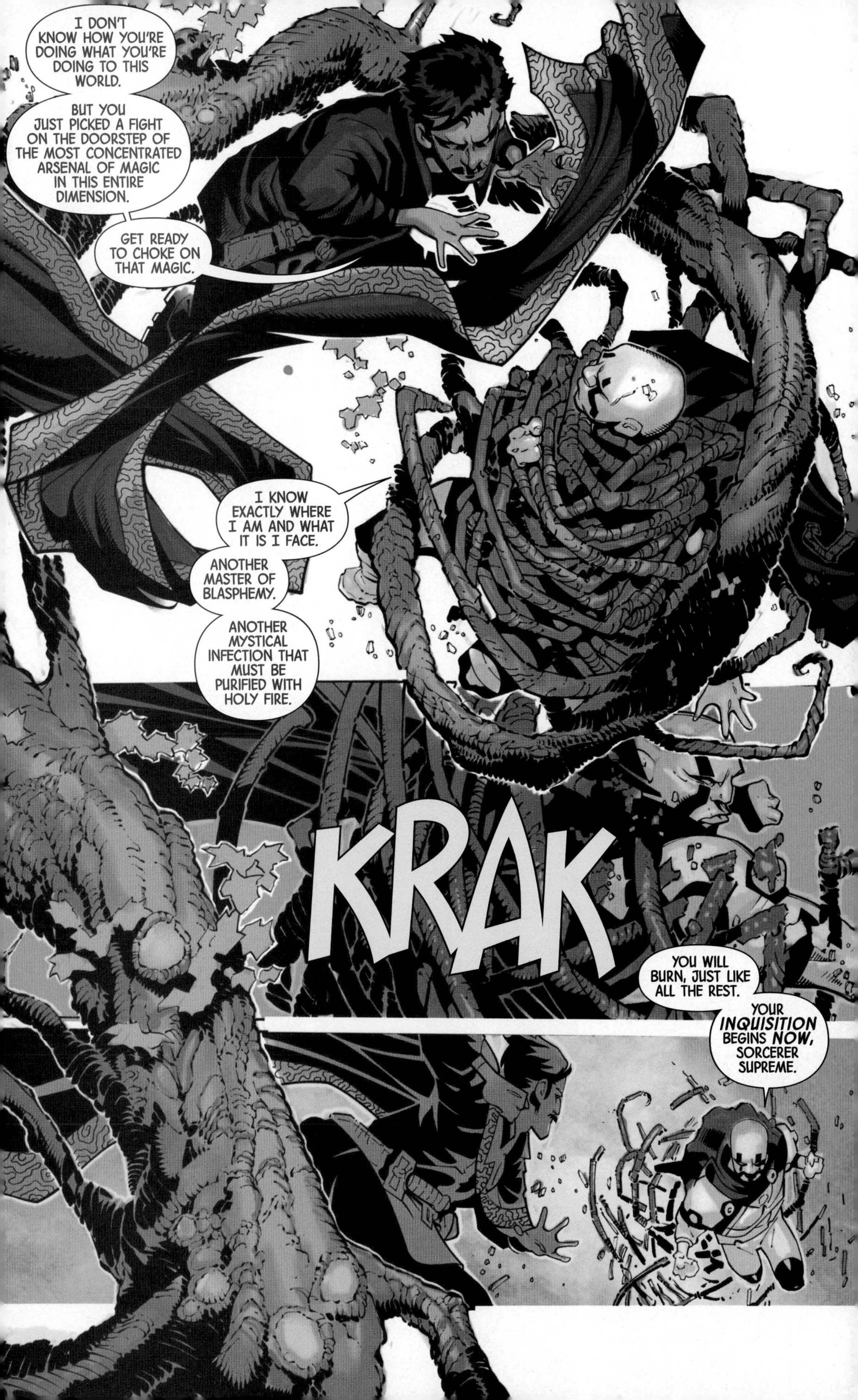
I DON'T KNOW HOW YOU'RE DOING WHAT YOU'RE DOING TO THIS WORLD.
BUT YOU JUST PICKED A FIGHT ON THE DOORSTEP OF THE MOST CONCENTRATED ARSENAL OF MAGIC IN THIS ENTIRE DIMENSION.
GET READY TO CHOKE ON THAT MAGIC.
I KNOW EXACTLY WHERE I AM AND WHAT IT IS I FACE.
ANOTHER MASTER OF BLASPHEMY.
ANOTHER MYSTICAL INFECTION THAT MUST BE PURIFIED WITH HOLY FIRE.
KRAK
YOU WILL BURN, JUST LIKE ALL THE REST.
YOUR INQUISITION BEGINS NOW, SORCERER SUPREME.

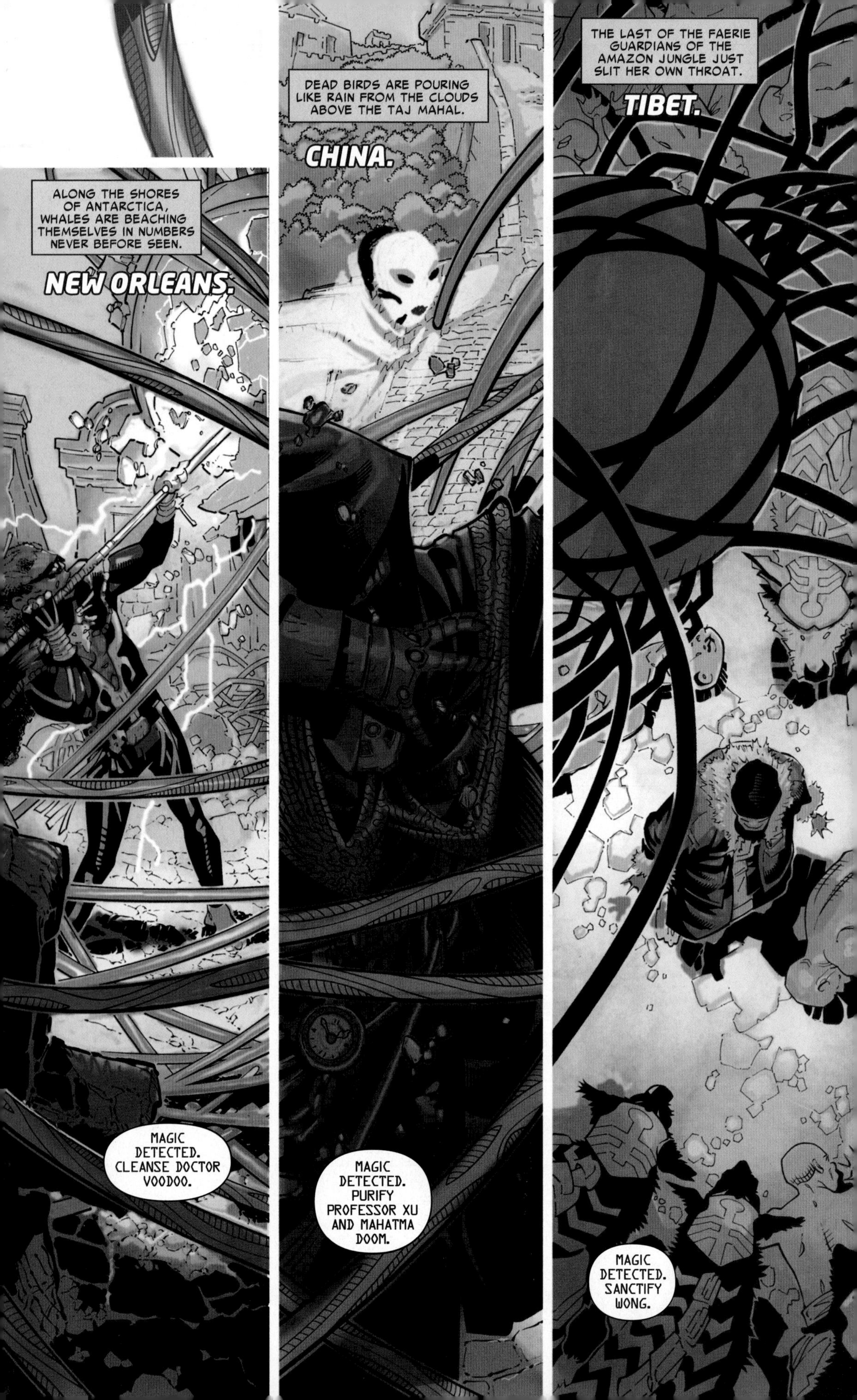
ALONG THE SHORES OF ANTARCTICA, WHALES ARE BEACHING THEMSELVES IN NUMBERS NEVER BEFORE SEEN.
NEW ORLEANS.
MAGIC DETECTED. CLEANSE DOCTOR VOODOO.
DEAD BIRDS ARE POURING LIKE RAIN FROM THE CLOUDS ABOVE THE TAJ MAHAL.
CHINA.
MAGIC DETECTED. PURIFY PROFESSOR XU AND MAHATMA DOOM.
THE LAST OF THE FAERIE GUARDIANS OF THE AMAZON JUNGLE JUST SLIT HER OWN THROAT.
TIBET.
MAGIC DETECTED. SANCTIFY WONG.

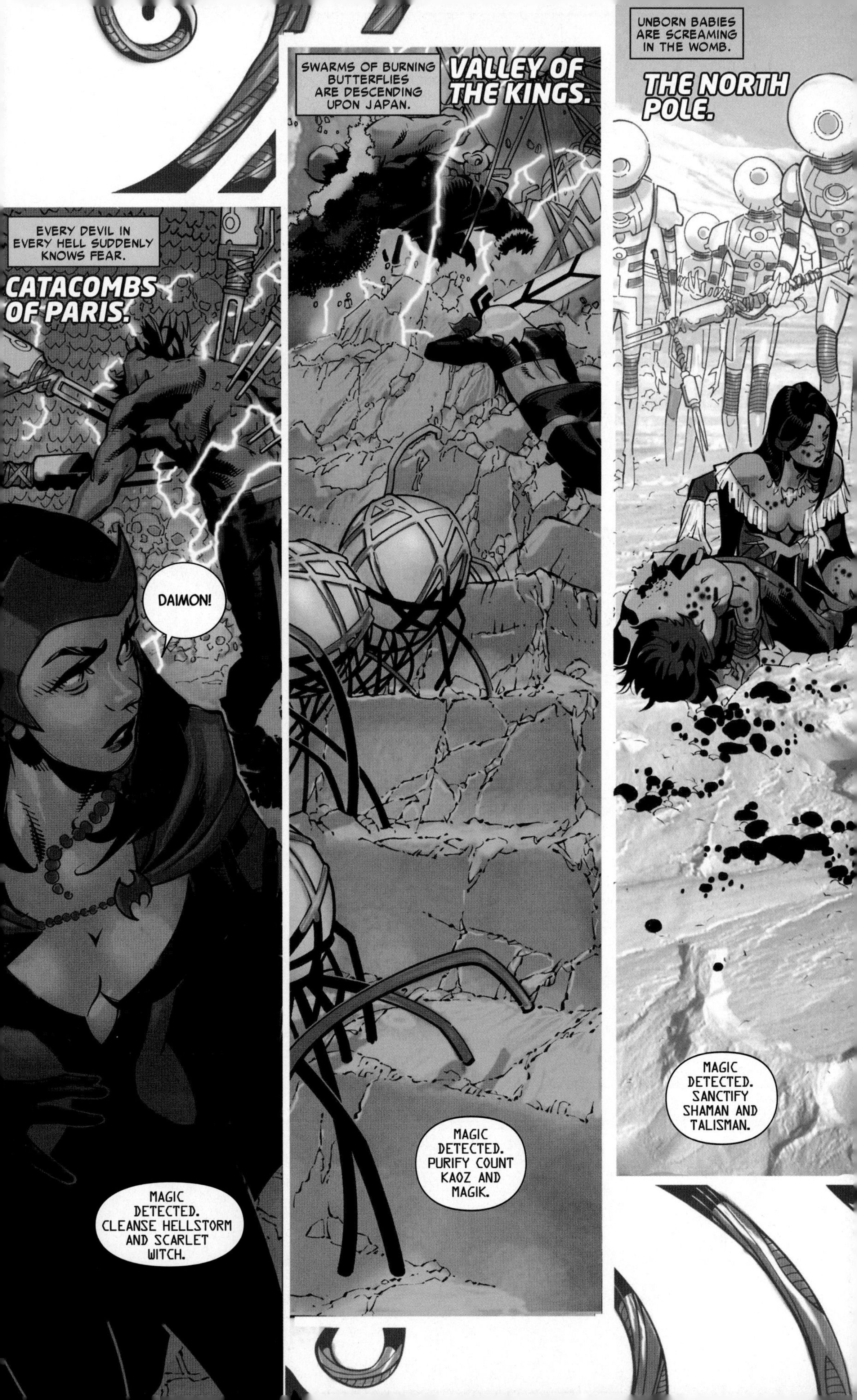
EVERY DEVIL IN EVERY HELL SUDDENLY KNOWS FEAR.
CATACOMBS OF PARIS.
DAIMON!
MAGIC DETECTED. CLEANSE HELLSTORM AND SCARLET WITCH.
SWARMS OF BURNING BUTTERFLIES ARE DESCENDING UPON JAPAN.
VALLEY OF THE KINGS.
MAGIC DETECTED. PURIFY COUNT KAOZ AND MAGIK.
UNBORN BABIES ARE SCREAMING IN THE WOMB.
THE NORTH POLE.
MAGIC DETECTED. SANCTIFY SHAMAN AND TALISMAN.

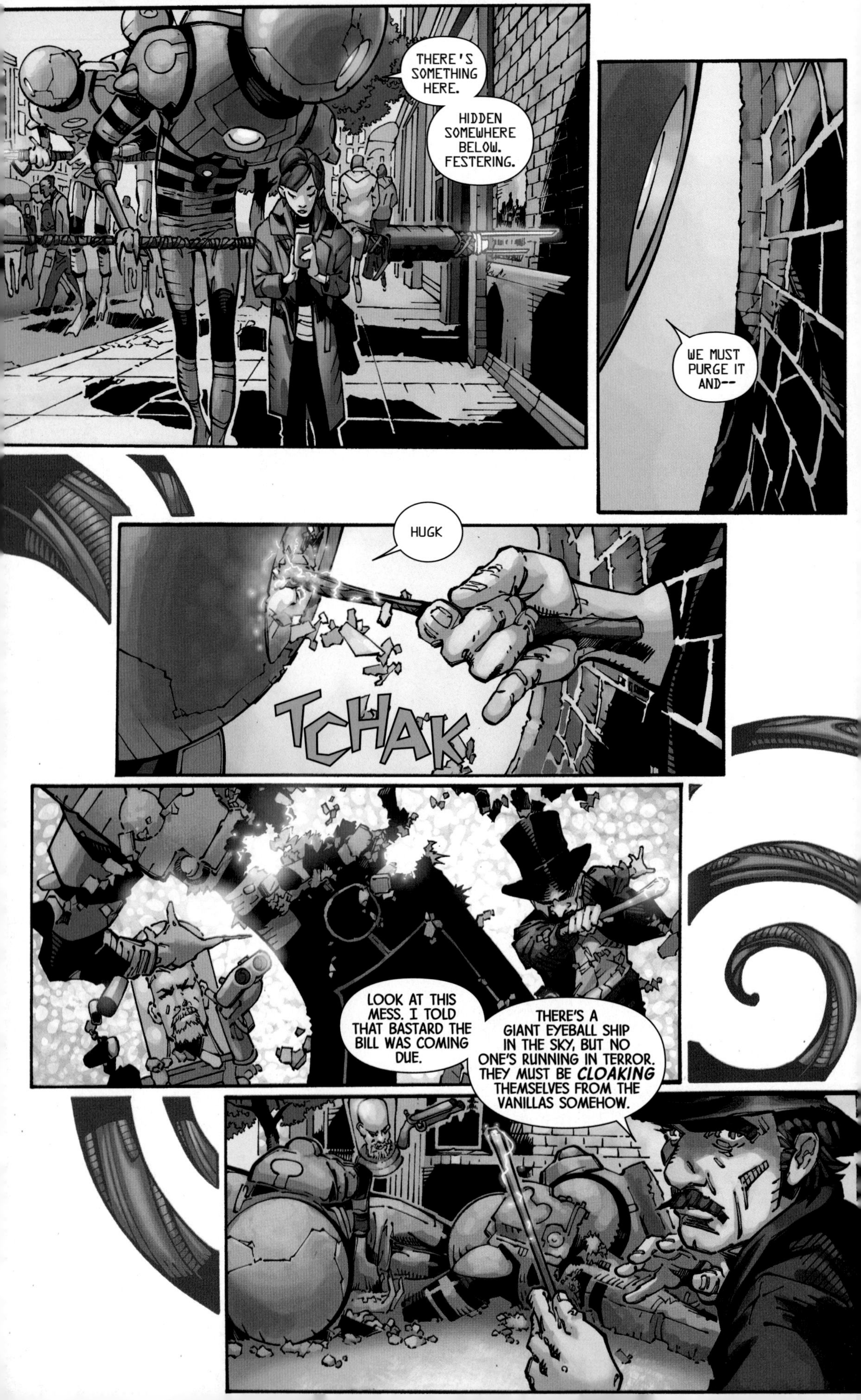
THERE'S SOMETHING HERE.
HIDDEN SOMEWHERE BELOW. FESTERING.
WE MUST PURGE IT AND--
HUGK
TCHAK
LOOK AT THIS MESS. I TOLD THAT BASTARD THE BILL WAS COMING DUE.
THERE'S A GIANT EYEBALL SHIP IN THE SKY, BUT NO ONE'S RUNNING IN TERROR. THEY MUST BE *CLOAKING* THEMSELVES FROM THE VANILLAS SOMEHOW.

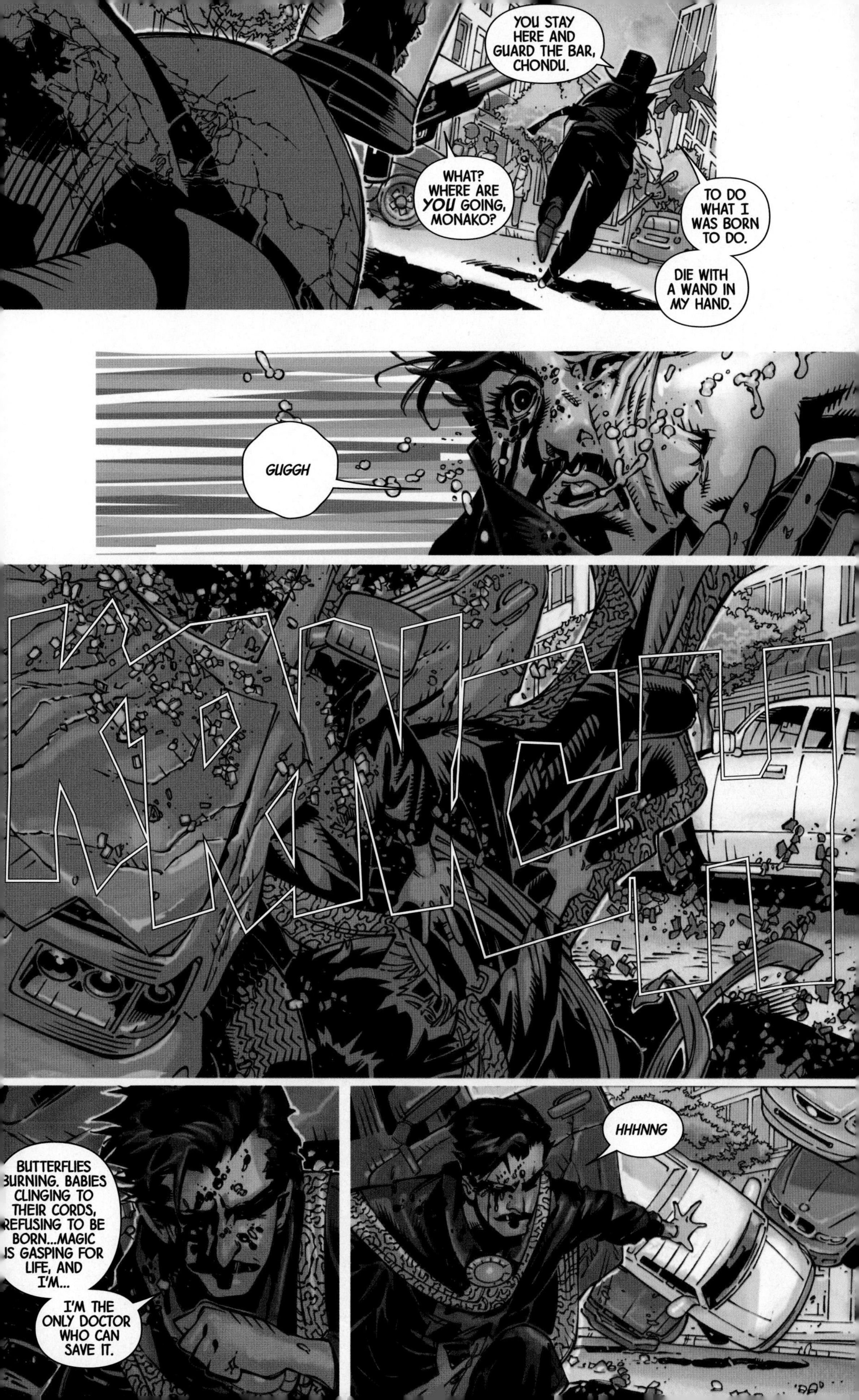

YOU STAY HERE AND GUARD THE BAR, CHONDU.
WHAT? WHERE ARE *YOU* GOING, MONAKO?
TO DO WHAT I WAS BORN TO DO.
DIE WITH A WAND IN MY HAND.
GUGGH
KRNCH
BUTTERFLIES BURNING. BABIES CLINGING TO THEIR CORDS, REFUSING TO BE BORN...MAGIC IS GASPING FOR LIFE, AND I'M...
I'M THE ONLY DOCTOR WHO CAN SAVE IT.
HHHNNG

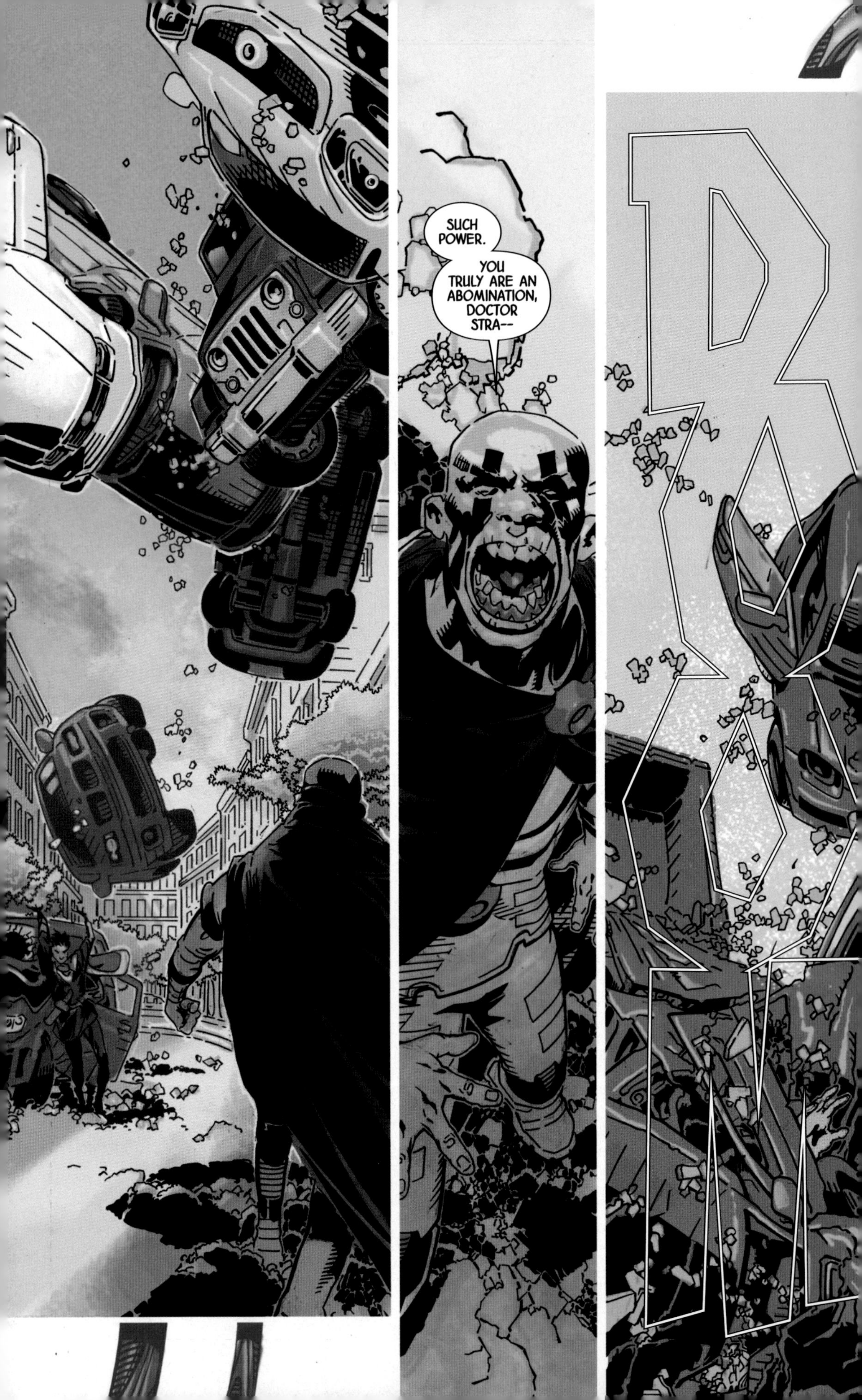
SUCH POWER.
YOU TRULY ARE AN ABOMINATION, DOCTOR STRA--

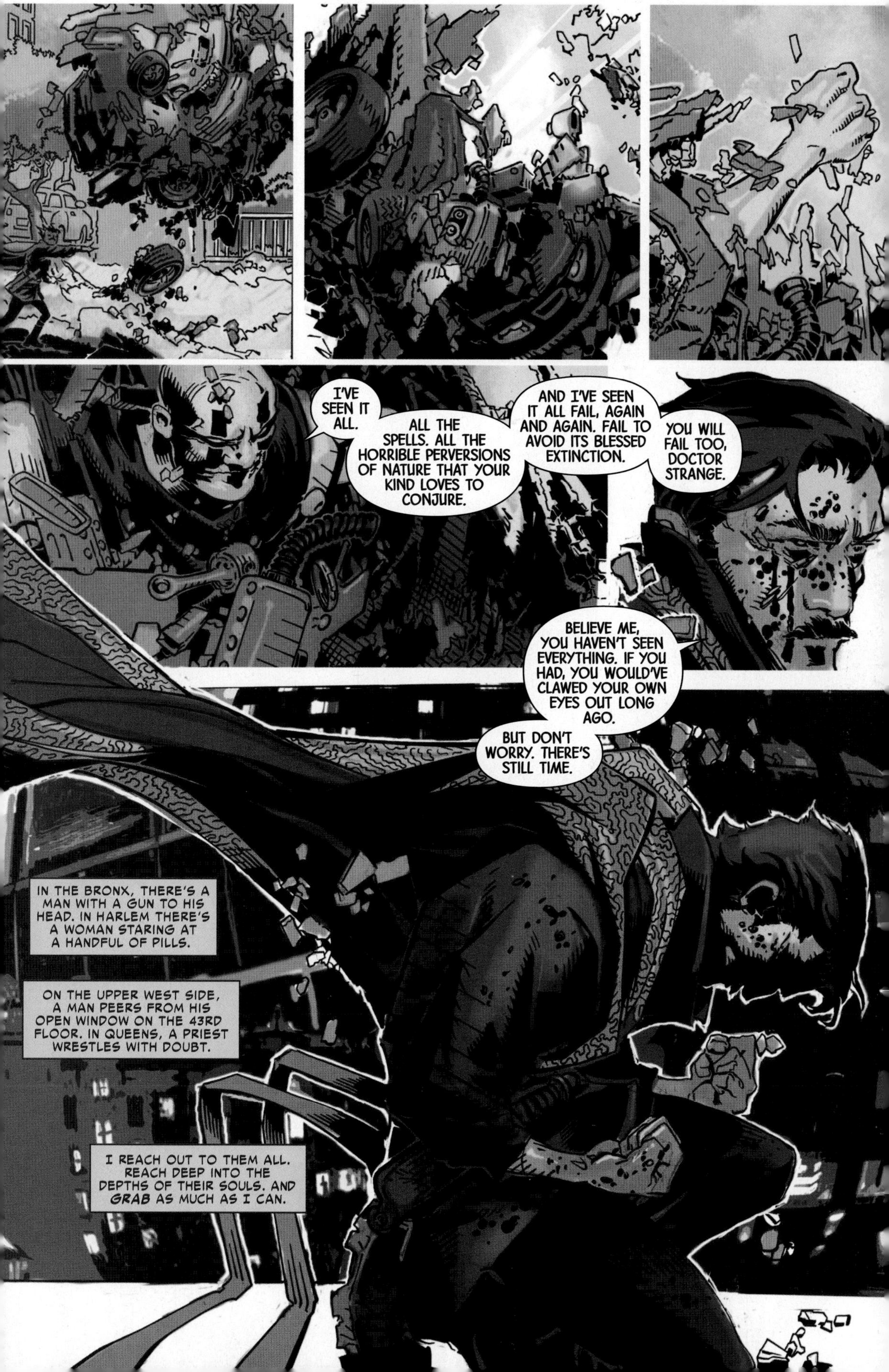
I'VE SEEN IT ALL.
ALL THE SPELLS. ALL THE HORRIBLE PERVERSIONS OF NATURE THAT YOUR KIND LOVES TO CONJURE.
AND I'VE SEEN IT ALL FAIL, AGAIN AND AGAIN. FAIL TO AVOID ITS BLESSED EXTINCTION.
YOU WILL FAIL TOO, DOCTOR STRANGE.
BELIEVE ME, YOU HAVEN'T SEEN EVERYTHING. IF YOU HAD, YOU WOULD'VE CLAWED YOUR OWN EYES OUT LONG AGO.
BUT DON'T WORRY. THERE'S STILL TIME.
IN THE BRONX, THERE'S A MAN WITH A GUN TO HIS HEAD. IN HARLEM THERE'S A WOMAN STARING AT A HANDFUL OF PILLS.
ON THE UPPER WEST SIDE, A MAN PEERS FROM HIS OPEN WINDOW ON THE 43RD FLOOR. IN QUEENS, A PRIEST WRESTLES WITH DOUBT.
I REACH OUT TO THEM ALL. REACH DEEP INTO THE DEPTHS OF THEIR SOULS. AND GRAB AS MUCH AS I CAN.

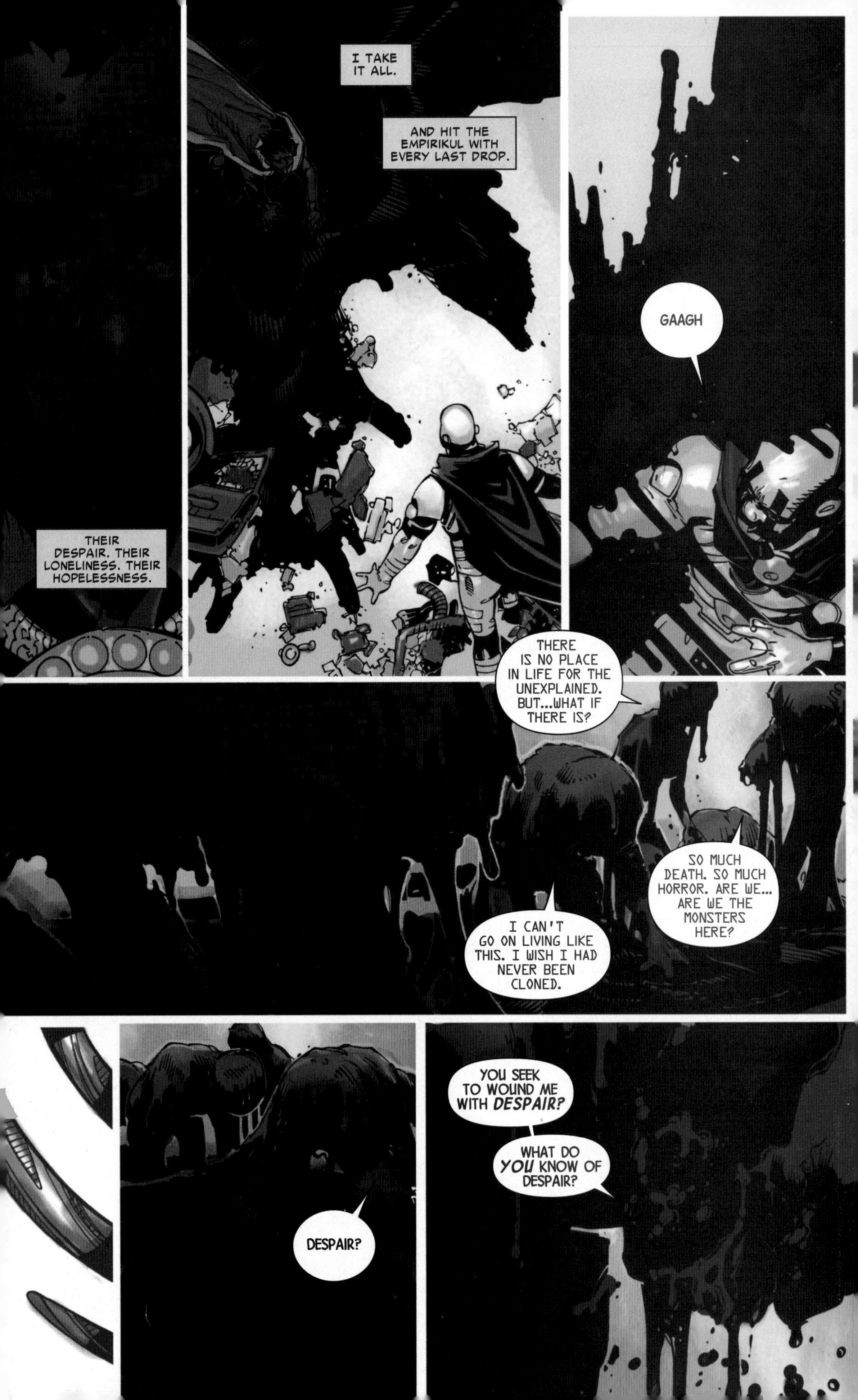
THEIR DESPAIR. THEIR LONELINESS. THEIR HOPELESSNESS.
I TAKE IT ALL.
AND HIT THE EMPIRIKUL WITH EVERY LAST DROP.
GAAGH
THERE IS NO PLACE IN LIFE FOR THE UNEXPLAINED. BUT...WHAT IF THERE IS?
SO MUCH DEATH. SO MUCH HORROR. ARE WE... ARE WE THE MONSTERS HERE?
I CAN'T GO ON LIVING LIKE THIS. I WISH I HAD NEVER BEEN CLONED.
DESPAIR?
YOU SEEK TO WOUND ME WITH DESPAIR?
WHAT DO YOU KNOW OF DESPAIR?

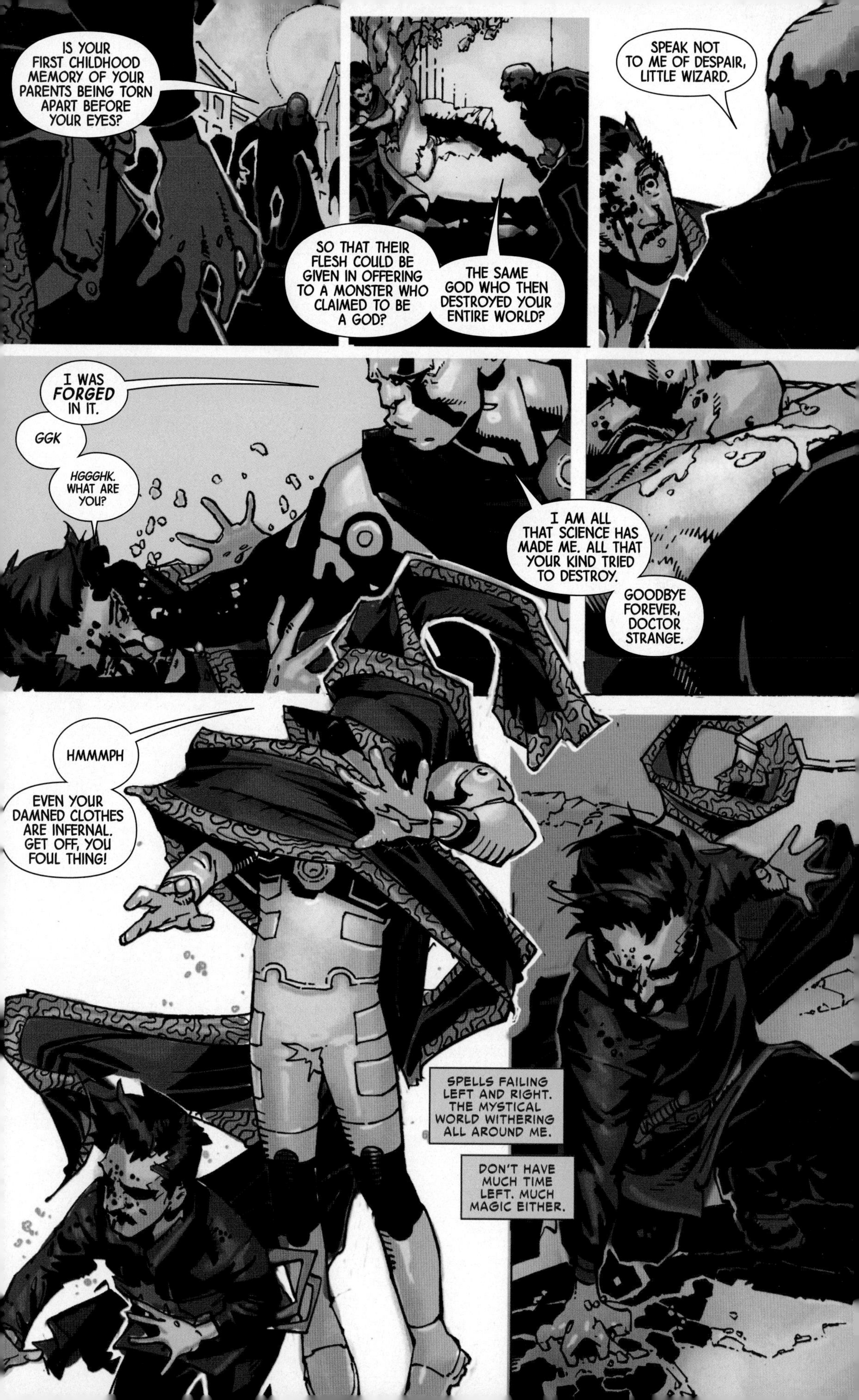
IS YOUR FIRST CHILDHOOD MEMORY OF YOUR PARENTS BEING TORN APART BEFORE YOUR EYES?
SO THAT THEIR FLESH COULD BE GIVEN IN OFFERING TO A MONSTER WHO CLAIMED TO BE A GOD?
THE SAME GOD WHO THEN DESTROYED YOUR ENTIRE WORLD?
SPEAK NOT TO ME OF DESPAIR, LITTLE WIZARD.
I WAS *FORGED* IN IT.
GGK
HGGGHK. WHAT ARE YOU?
I AM ALL THAT SCIENCE HAS MADE ME. ALL THAT YOUR KIND TRIED TO DESTROY.
GOODBYE FOREVER, DOCTOR STRANGE.
HMMMPH
EVEN YOUR DAMNED CLOTHES ARE INFERNAL. GET OFF, YOU FOUL THING!
SPELLS FAILING LEFT AND RIGHT. THE MYSTICAL WORLD WITHERING ALL AROUND ME.
DON'T HAVE MUCH TIME LEFT. MUCH MAGIC EITHER.

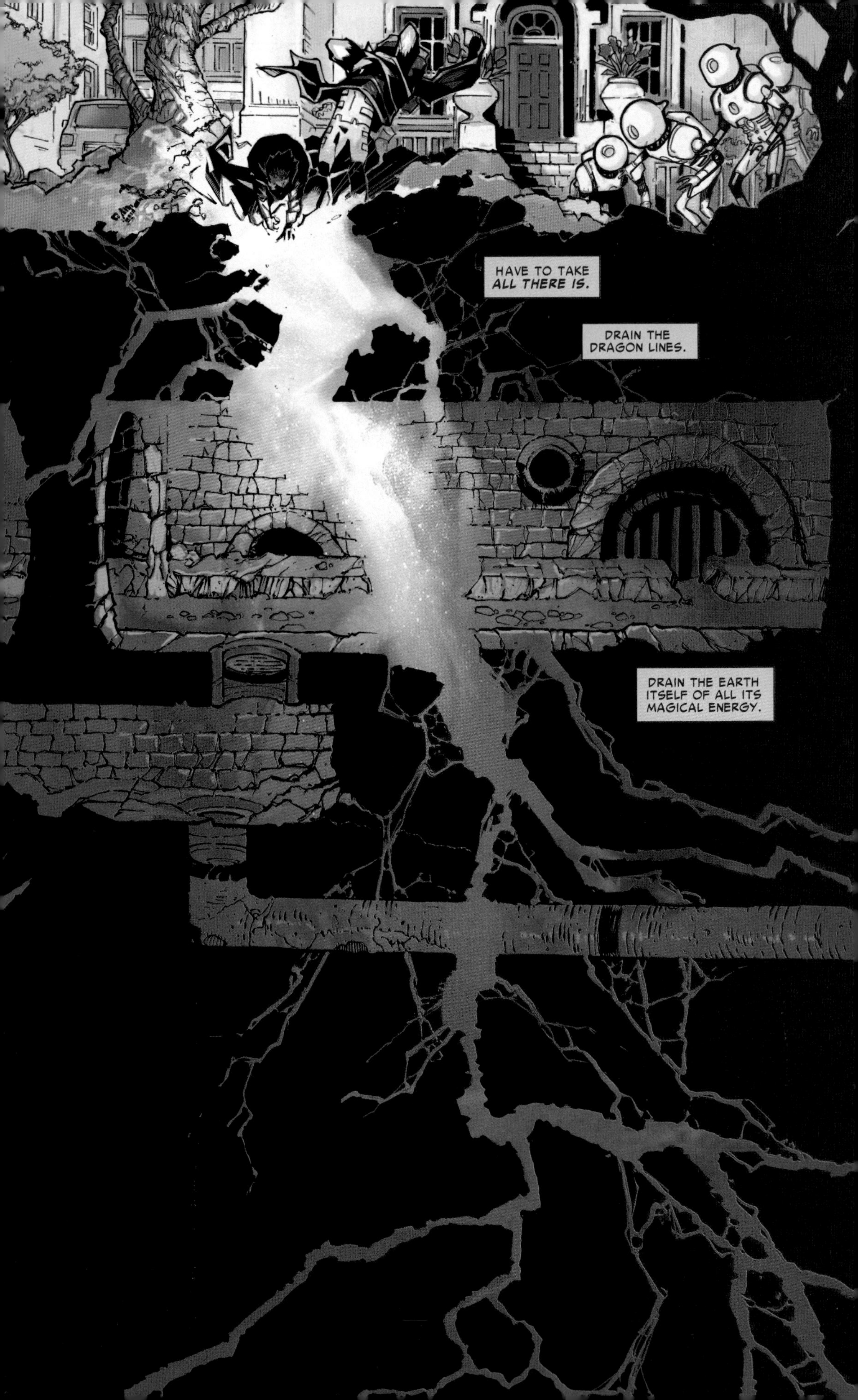
HAVE TO TAKE
ALL THERE IS.
DRAIN THE
DRAGON LINES.
DRAIN THE EARTH
ITSELF OF ALL ITS
MAGICAL ENERGY.

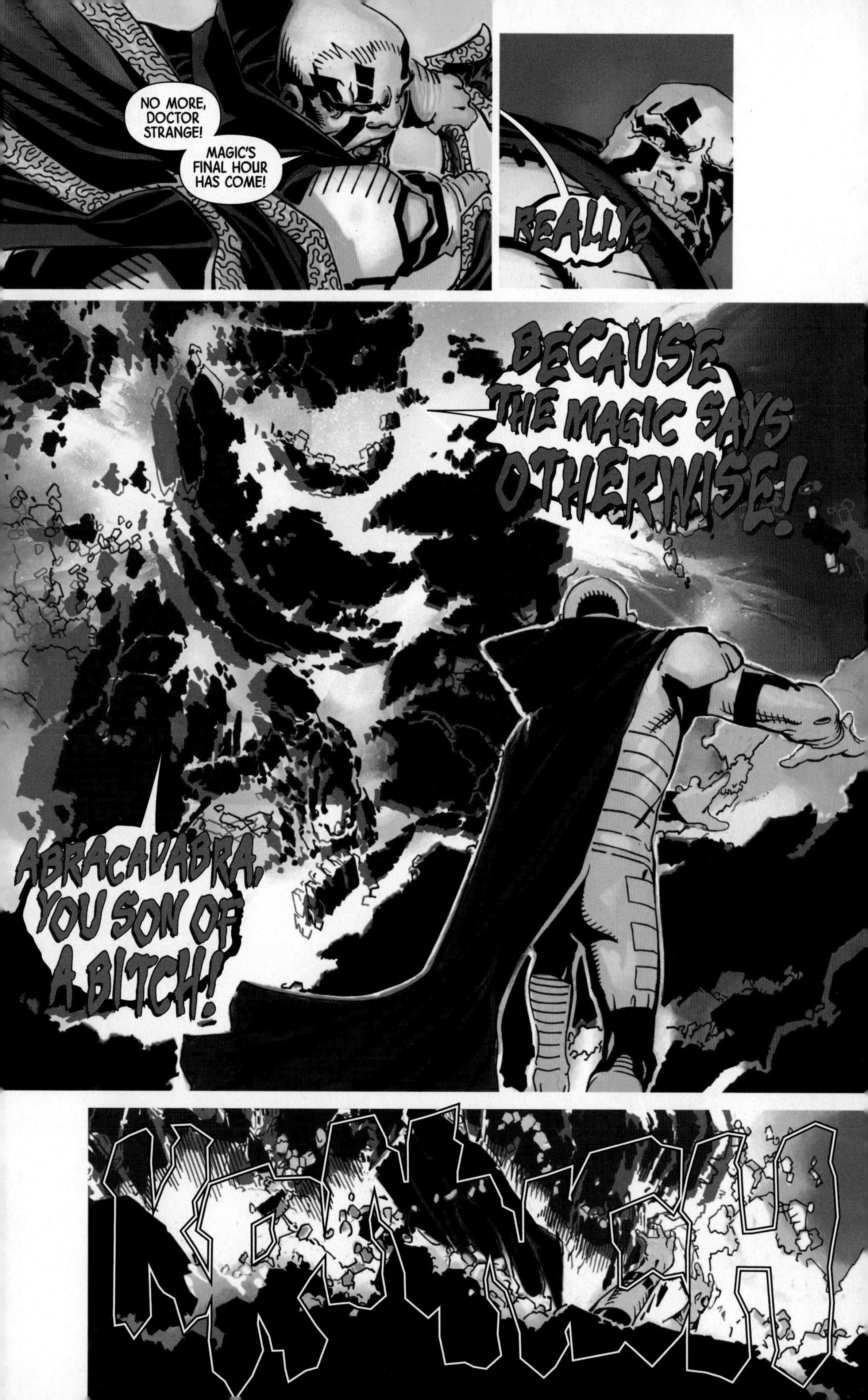
NO MORE, DOCTOR STRANGE!
MAGIC'S FINAL HOUR HAS COME!
REALLY?
BECAUSE THE MAGIC SAYS OTHERWISE!
ABRACADABRA, YOU SON OF A BITCH!

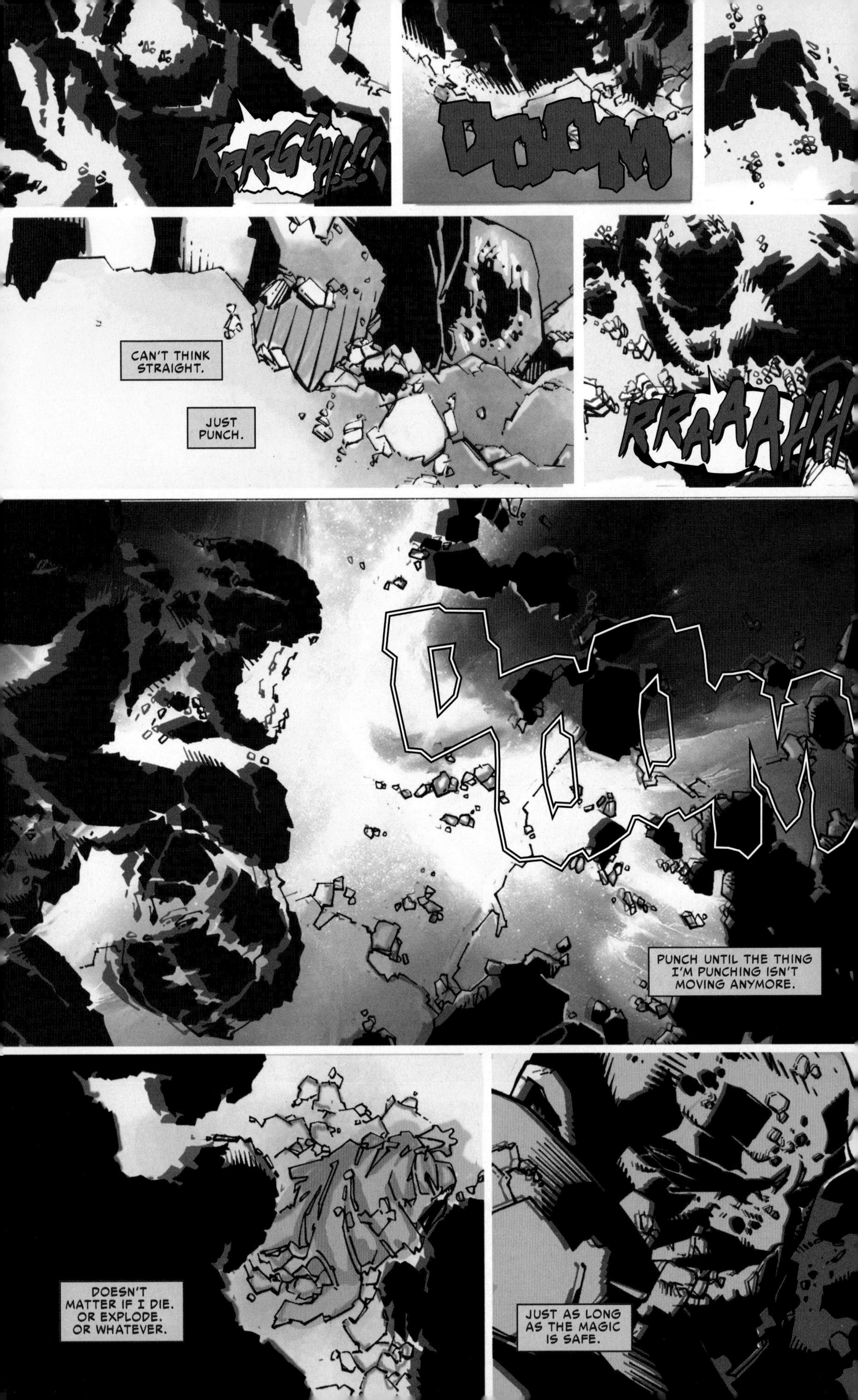
RRRGGH!!!
DOOM
CAN'T THINK STRAIGHT.
JUST PUNCH.
RRAAAAHH
DOOM
PUNCH UNTIL THE THING I'M PUNCHING ISN'T MOVING ANYMORE.
DOESN'T MATTER IF I DIE. OR EXPLODE. OR WHATEVER.
JUST AS LONG AS THE MAGIC IS SAFE.

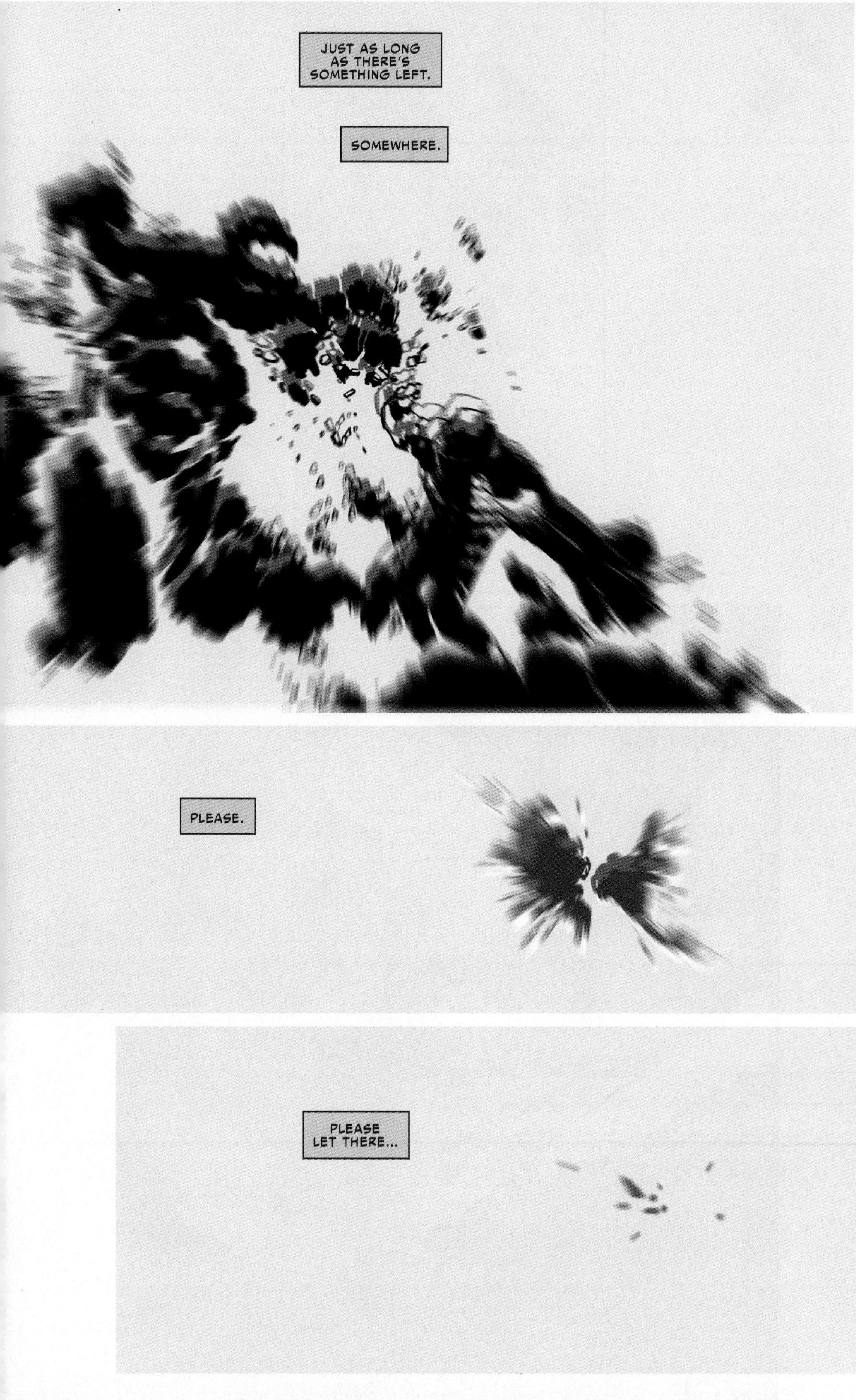
JUST AS LONG AS THERE'S SOMETHING LEFT.
SOMEWHERE.
PLEASE.
PLEASE LET THERE...

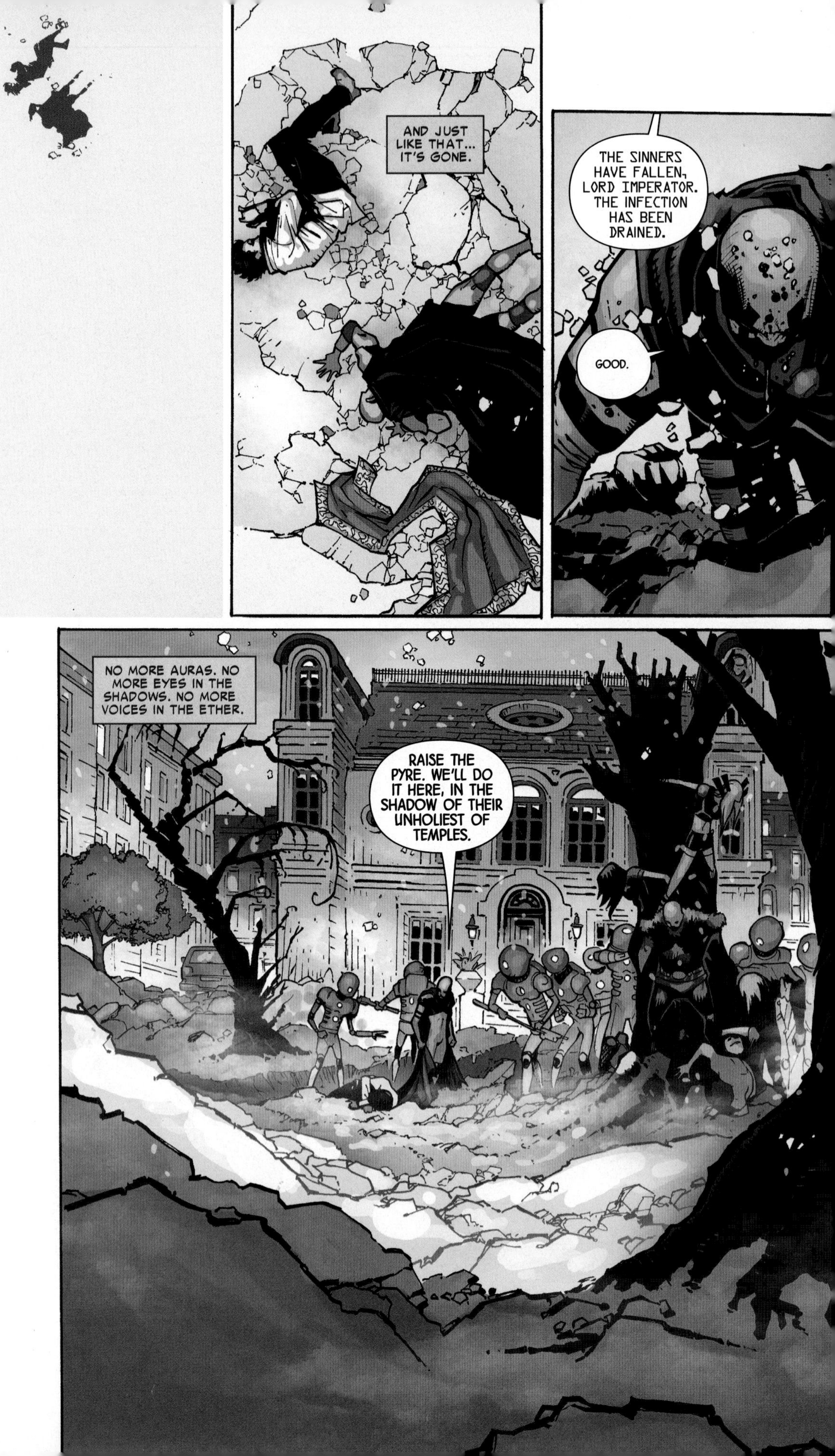
AND JUST LIKE THAT... IT'S GONE.
THE SINNERS HAVE FALLEN, LORD IMPERATOR. THE INFECTION HAS BEEN DRAINED.
GOOD.
NO MORE AURAS. NO MORE EYES IN THE SHADOWS. NO MORE VOICES IN THE ETHER.
RAISE THE PYRE. WE'LL DO IT HERE, IN THE SHADOW OF THEIR UNHOLIEST OF TEMPLES.

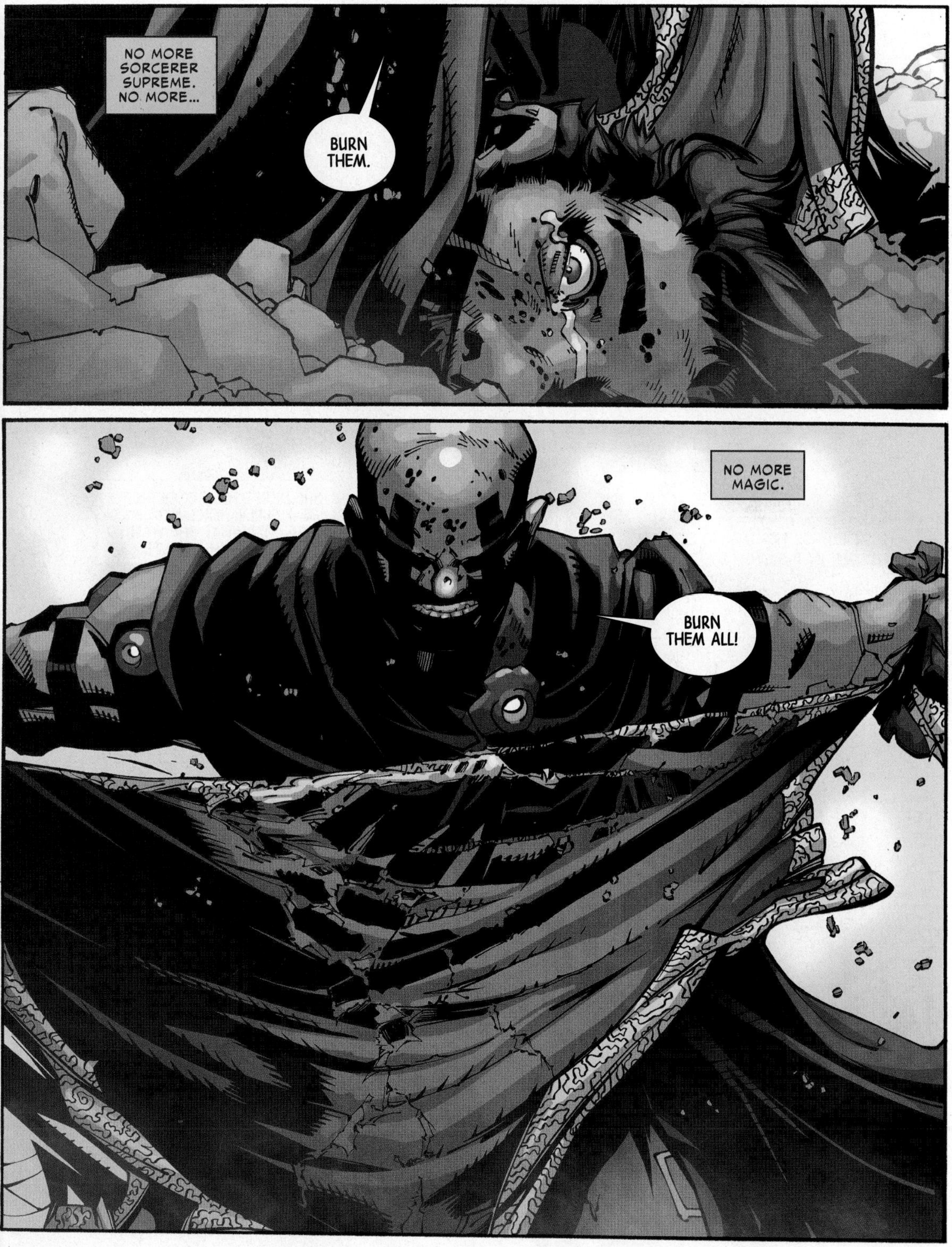
NO MORE SORCERER SUPREME. NO MORE...
BURN THEM.
NO MORE MAGIC.
BURN THEM ALL!

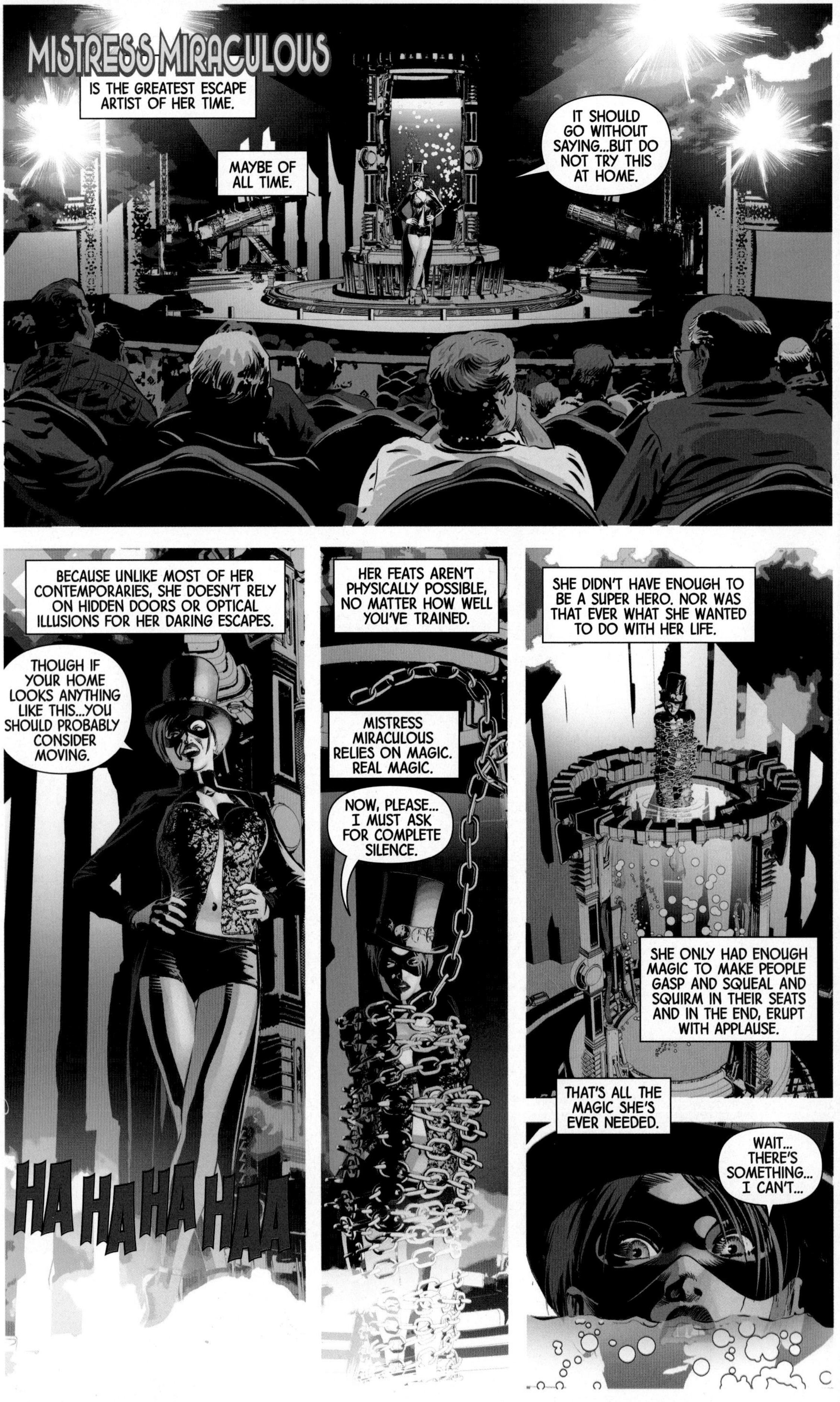
MISTRESS MIRACULOUS
IS THE GREATEST ESCAPE ARTIST OF HER TIME.
MAYBE OF ALL TIME.
IT SHOULD GO WITHOUT SAYING...BUT DO NOT TRY THIS AT HOME.
BECAUSE UNLIKE MOST OF HER CONTEMPORARIES, SHE DOESN'T RELY ON HIDDEN DOORS OR OPTICAL ILLUSIONS FOR HER DARING ESCAPES.
THOUGH IF YOUR HOME LOOKS ANYTHING LIKE THIS...YOU SHOULD PROBABLY CONSIDER MOVING.
HA HA HA HAA
HER FEATS AREN'T PHYSICALLY POSSIBLE, NO MATTER HOW WELL YOU'VE TRAINED.
MISTRESS MIRACULOUS RELIES ON MAGIC. REAL MAGIC.
NOW, PLEASE... I MUST ASK FOR COMPLETE SILENCE.
SHE DIDN'T HAVE ENOUGH TO BE A SUPER HERO. NOR WAS THAT EVER WHAT SHE WANTED TO DO WITH HER LIFE.
SHE ONLY HAD ENOUGH MAGIC TO MAKE PEOPLE GASP AND SQUEAL AND SQUIRM IN THEIR SEATS AND IN THE END, ERUPT WITH APPLAUSE.
THAT'S ALL THE MAGIC SHE'S EVER NEEDED.
WAIT... THERE'S SOMETHING... I CAN'T...

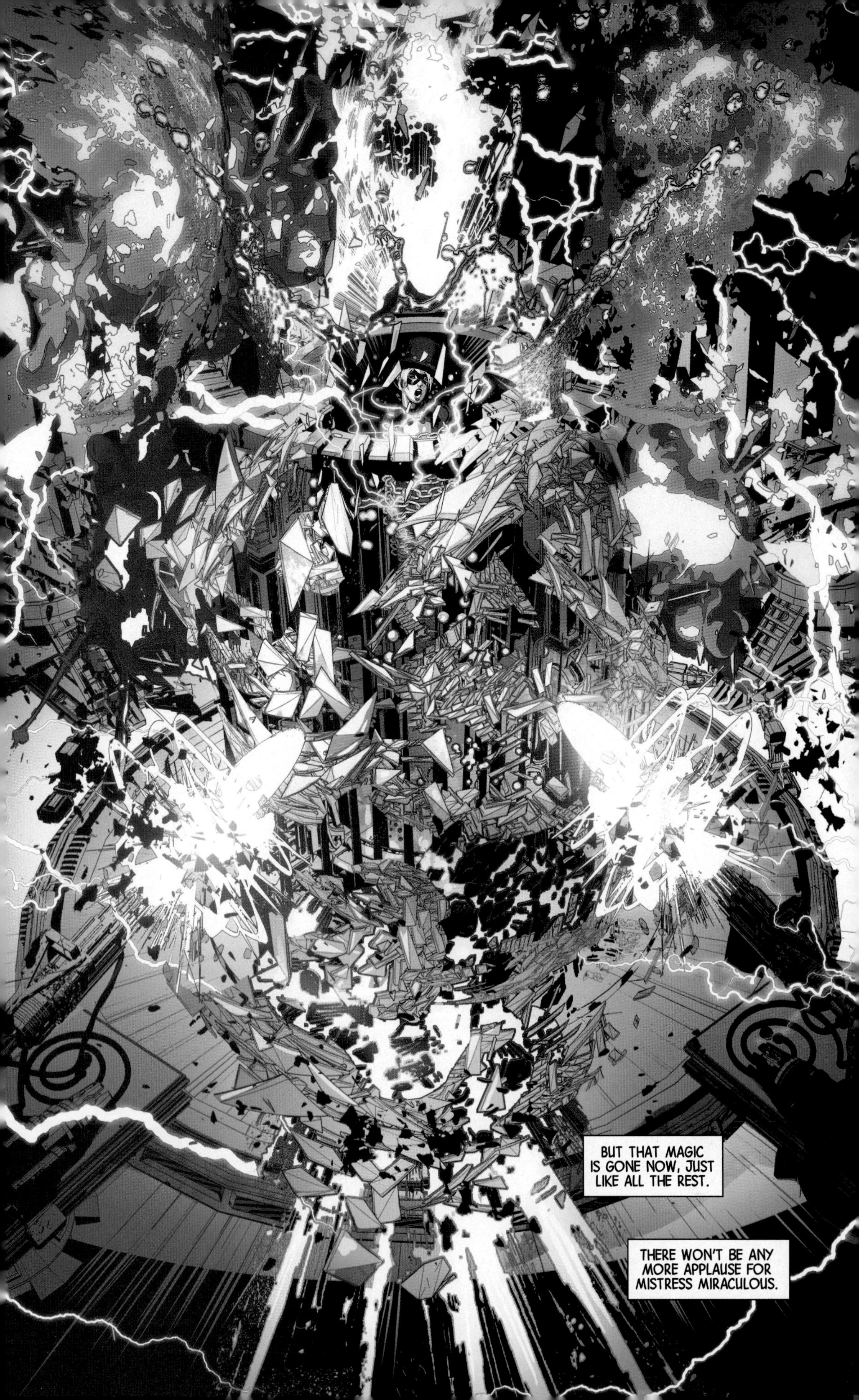
BUT THAT MAGIC
IS GONE NOW, JUST
LIKE ALL THE REST.
THERE WON'T BE ANY
MORE APPLAUSE FOR
MISTRESS MIRACULOUS.

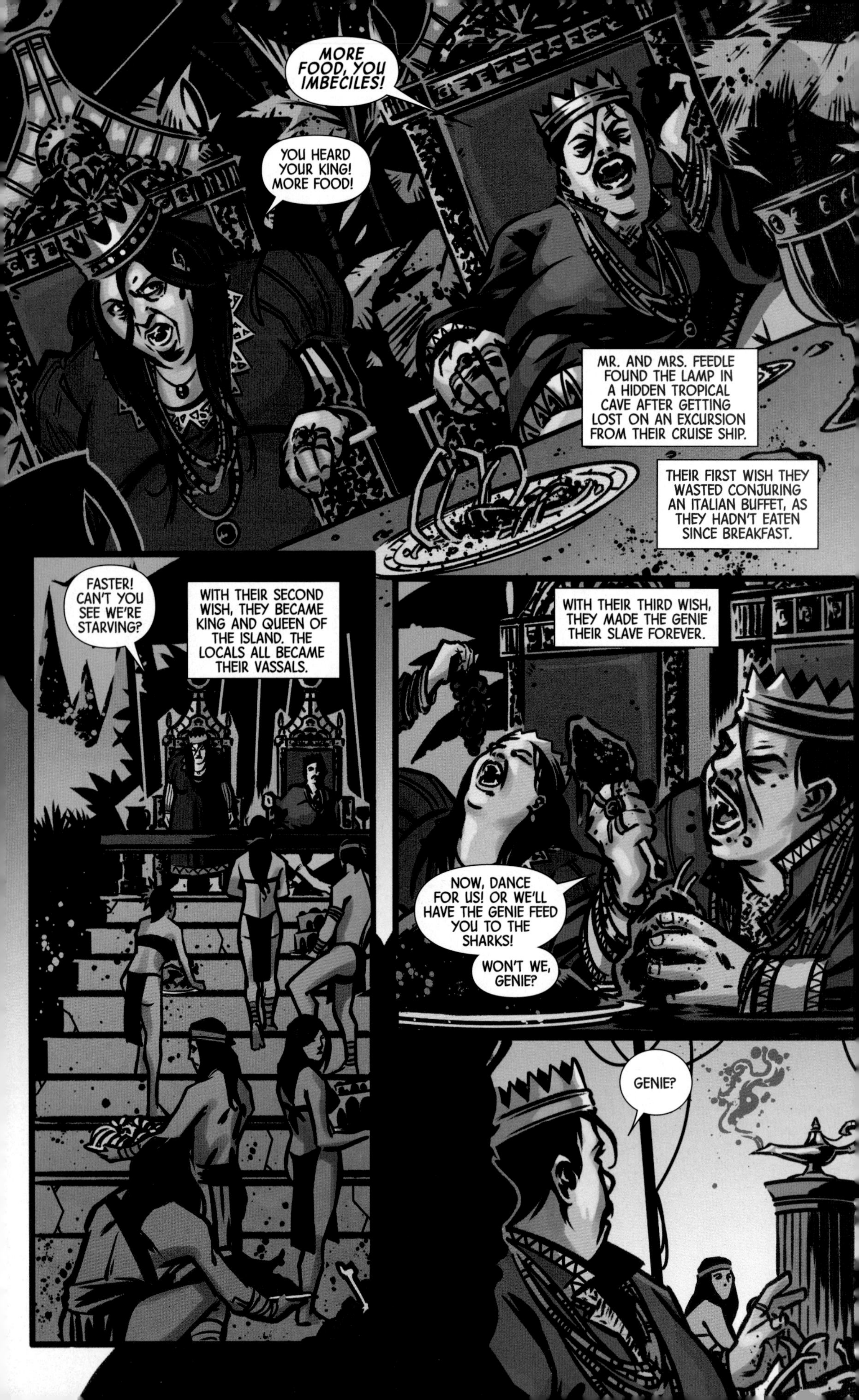
MORE FOOD, YOU IMBECILES!
YOU HEARD YOUR KING! MORE FOOD!
MR. AND MRS. FEEDLE FOUND THE LAMP IN A HIDDEN TROPICAL CAVE AFTER GETTING LOST ON AN EXCURSION FROM THEIR CRUISE SHIP.
THEIR FIRST WISH THEY WASTED CONJURING AN ITALIAN BUFFET, AS THEY HADN'T EATEN SINCE BREAKFAST.
FASTER! CAN'T YOU SEE WE'RE STARVING?
WITH THEIR SECOND WISH, THEY BECAME KING AND QUEEN OF THE ISLAND. THE LOCALS ALL BECAME THEIR VASSALS.
WITH THEIR THIRD WISH, THEY MADE THE GENIE THEIR SLAVE FOREVER.
NOW, DANCE FOR US! OR WE'LL HAVE THE GENIE FEED YOU TO THE SHARKS!
WON'T WE, GENIE?
GENIE?

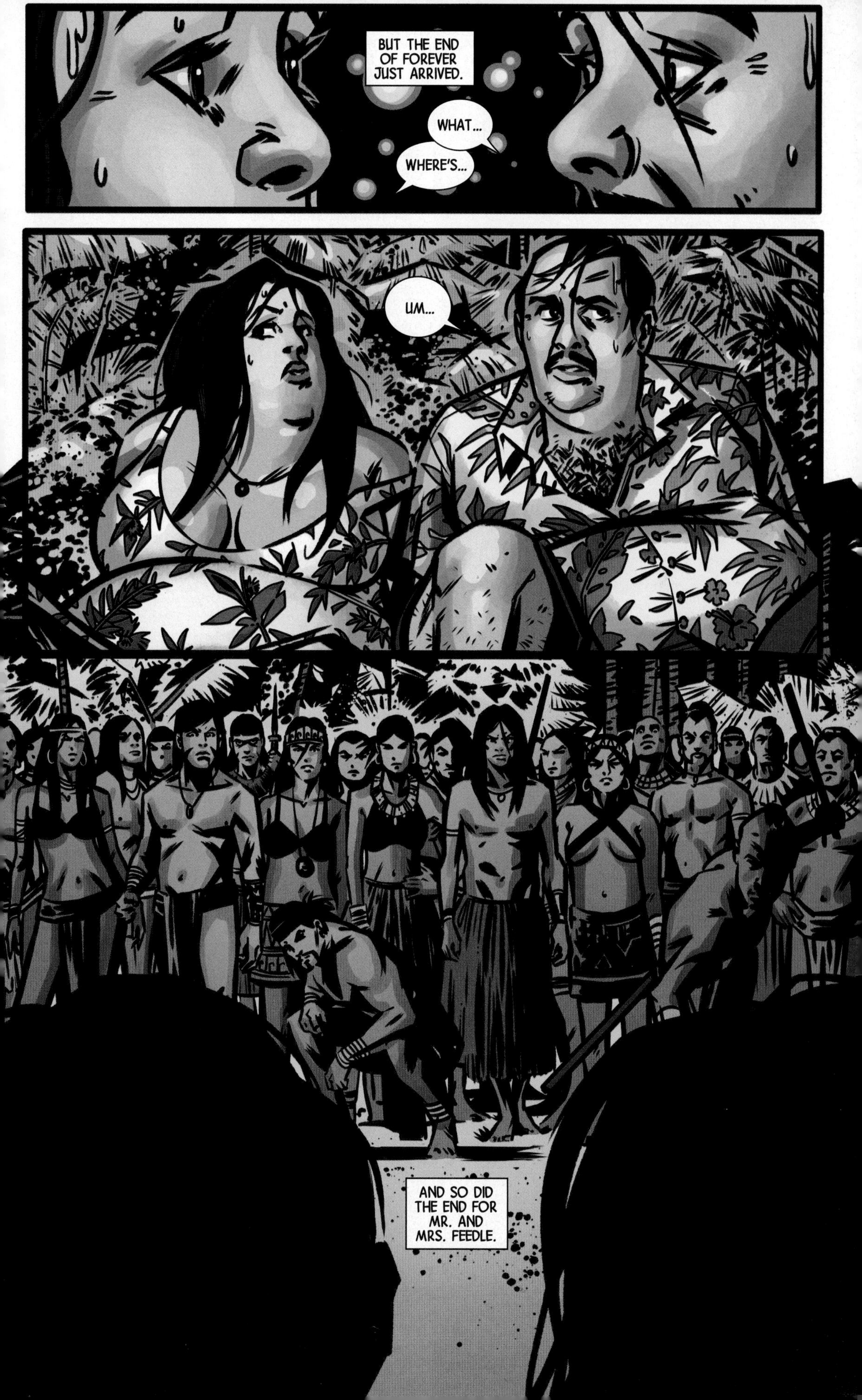
BUT THE END OF FOREVER JUST ARRIVED.
WHAT...
WHERE'S...
UM...
AND SO DID THE END FOR MR. AND MRS. FEEDLE.

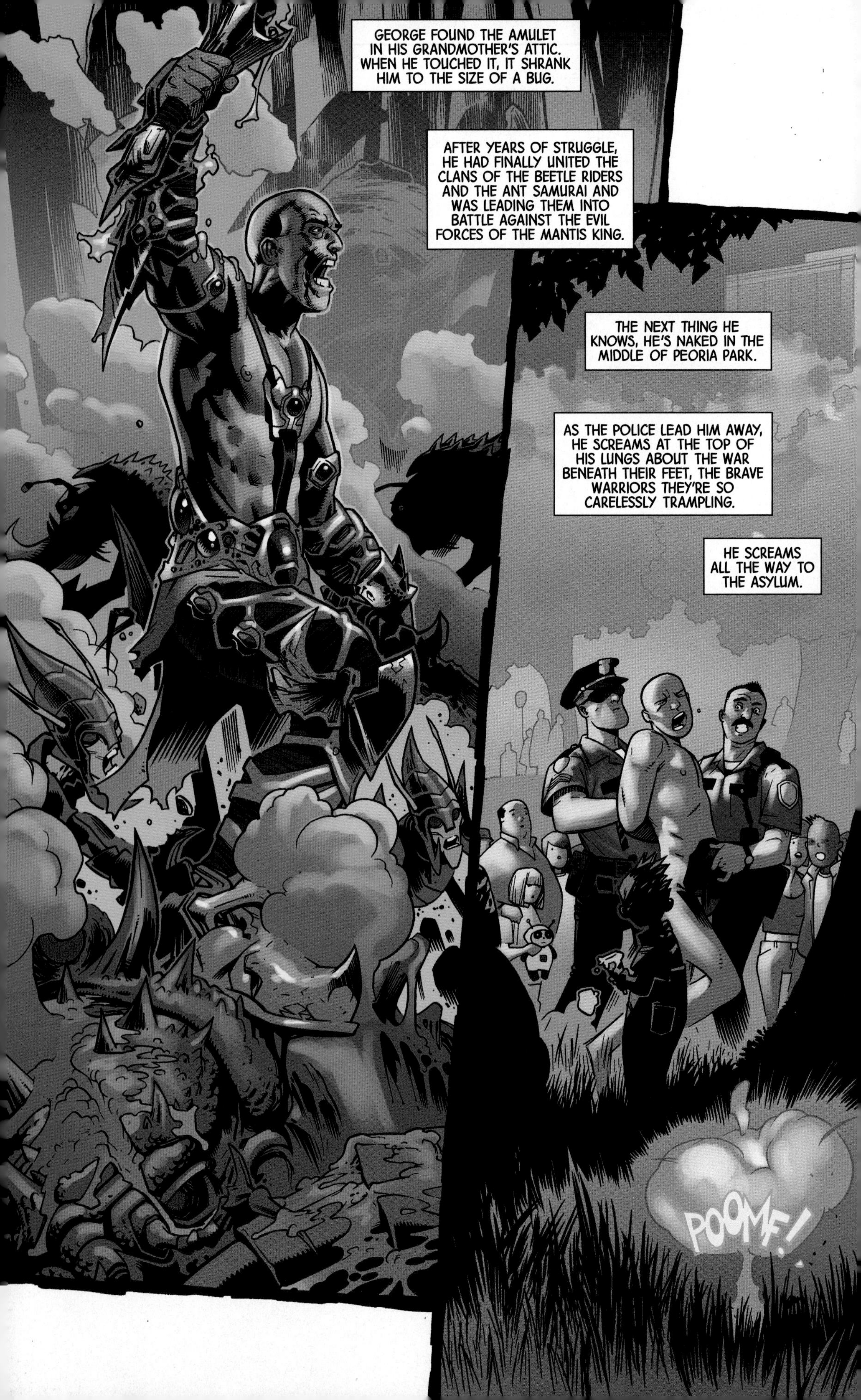
GEORGE FOUND THE AMULET IN HIS GRANDMOTHER'S ATTIC. WHEN HE TOUCHED IT, IT SHRANK HIM TO THE SIZE OF A BUG.
AFTER YEARS OF STRUGGLE, HE HAD FINALLY UNITED THE CLANS OF THE BEETLE RIDERS AND THE ANT SAMURAI AND WAS LEADING THEM INTO BATTLE AGAINST THE EVIL FORCES OF THE MANTIS KING.
THE NEXT THING HE KNOWS, HE'S NAKED IN THE MIDDLE OF PEORIA PARK.
AS THE POLICE LEAD HIM AWAY, HE SCREAMS AT THE TOP OF HIS LUNGS ABOUT THE WAR BENEATH THEIR FEET, THE BRAVE WARRIORS THEY'RE SO CARELESSLY TRAMPLING.
HE SCREAMS ALL THE WAY TO THE ASYLUM.
POOMF!

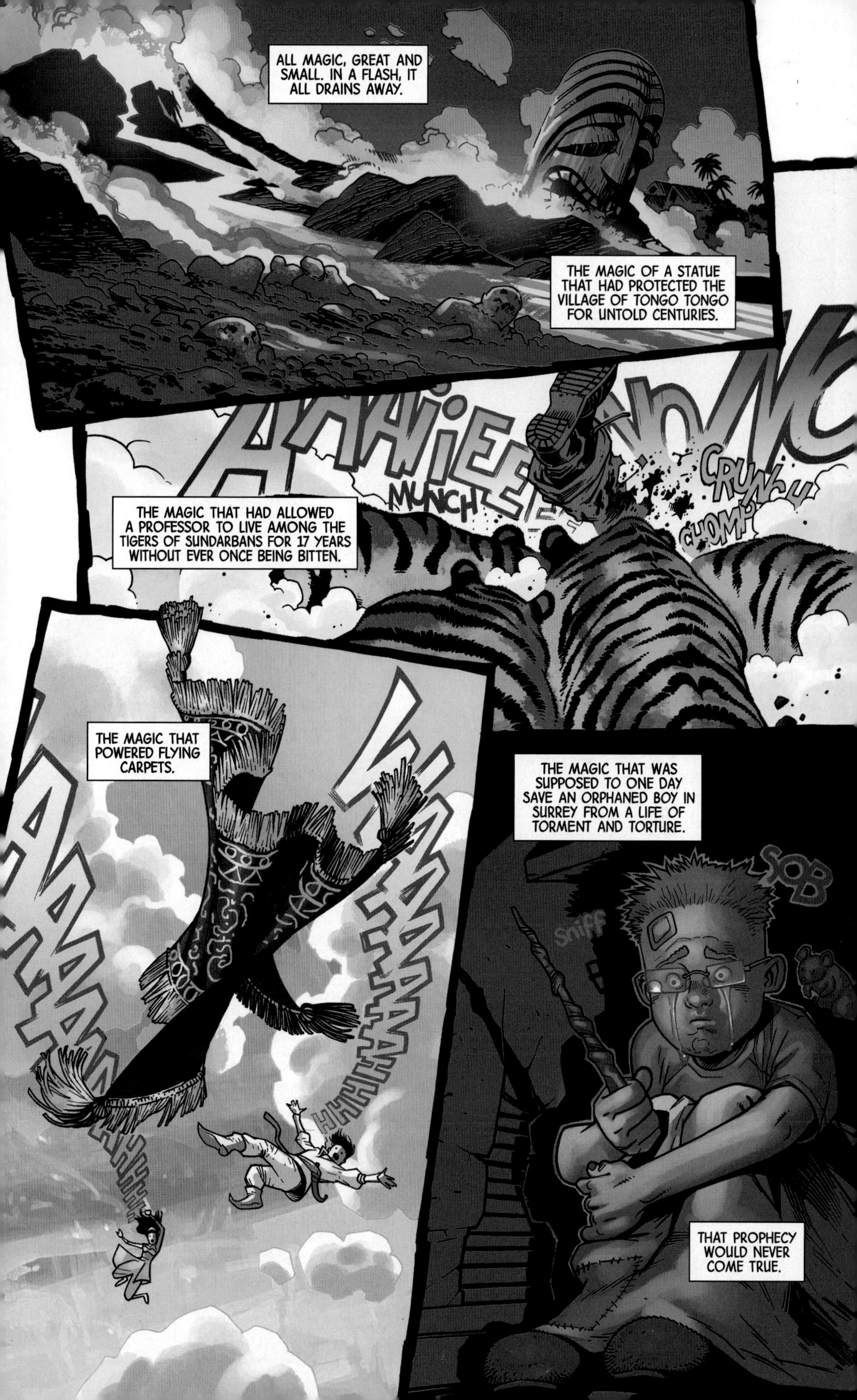
ALL MAGIC, GREAT AND SMALL. IN A FLASH, IT ALL DRAINS AWAY.
THE MAGIC OF A STATUE THAT HAD PROTECTED THE VILLAGE OF TONGO TONGO FOR UNTOLD CENTURIES.
THE MAGIC THAT HAD ALLOWED A PROFESSOR TO LIVE AMONG THE TIGERS OF SUNDARBANS FOR 17 YEARS WITHOUT EVER ONCE BEING BITTEN.
MUNCH
CRUNCH
CHOMP
THE MAGIC THAT POWERED FLYING CARPETS.
THE MAGIC THAT WAS SUPPOSED TO ONE DAY SAVE AN ORPHANED BOY IN SURREY FROM A LIFE OF TORMENT AND TORTURE.
SOB
SNIFF
THAT PROPHECY WOULD NEVER COME TRUE.

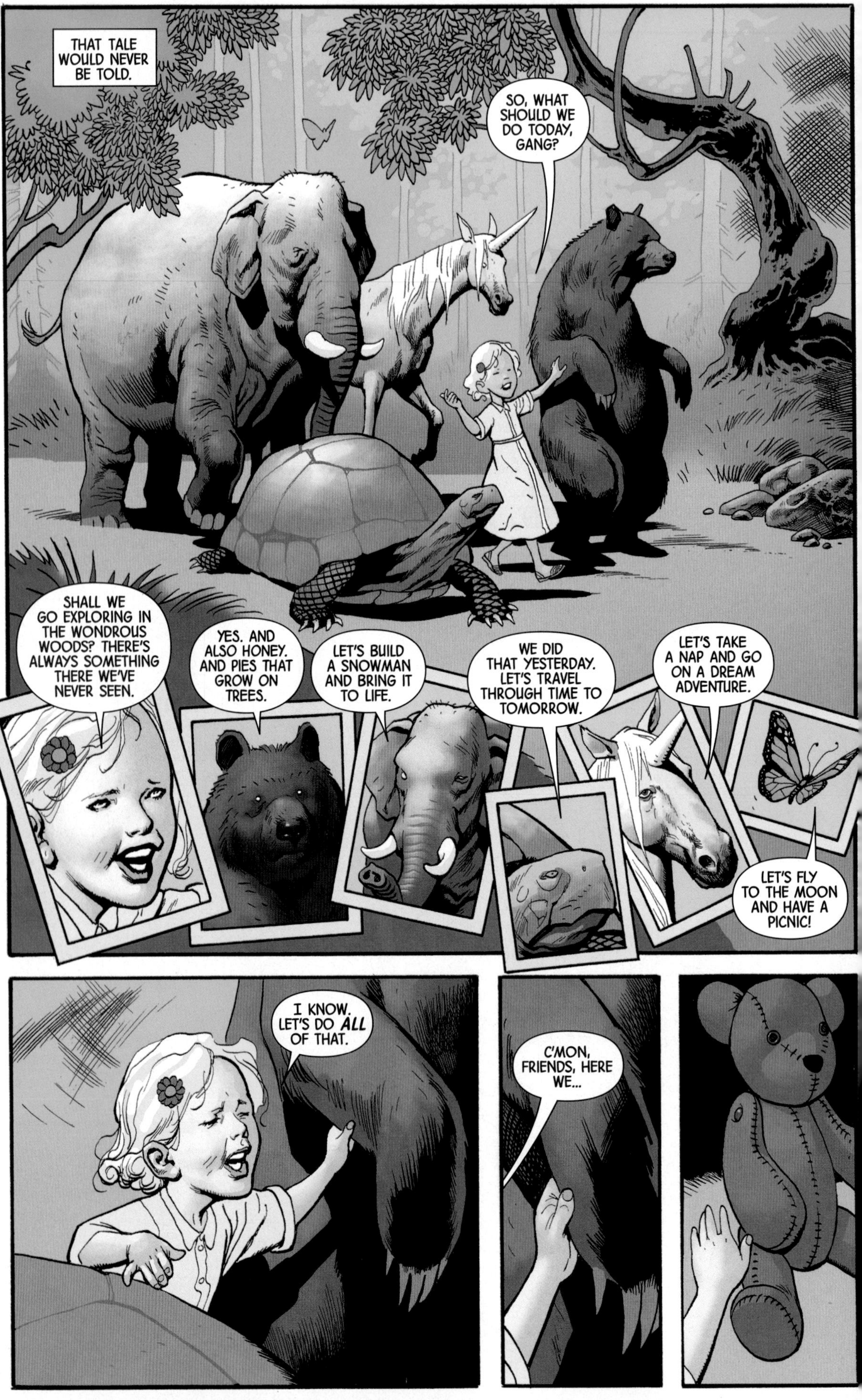

THAT TALE WOULD NEVER BE TOLD.
SO, WHAT SHOULD WE DO TODAY, GANG?
SHALL WE GO EXPLORING IN THE WONDROUS WOODS? THERE'S ALWAYS SOMETHING THERE WE'VE NEVER SEEN.
YES. AND ALSO HONEY. AND PIES THAT GROW ON TREES.
LET'S BUILD A SNOWMAN AND BRING IT TO LIFE.
WE DID THAT YESTERDAY. LET'S TRAVEL THROUGH TIME TO TOMORROW.
LET'S TAKE A NAP AND GO ON A DREAM ADVENTURE.
LET'S FLY TO THE MOON AND HAVE A PICNIC!
I KNOW. LET'S DO *ALL* OF THAT.
C'MON, FRIENDS, HERE WE...

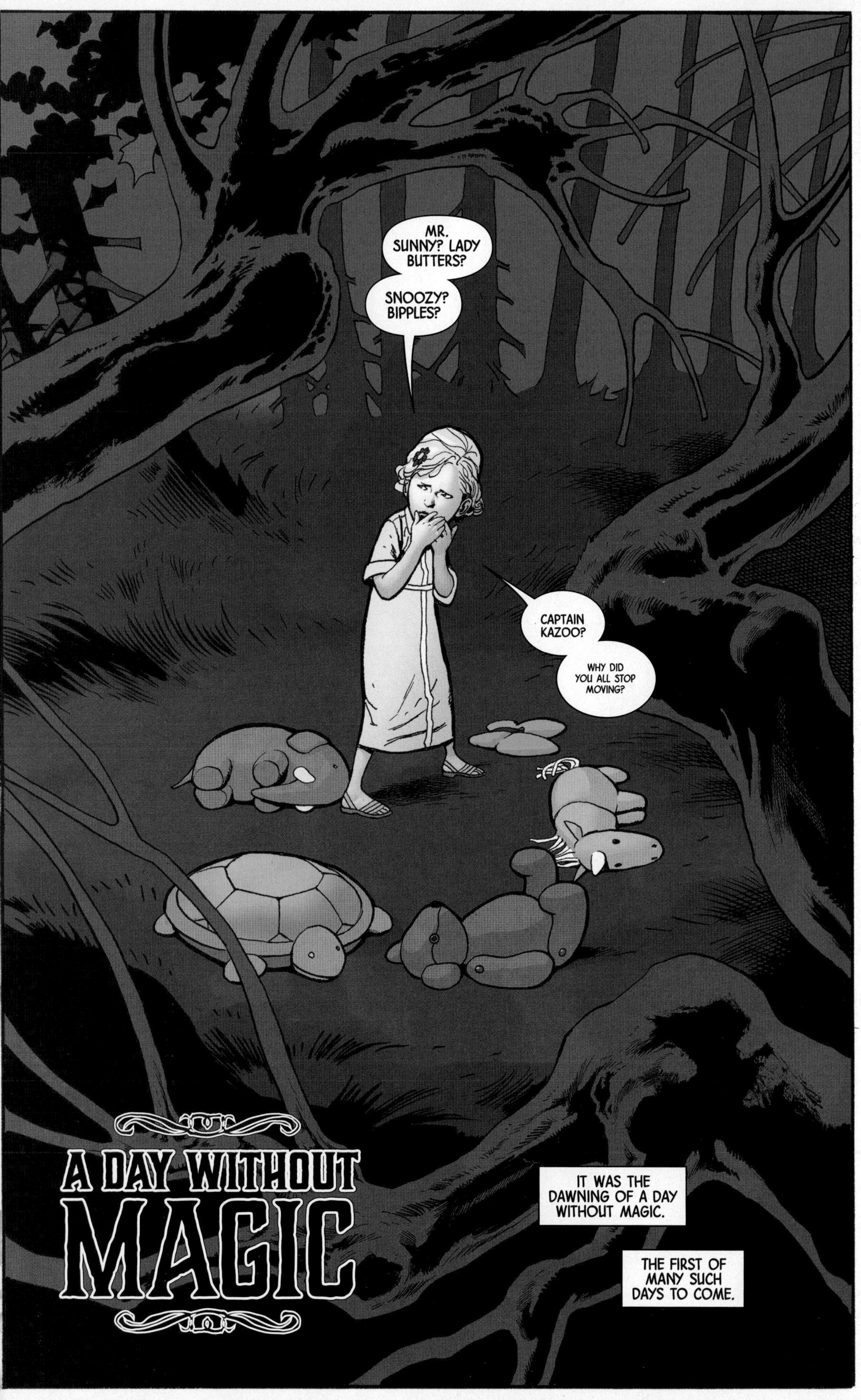
MR. SUNNY? LADY BUTTERS?
SNOOZY? BIPPLES?
CAPTAIN KAZOO?
WHY DID YOU ALL STOP MOVING?
A DAY WITHOUT MAGIC
IT WAS THE DAWNING OF A DAY WITHOUT MAGIC.
THE FIRST OF MANY SUCH DAYS TO COME.

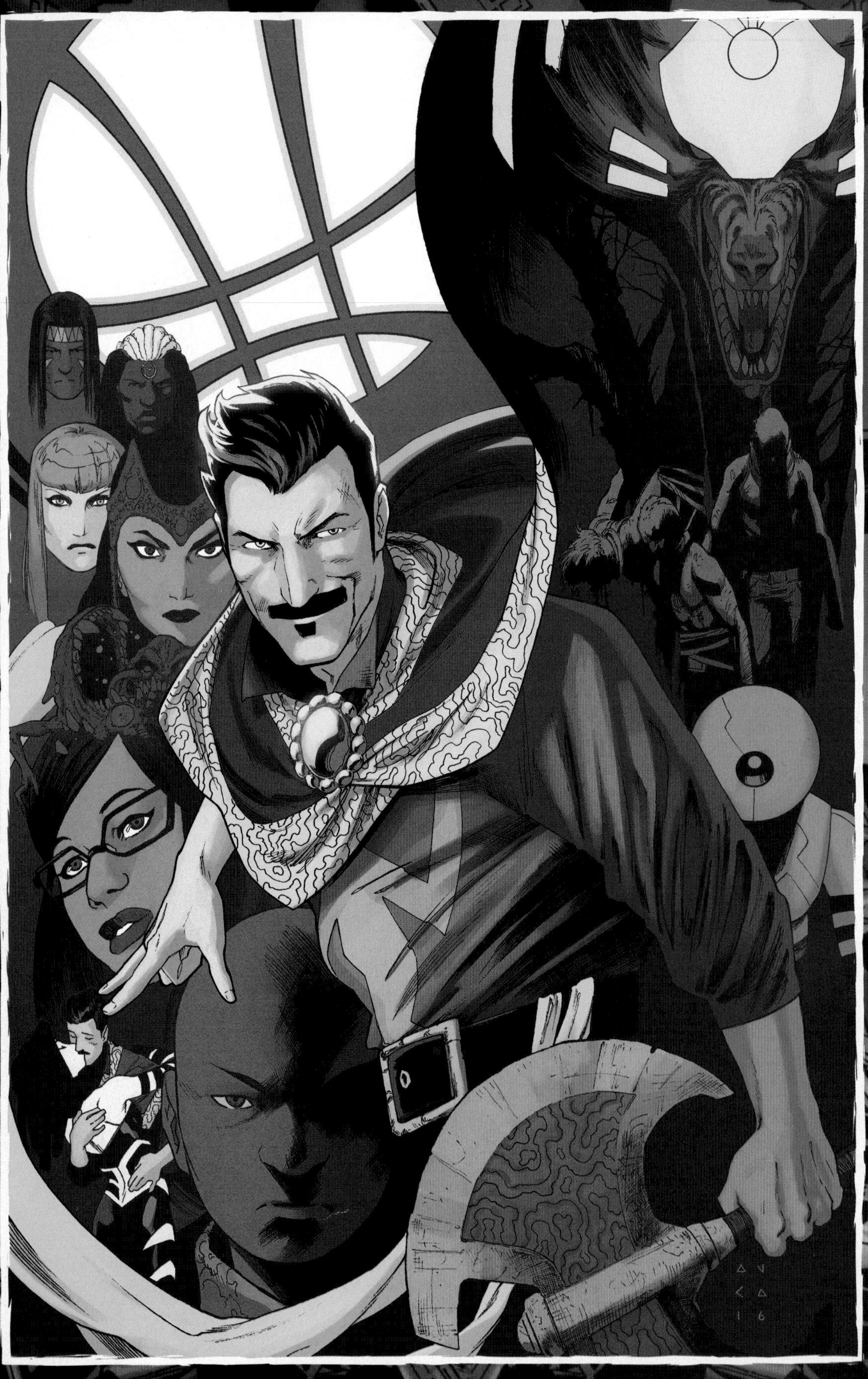

#6 STORY THUS FAR VARIANT BY **KRIS ANKA**

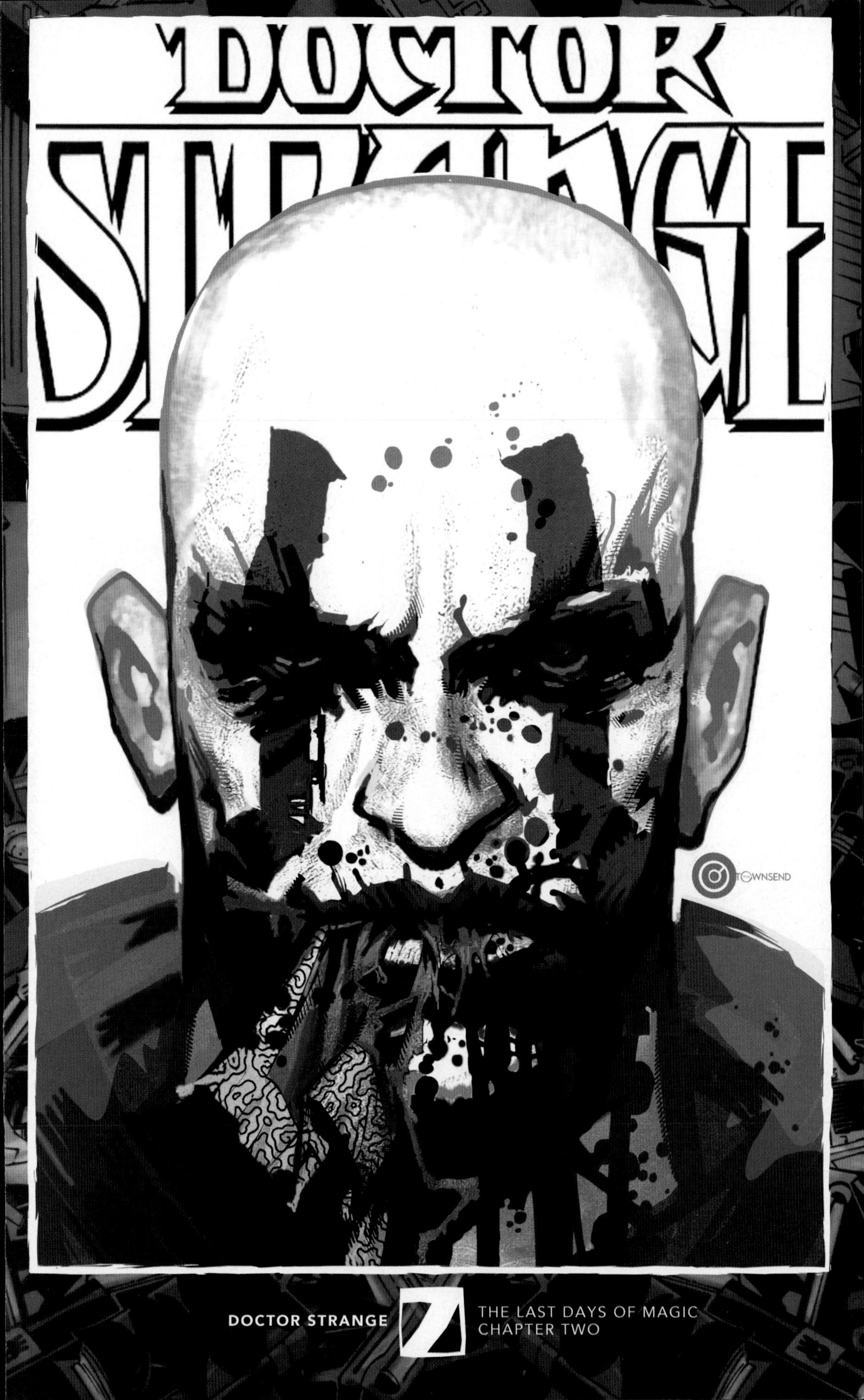
DOCTOR
STRANGE
TOWNSEND

DOCTOR STRANGE 7 THE LAST DAYS OF MAGIC
CHAPTER TWO

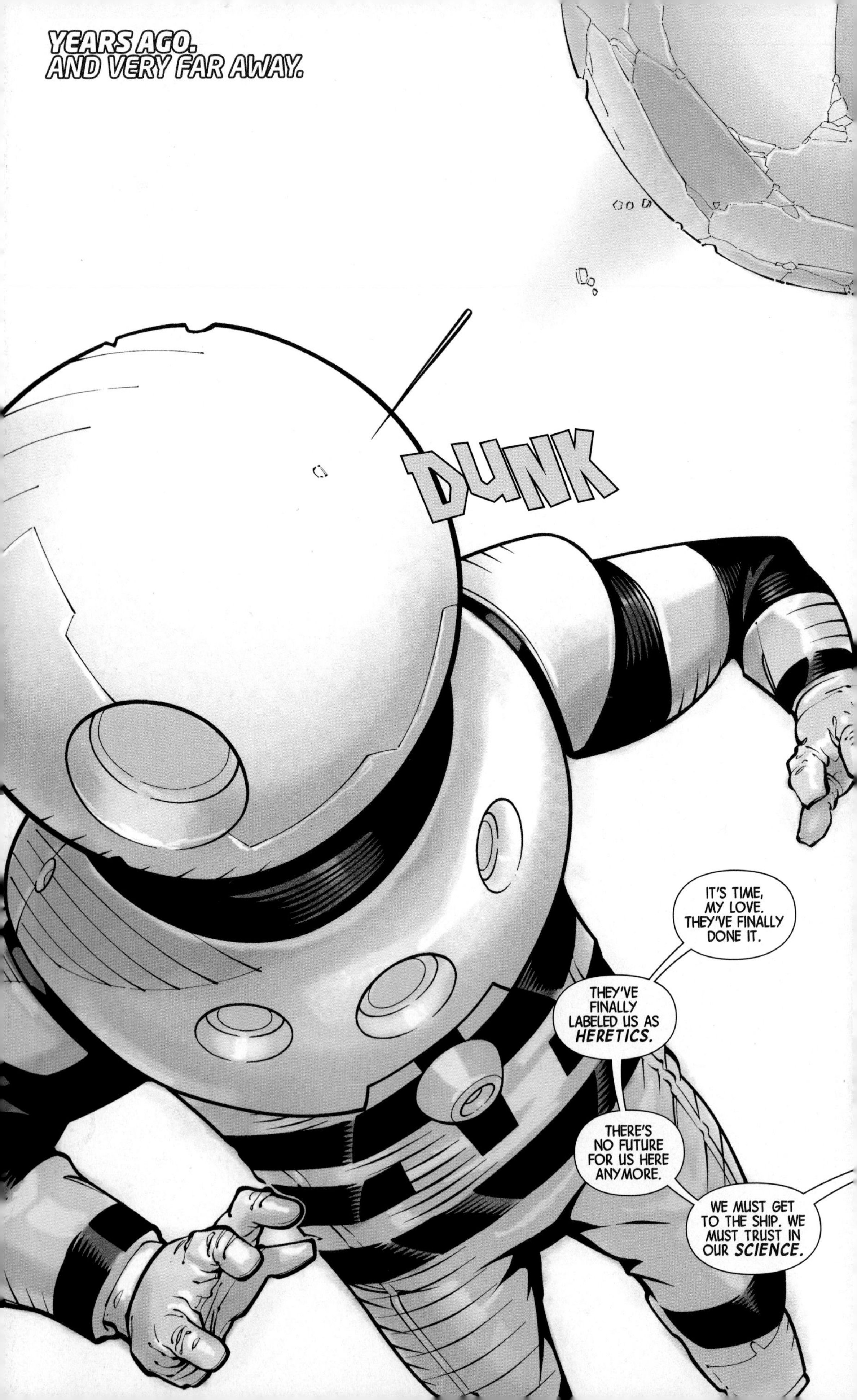
YEARS AGO.
AND VERY FAR AWAY.
DUNK
IT'S TIME, MY LOVE. THEY'VE FINALLY DONE IT.
THEY'VE FINALLY LABELED US AS HERETICS.
THERE'S NO FUTURE FOR US HERE ANYMORE.
WE MUST GET TO THE SHIP. WE MUST TRUST IN OUR SCIENCE.

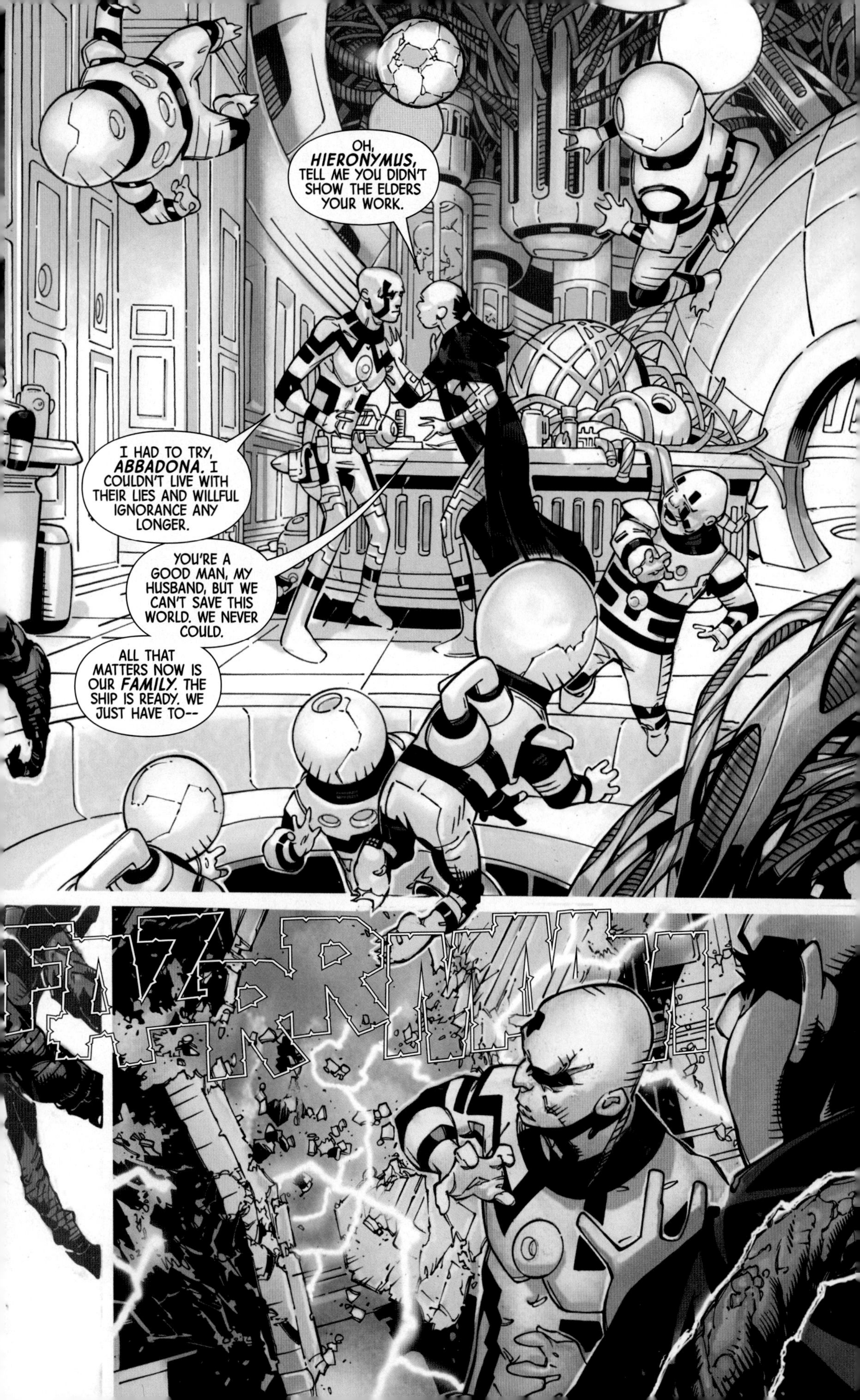
OH, *HIERONYMUS,* TELL ME YOU DIDN'T SHOW THE ELDERS YOUR WORK.
I HAD TO TRY, *ABBADONA.* I COULDN'T LIVE WITH THEIR LIES AND WILLFUL IGNORANCE ANY LONGER.
YOU'RE A GOOD MAN, MY HUSBAND, BUT WE CAN'T SAVE THIS WORLD. WE NEVER COULD.
ALL THAT MATTERS NOW IS OUR *FAMILY*. THE SHIP IS READY. WE JUST HAVE TO--

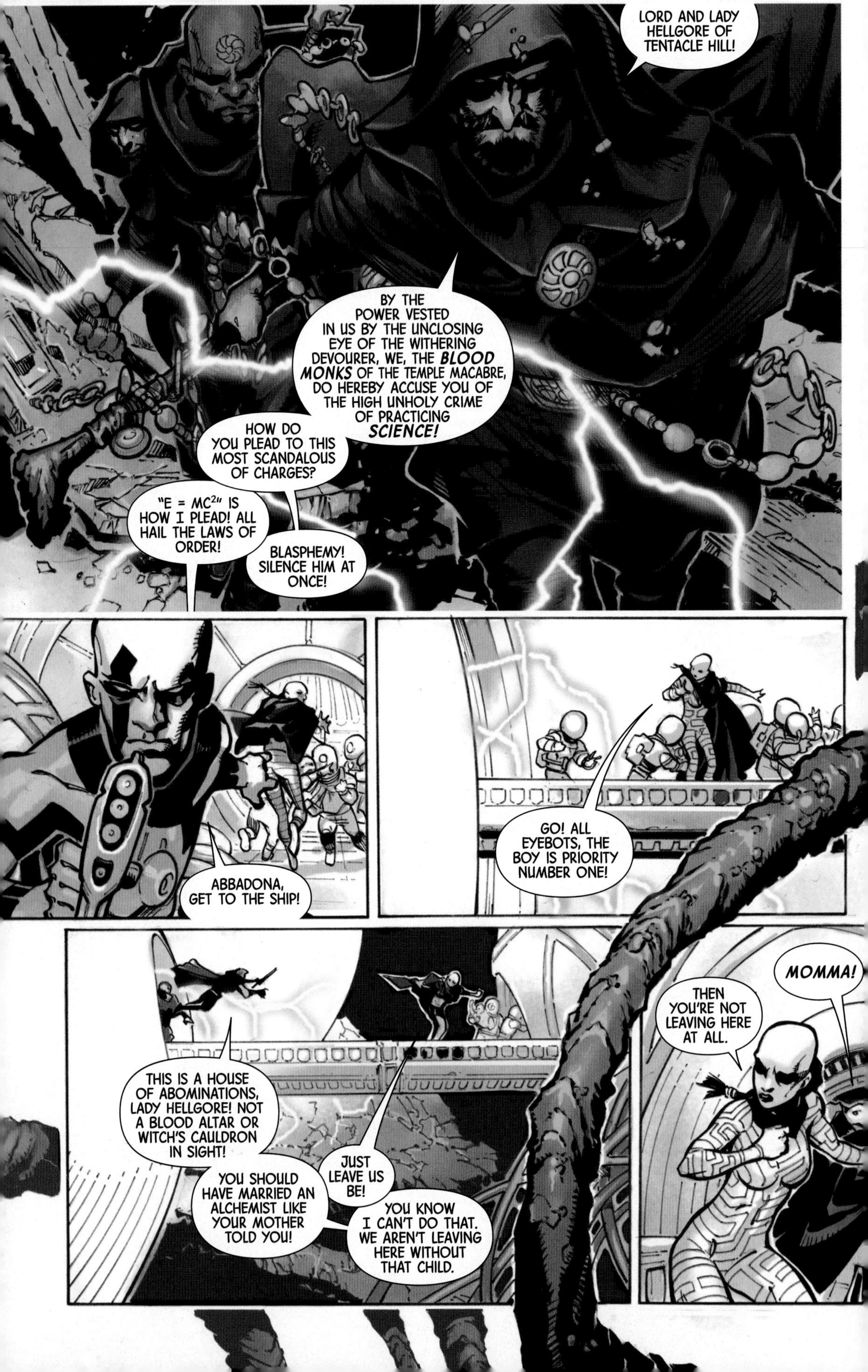
LORD AND LADY HELLGORE OF TENTACLE HILL!
BY THE POWER VESTED IN US BY THE UNCLOSING EYE OF THE WITHERING DEVOURER, WE, THE BLOOD MONKS OF THE TEMPLE MACABRE, DO HEREBY ACCUSE YOU OF THE HIGH UNHOLY CRIME OF PRACTICING SCIENCE!
HOW DO YOU PLEAD TO THIS MOST SCANDALOUS OF CHARGES?
"E = MC²" IS HOW I PLEAD! ALL HAIL THE LAWS OF ORDER!
BLASPHEMY! SILENCE HIM AT ONCE!
ABBADONA, GET TO THE SHIP!
GO! ALL EYEBOTS, THE BOY IS PRIORITY NUMBER ONE!
THIS IS A HOUSE OF ABOMINATIONS, LADY HELLGORE! NOT A BLOOD ALTAR OR WITCH'S CAULDRON IN SIGHT!
YOU SHOULD HAVE MARRIED AN ALCHEMIST LIKE YOUR MOTHER TOLD YOU!
JUST LEAVE US BE!
YOU KNOW I CAN'T DO THAT. WE AREN'T LEAVING HERE WITHOUT THAT CHILD.
THEN YOU'RE NOT LEAVING HERE AT ALL.
MOMMA!

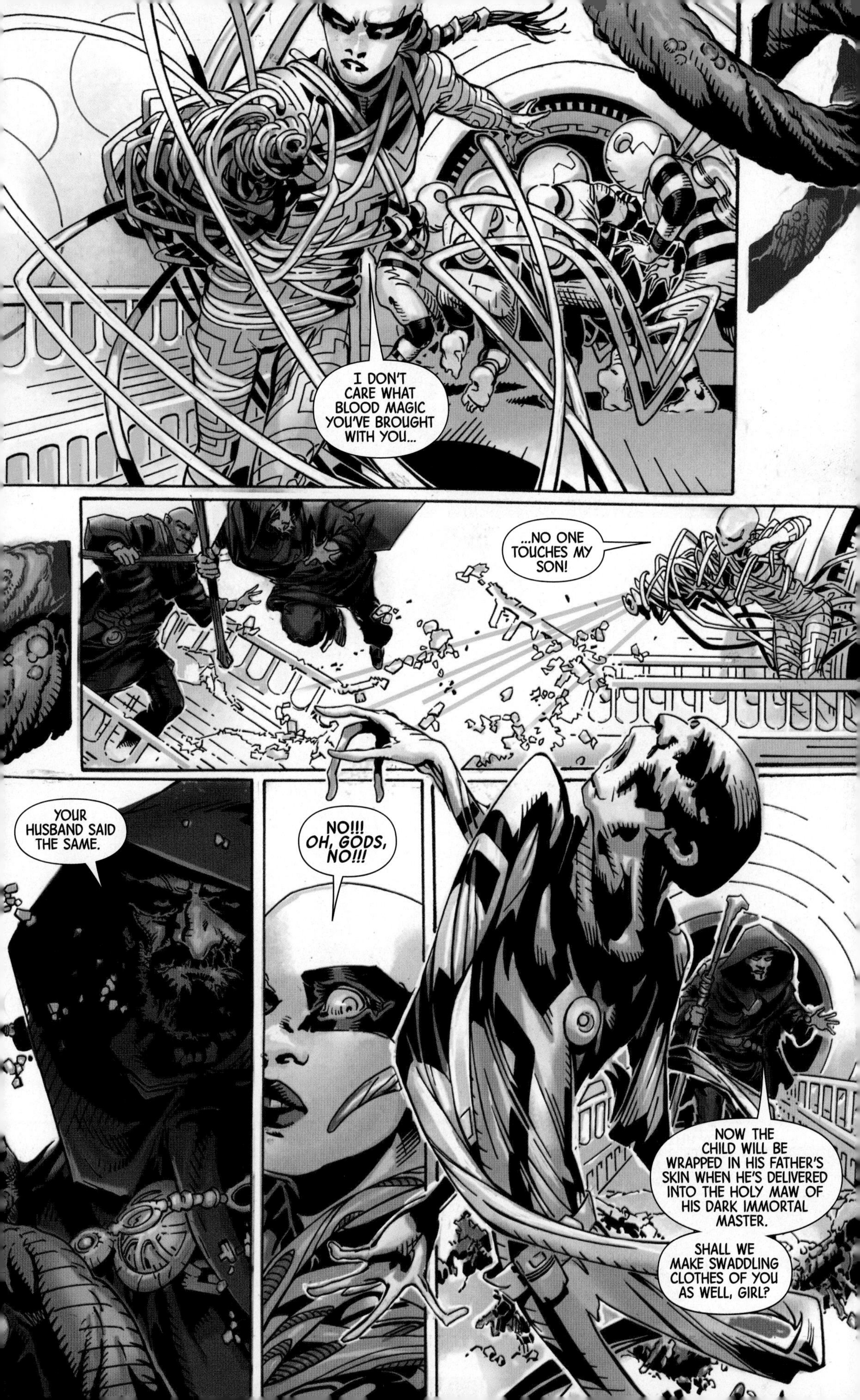
I DON'T CARE WHAT BLOOD MAGIC YOU'VE BROUGHT WITH YOU...
...NO ONE TOUCHES MY SON!
YOUR HUSBAND SAID THE SAME.
NO!!! OH, GODS, NO!!!
NOW THE CHILD WILL BE WRAPPED IN HIS FATHER'S SKIN WHEN HE'S DELIVERED INTO THE HOLY MAW OF HIS DARK IMMORTAL MASTER.
SHALL WE MAKE SWADDLING CLOTHES OF YOU AS WELL, GIRL?

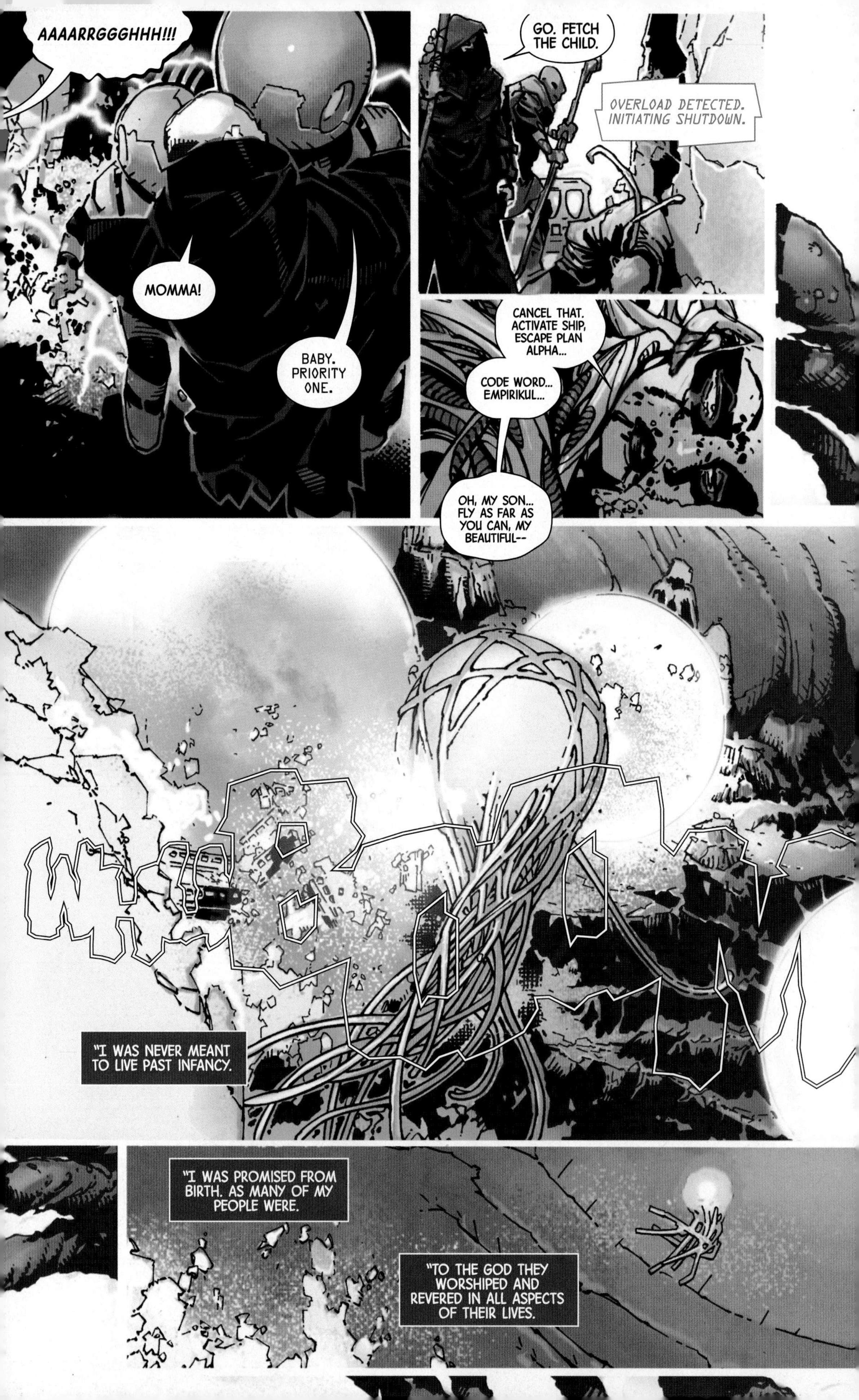
AAAARRGGGHHH!!!
MOMMA!
BABY. PRIORITY ONE.
GO. FETCH THE CHILD.
OVERLOAD DETECTED. INITIATING SHUTDOWN.
CANCEL THAT. ACTIVATE SHIP, ESCAPE PLAN ALPHA...
CODE WORD... EMPIRIKUL...
OH, MY SON... FLY AS FAR AS YOU CAN, MY BEAUTIFUL--
"I WAS NEVER MEANT TO LIVE PAST INFANCY.
"I WAS PROMISED FROM BIRTH. AS MANY OF MY PEOPLE WERE.
"TO THE GOD THEY WORSHIPED AND REVERED IN ALL ASPECTS OF THEIR LIVES.

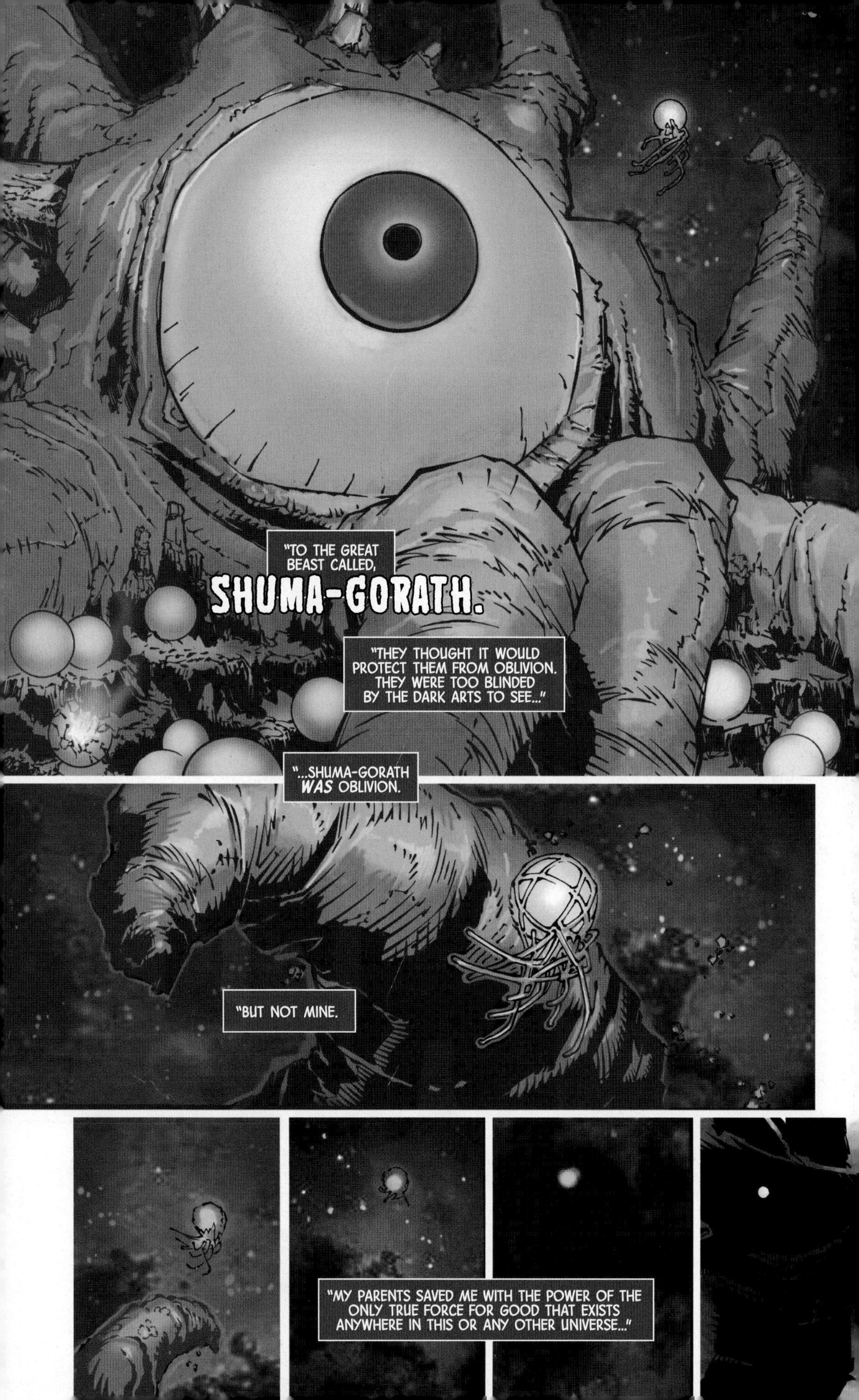
"TO THE GREAT BEAST CALLED,
SHUMA-GORATH.
"THEY THOUGHT IT WOULD PROTECT THEM FROM OBLIVION. THEY WERE TOO BLINDED BY THE DARK ARTS TO SEE..."
"...SHUMA-GORATH *WAS* OBLIVION.
"BUT NOT MINE.
"MY PARENTS SAVED ME WITH THE POWER OF THE ONLY TRUE FORCE FOR GOOD THAT EXISTS ANYWHERE IN THIS OR ANY OTHER UNIVERSE..."

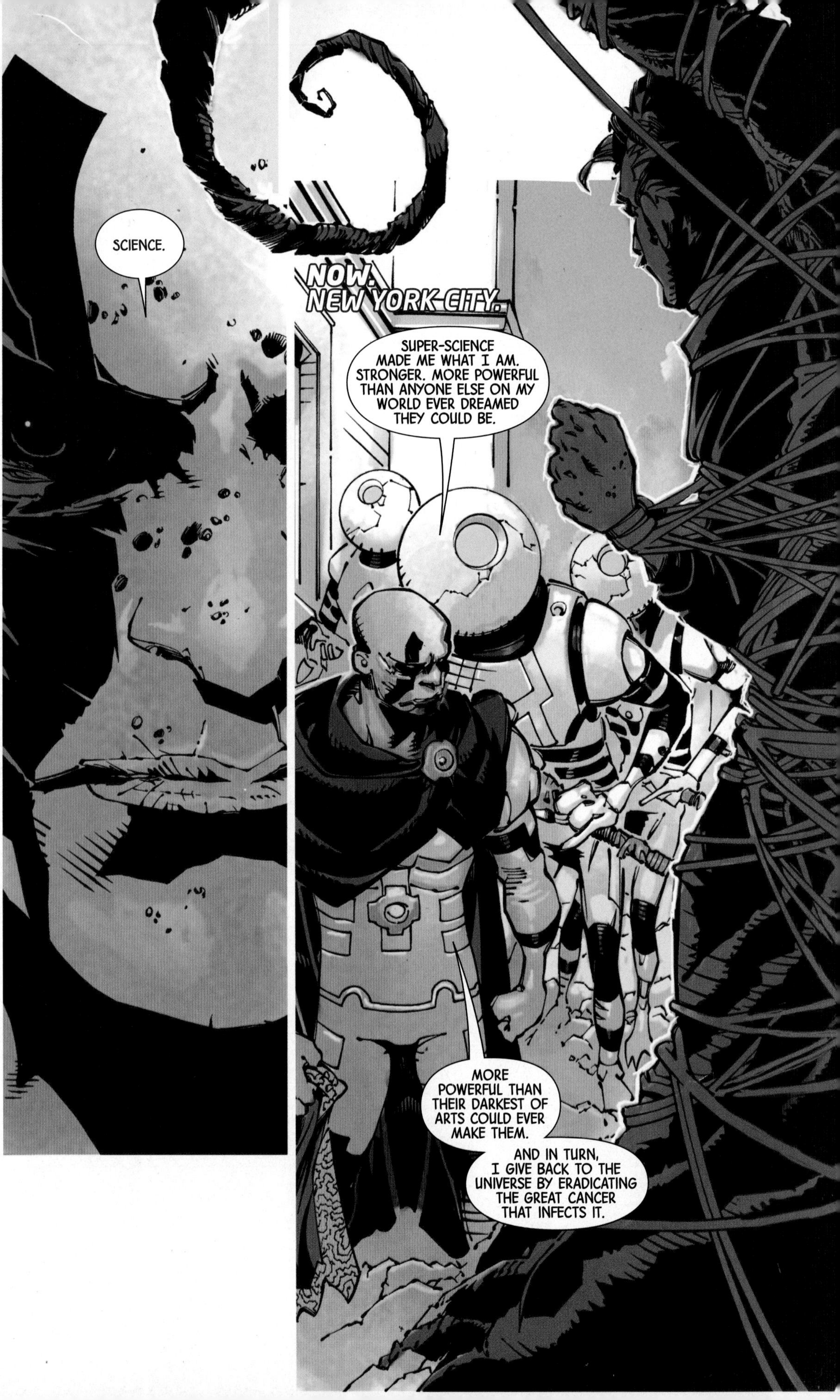
SCIENCE.
NOW. NEW YORK CITY.
SUPER-SCIENCE MADE ME WHAT I AM. STRONGER. MORE POWERFUL THAN ANYONE ELSE ON MY WORLD EVER DREAMED THEY COULD BE.
MORE POWERFUL THAN THEIR DARKEST OF ARTS COULD EVER MAKE THEM.
AND IN TURN, I GIVE BACK TO THE UNIVERSE BY ERADICATING THE GREAT CANCER THAT INFECTS IT.

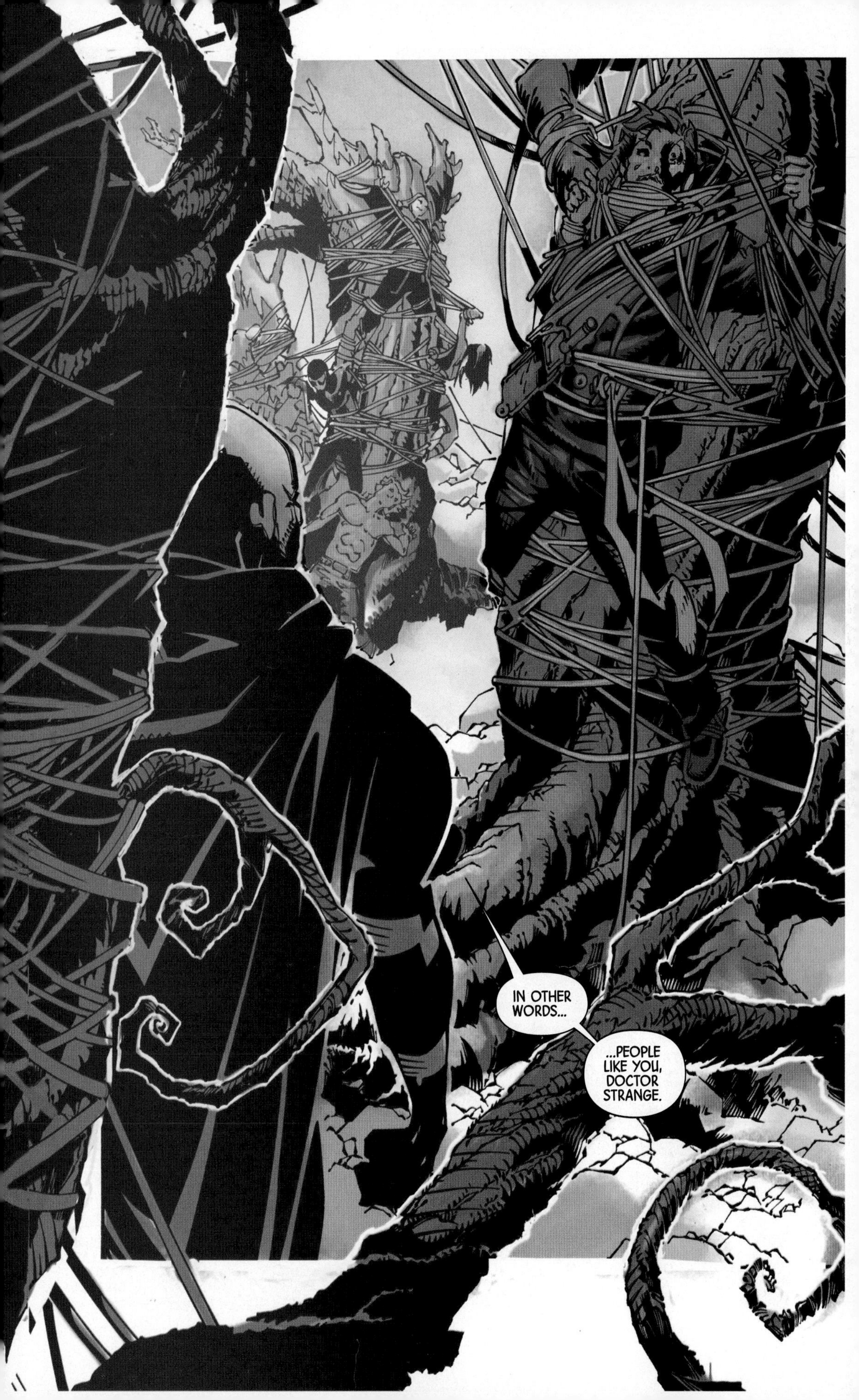
IN OTHER WORDS...
...PEOPLE LIKE YOU, DOCTOR STRANGE.

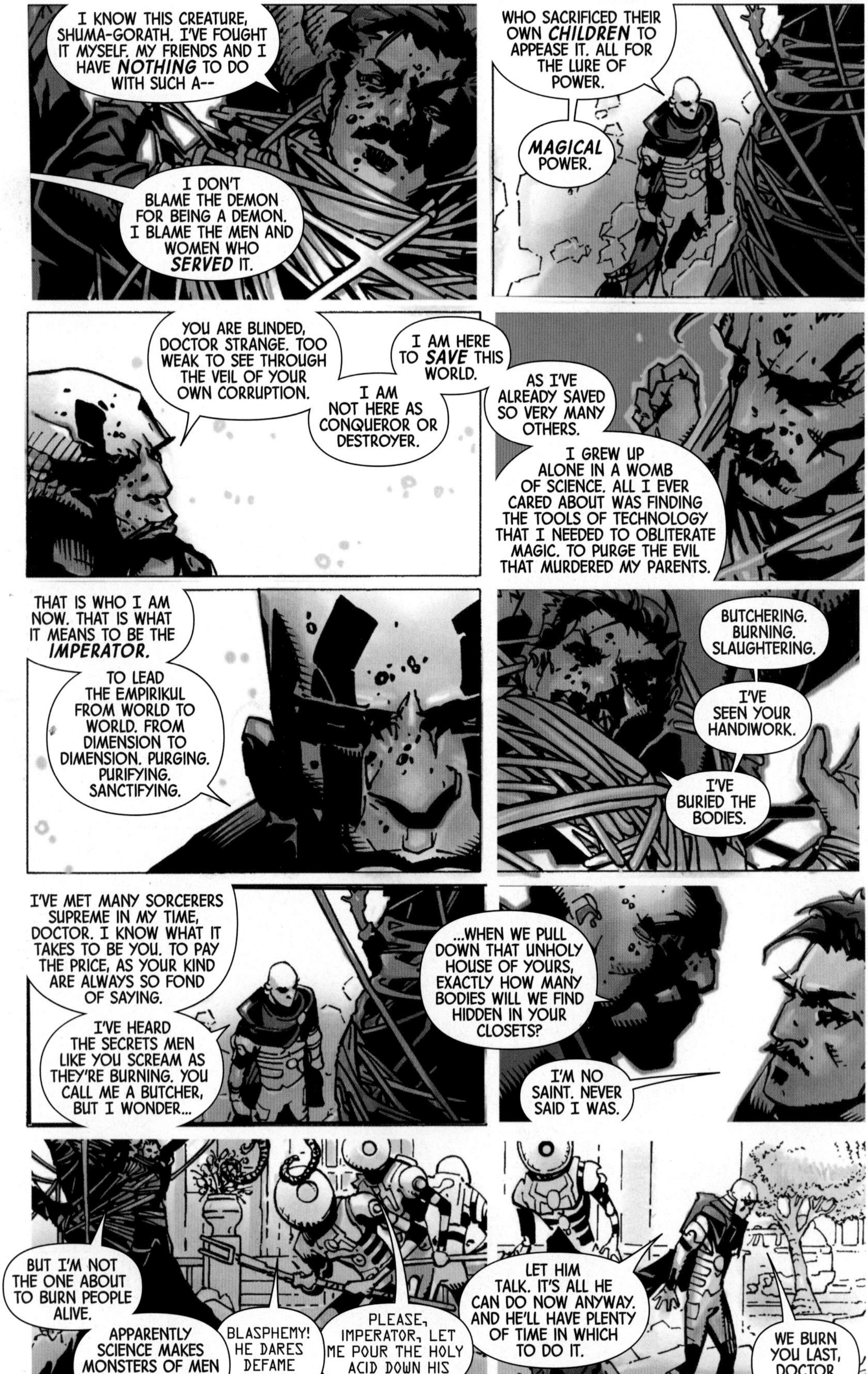
I KNOW THIS CREATURE, SHUMA-GORATH. I'VE FOUGHT IT MYSELF. MY FRIENDS AND I HAVE NOTHING TO DO WITH SUCH A--
I DON'T BLAME THE DEMON FOR BEING A DEMON. I BLAME THE MEN AND WOMEN WHO SERVED IT.
WHO SACRIFICED THEIR OWN CHILDREN TO APPEASE IT. ALL FOR THE LURE OF POWER.
MAGICAL POWER.
YOU ARE BLINDED, DOCTOR STRANGE. TOO WEAK TO SEE THROUGH THE VEIL OF YOUR OWN CORRUPTION.
I AM NOT HERE AS CONQUEROR OR DESTROYER.
I AM HERE TO SAVE THIS WORLD.
AS I'VE ALREADY SAVED SO VERY MANY OTHERS.
I GREW UP ALONE IN A WOMB OF SCIENCE. ALL I EVER CARED ABOUT WAS FINDING THE TOOLS OF TECHNOLOGY THAT I NEEDED TO OBLITERATE MAGIC. TO PURGE THE EVIL THAT MURDERED MY PARENTS.
THAT IS WHO I AM NOW. THAT IS WHAT IT MEANS TO BE THE IMPERATOR.
TO LEAD THE EMPIRIKUL FROM WORLD TO WORLD. FROM DIMENSION TO DIMENSION. PURGING. PURIFYING. SANCTIFYING.
BUTCHERING. BURNING. SLAUGHTERING.
I'VE SEEN YOUR HANDIWORK.
I'VE BURIED THE BODIES.
I'VE MET MANY SORCERERS SUPREME IN MY TIME, DOCTOR. I KNOW WHAT IT TAKES TO BE YOU. TO PAY THE PRICE, AS YOUR KIND ARE ALWAYS SO FOND OF SAYING.
I'VE HEARD THE SECRETS MEN LIKE YOU SCREAM AS THEY'RE BURNING. YOU CALL ME A BUTCHER, BUT I WONDER...
...WHEN WE PULL DOWN THAT UNHOLY HOUSE OF YOURS, EXACTLY HOW MANY BODIES WILL WE FIND HIDDEN IN YOUR CLOSETS?
I'M NO SAINT. NEVER SAID I WAS.
BUT I'M NOT THE ONE ABOUT TO BURN PEOPLE ALIVE.
APPARENTLY SCIENCE MAKES MONSTERS OF MEN JUST AS EASILY AS MAGIC.
BLASPHEMY! HE DARES DEFAME SCIENCE!
PLEASE, IMPERATOR, LET ME POUR THE HOLY ACID DOWN HIS THROAT!
LET HIM TALK. IT'S ALL HE CAN DO NOW ANYWAY. AND HE'LL HAVE PLENTY OF TIME IN WHICH TO DO IT.
WE BURN YOU LAST, DOCTOR STRANGE.

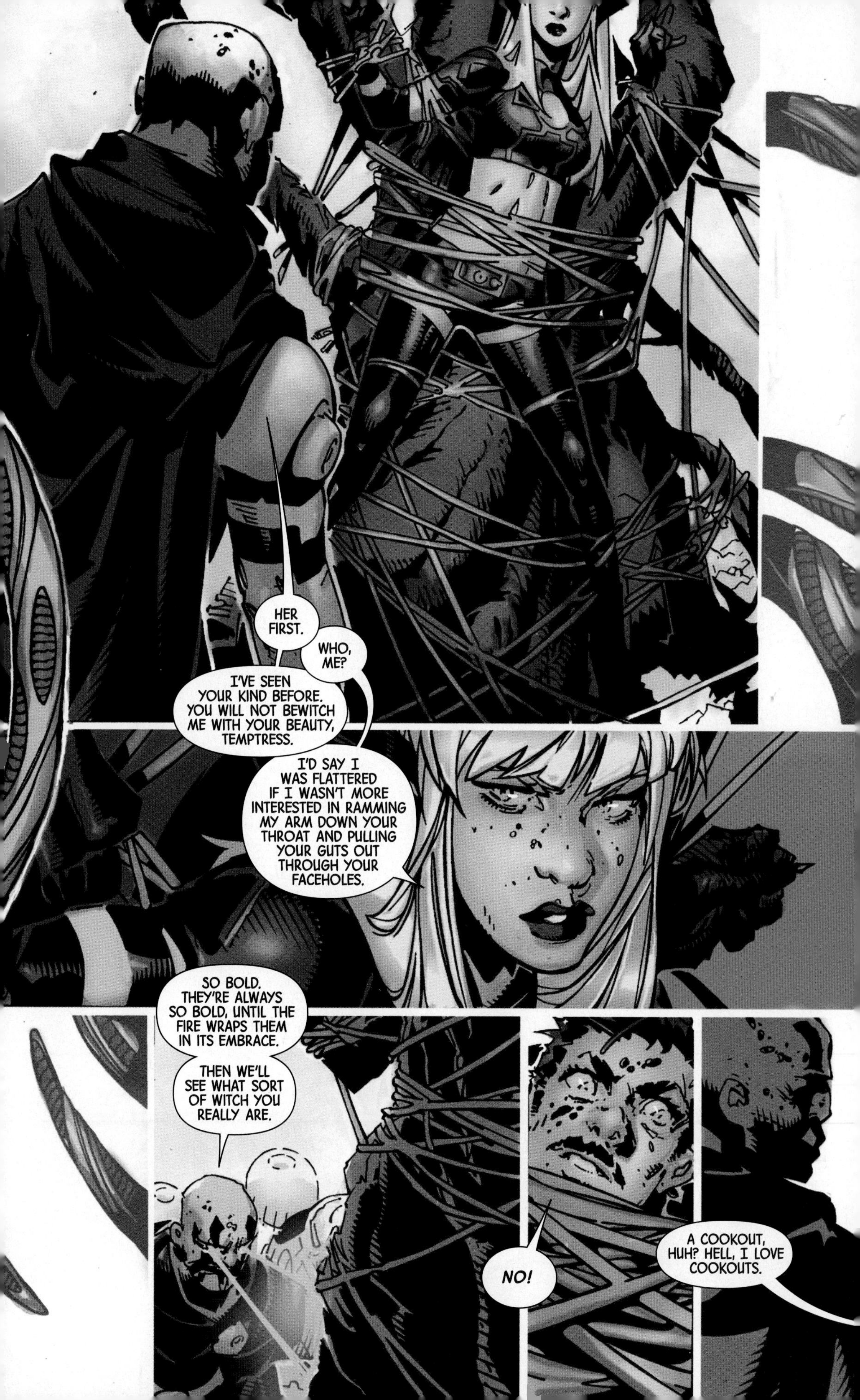
HER FIRST.
WHO, ME?
I'VE SEEN YOUR KIND BEFORE. YOU WILL NOT BEWITCH ME WITH YOUR BEAUTY, TEMPTRESS.
I'D SAY I WAS FLATTERED IF I WASN'T MORE INTERESTED IN RAMMING MY ARM DOWN YOUR THROAT AND PULLING YOUR GUTS OUT THROUGH YOUR FACEHOLES.
SO BOLD. THEY'RE ALWAYS SO BOLD, UNTIL THE FIRE WRAPS THEM IN ITS EMBRACE.
THEN WE'LL SEE WHAT SORT OF WITCH YOU REALLY ARE.
NO!
A COOKOUT, HUH? HELL, I LOVE COOKOUTS.

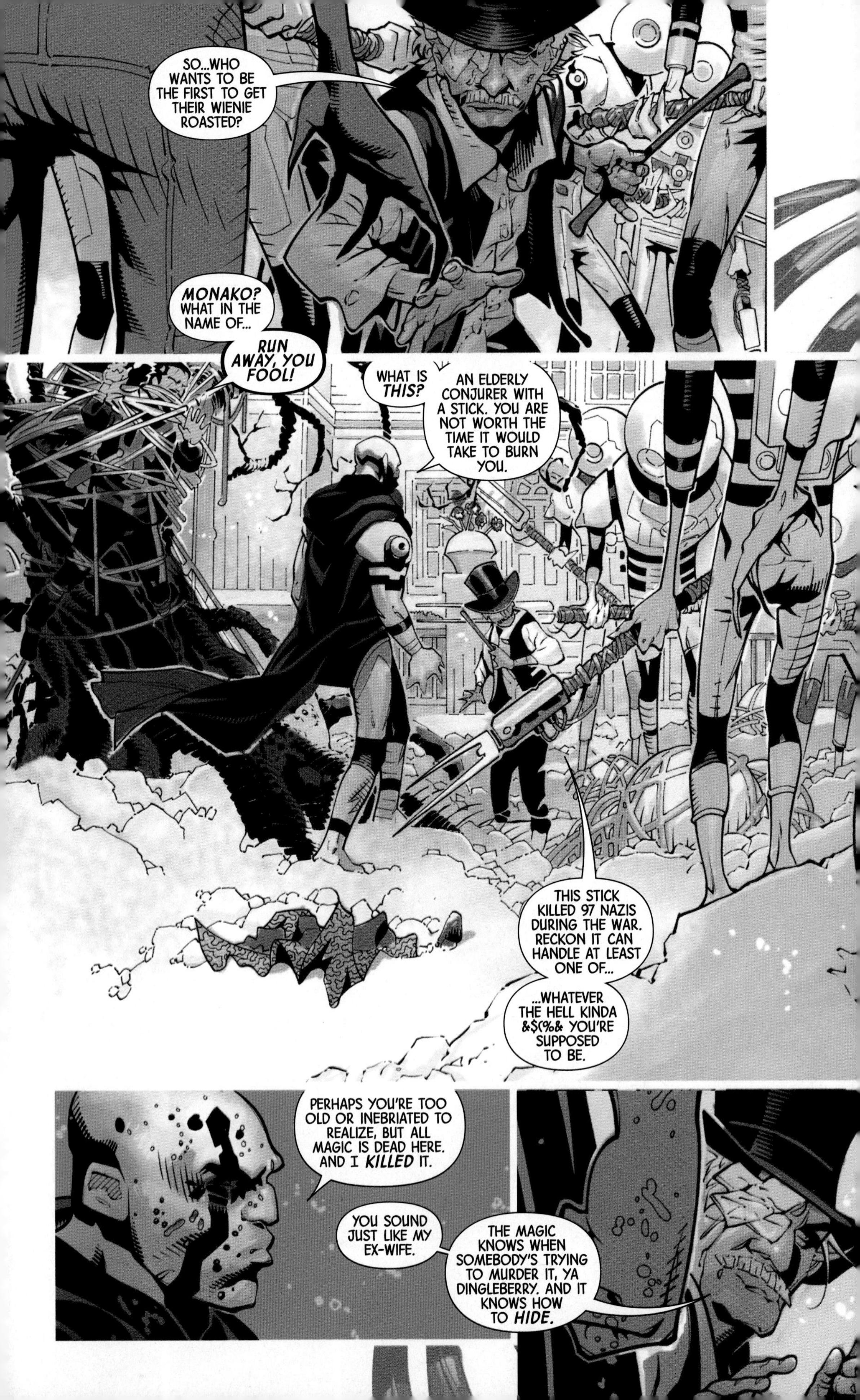
SO...WHO WANTS TO BE THE FIRST TO GET THEIR WIENIE ROASTED?
MONAKO? WHAT IN THE NAME OF...
RUN AWAY, YOU FOOL!
WHAT IS THIS?
AN ELDERLY CONJURER WITH A STICK. YOU ARE NOT WORTH THE TIME IT WOULD TAKE TO BURN YOU.
THIS STICK KILLED 97 NAZIS DURING THE WAR. RECKON IT CAN HANDLE AT LEAST ONE OF...
...WHATEVER THE HELL KINDA &$(%& YOU'RE SUPPOSED TO BE.
PERHAPS YOU'RE TOO OLD OR INEBRIATED TO REALIZE, BUT ALL MAGIC IS DEAD HERE. AND I KILLED IT.
YOU SOUND JUST LIKE MY EX-WIFE.
THE MAGIC KNOWS WHEN SOMEBODY'S TRYING TO MURDER IT, YA DINGLEBERRY. AND IT KNOWS HOW TO HIDE.

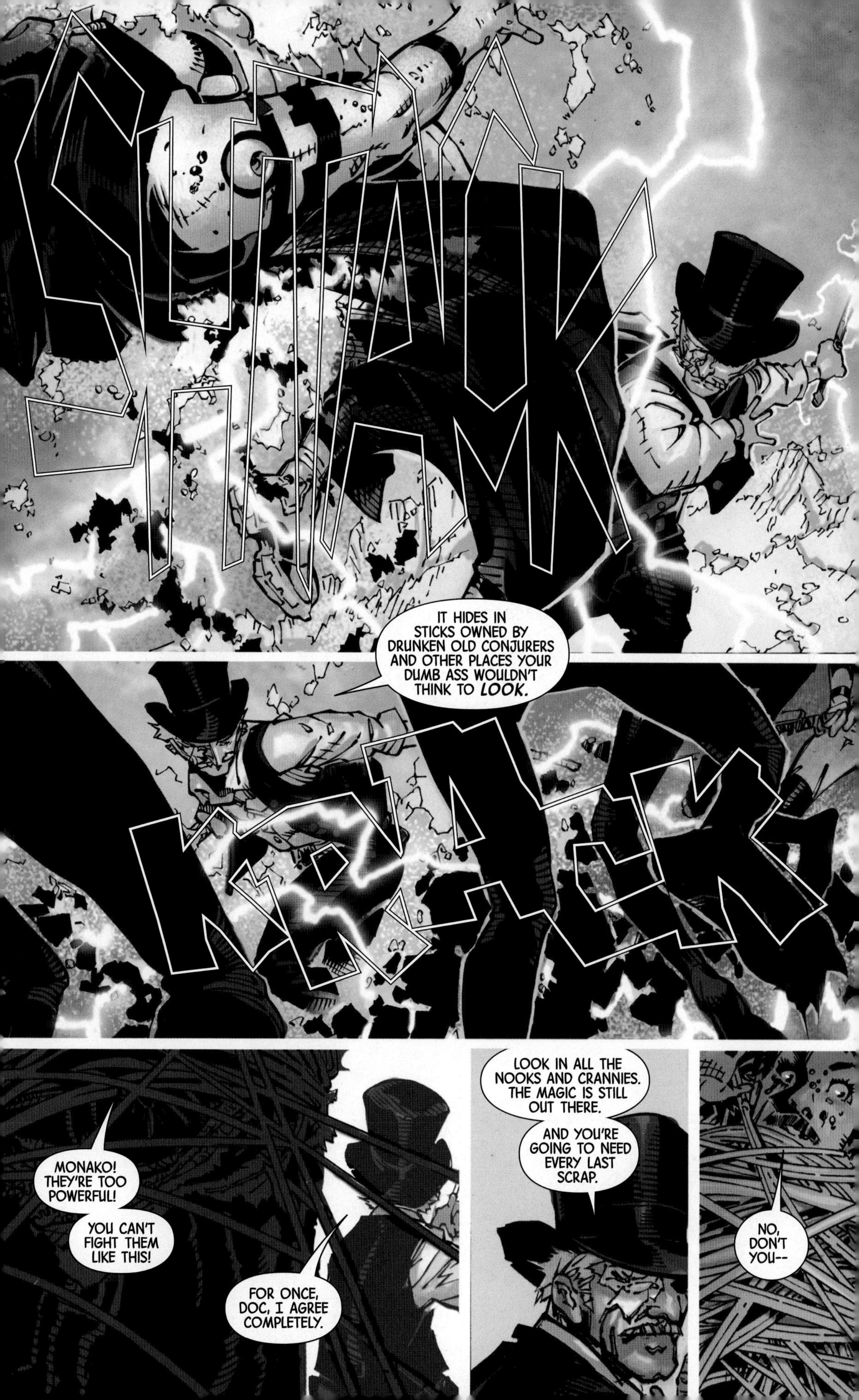
IT HIDES IN STICKS OWNED BY DRUNKEN OLD CONJURERS AND OTHER PLACES YOUR DUMB ASS WOULDN'T THINK TO *LOOK.*
MONAKO! THEY'RE TOO POWERFUL!
YOU CAN'T FIGHT THEM LIKE THIS!
FOR ONCE, DOC, I AGREE COMPLETELY.
LOOK IN ALL THE NOOKS AND CRANNIES. THE MAGIC IS STILL OUT THERE.
AND YOU'RE GOING TO NEED EVERY LAST SCRAP.
NO, DON'T YOU--

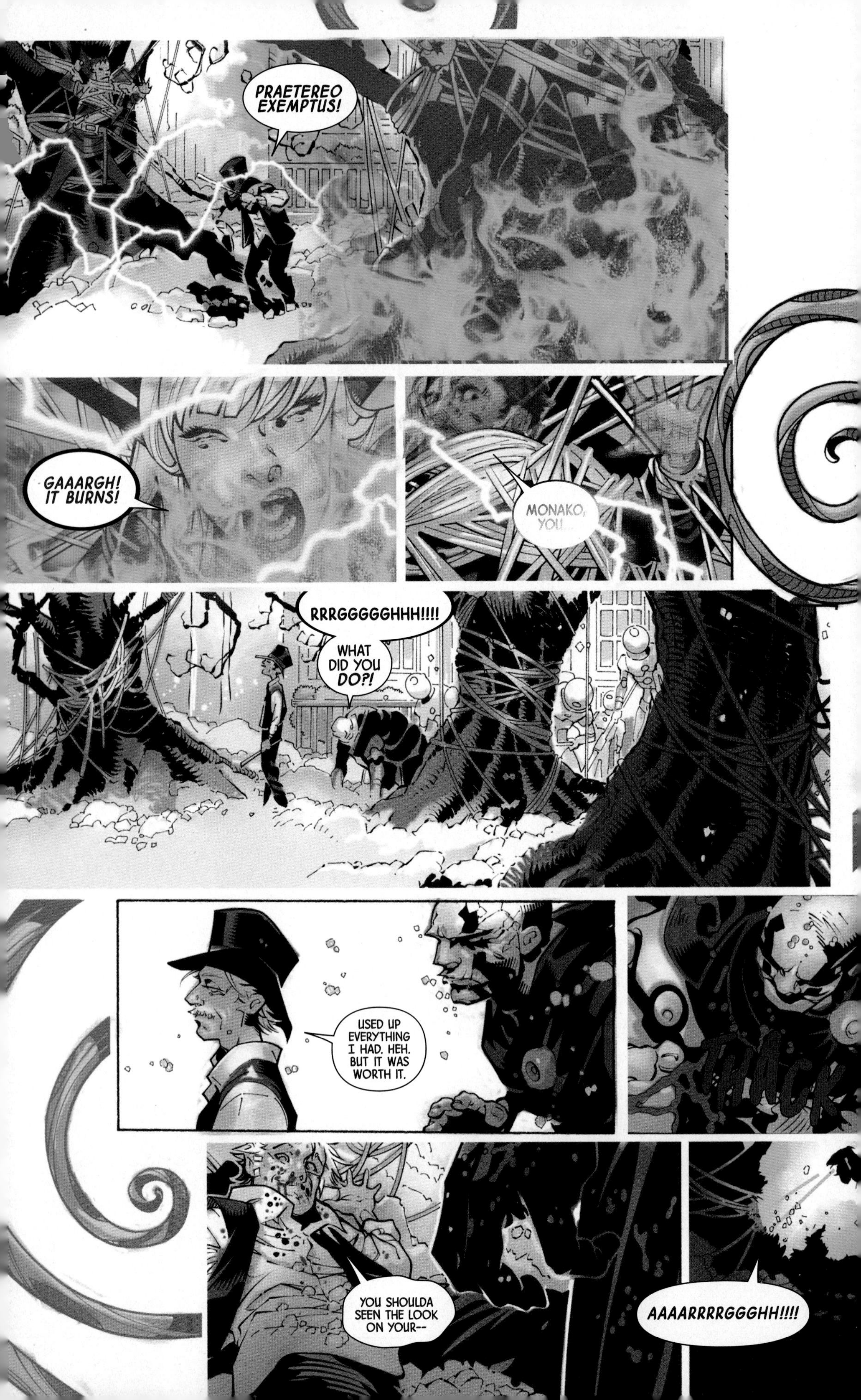
PRAETEREO EXEMPTUS!
GAAARGH! IT BURNS!
MONAKO, YOU...
RRRGGGGGHH!!!!
WHAT DID YOU DO?!
USED UP EVERYTHING I HAD. HEH. BUT IT WAS WORTH IT.
THACK
YOU SHOULDA SEEN THE LOOK ON YOUR--
AAAARRRRGGGHH!!!!

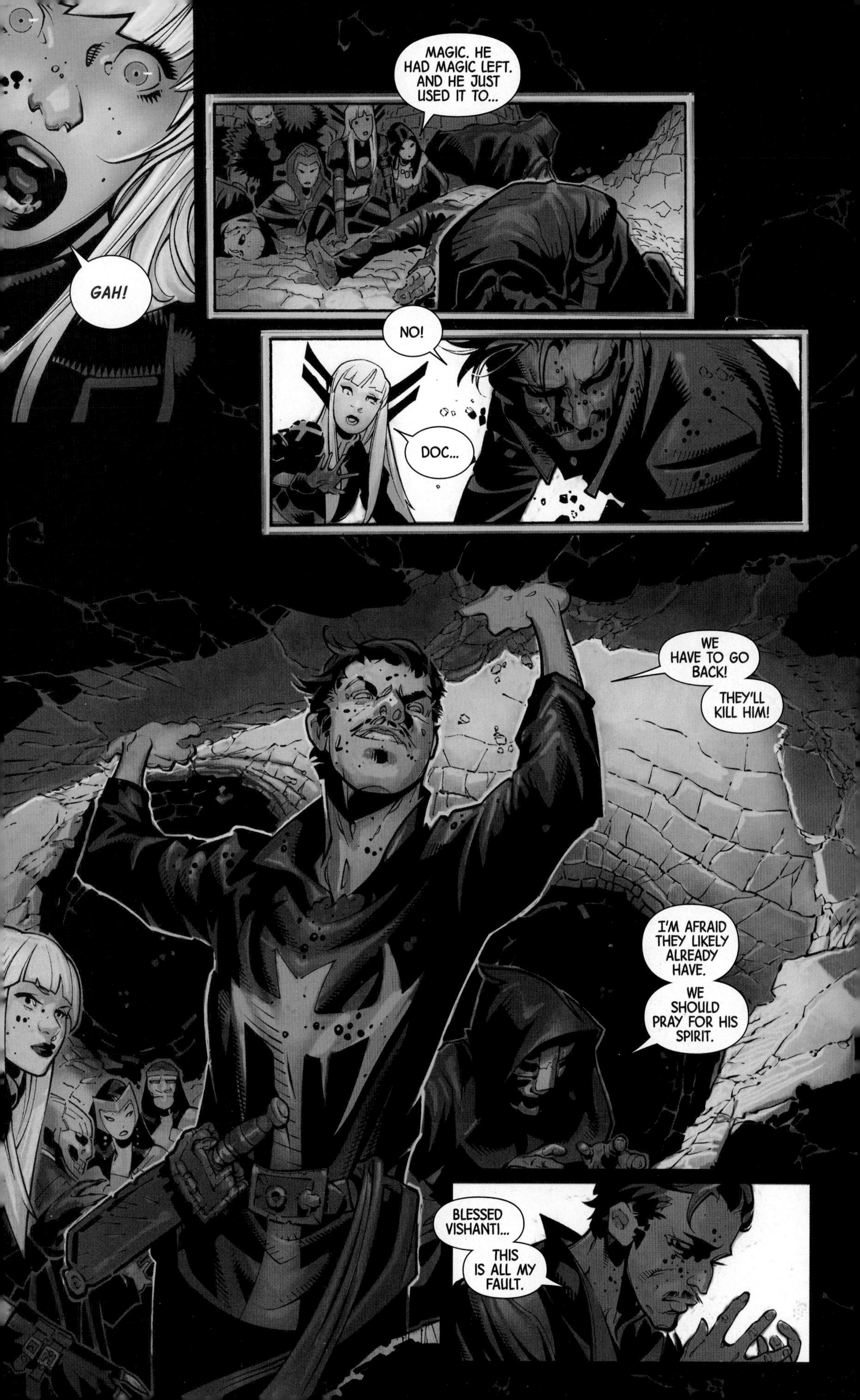
GAH!
MAGIC. HE HAD MAGIC LEFT. AND HE JUST USED IT TO...
NO!
DOC...
WE HAVE TO GO BACK!
THEY'LL KILL HIM!
I'M AFRAID THEY LIKELY ALREADY HAVE.
WE SHOULD PRAY FOR HIS SPIRIT.
BLESSED VISHANTI...
THIS IS ALL MY FAULT.

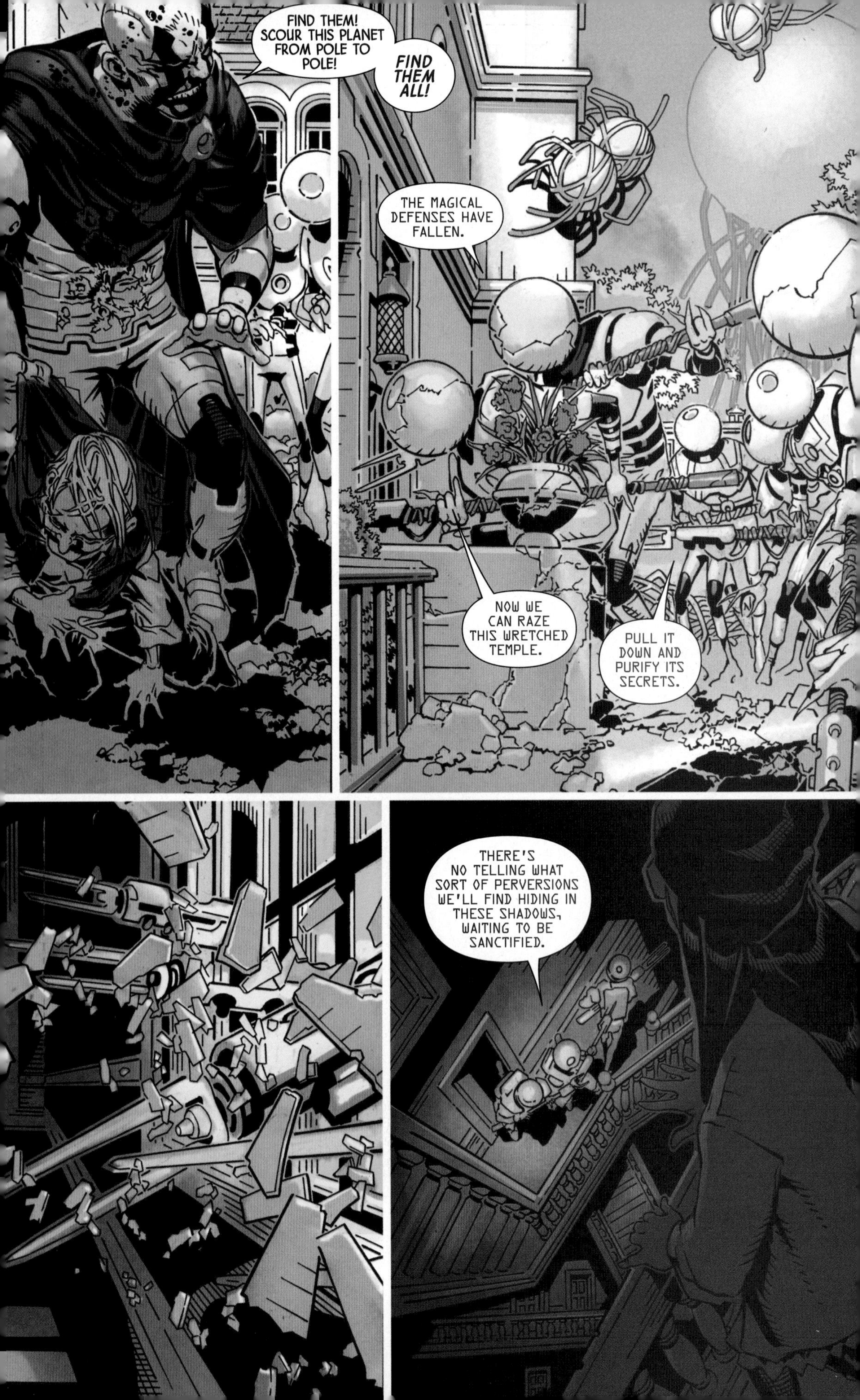
FIND THEM! SCOUR THIS PLANET FROM POLE TO POLE!
FIND THEM ALL!
THE MAGICAL DEFENSES HAVE FALLEN.
NOW WE CAN RAZE THIS WRETCHED TEMPLE.
PULL IT DOWN AND PURIFY ITS SECRETS.
THERE'S NO TELLING WHAT SORT OF PERVERSIONS WE'LL FIND HIDING IN THESE SHADOWS, WAITING TO BE SANCTIFIED.

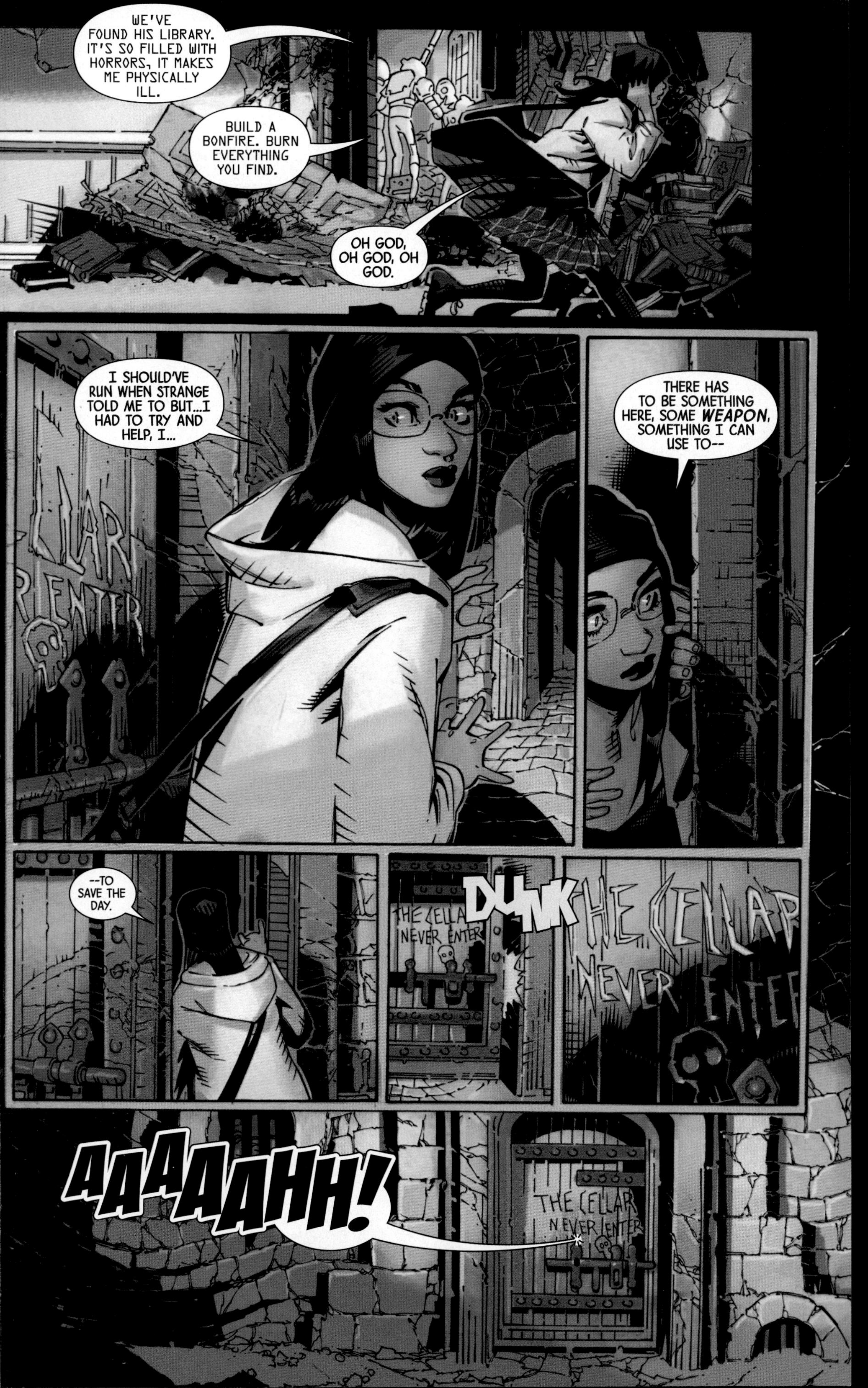

WE'VE FOUND HIS LIBRARY. IT'S SO FILLED WITH HORRORS, IT MAKES ME PHYSICALLY ILL.
BUILD A BONFIRE. BURN EVERYTHING YOU FIND.
OH GOD, OH GOD, OH GOD.
I SHOULD'VE RUN WHEN STRANGE TOLD ME TO BUT...I HAD TO TRY AND HELP, I...
THERE HAS TO BE SOMETHING HERE, SOME WEAPON, SOMETHING I CAN USE TO--
--TO SAVE THE DAY.
THE CELLAR NEVER ENTER
DUNK
THE CELLAR NEVER ENTER
AAAAAHH!
THE CELLAR NEVER ENTER

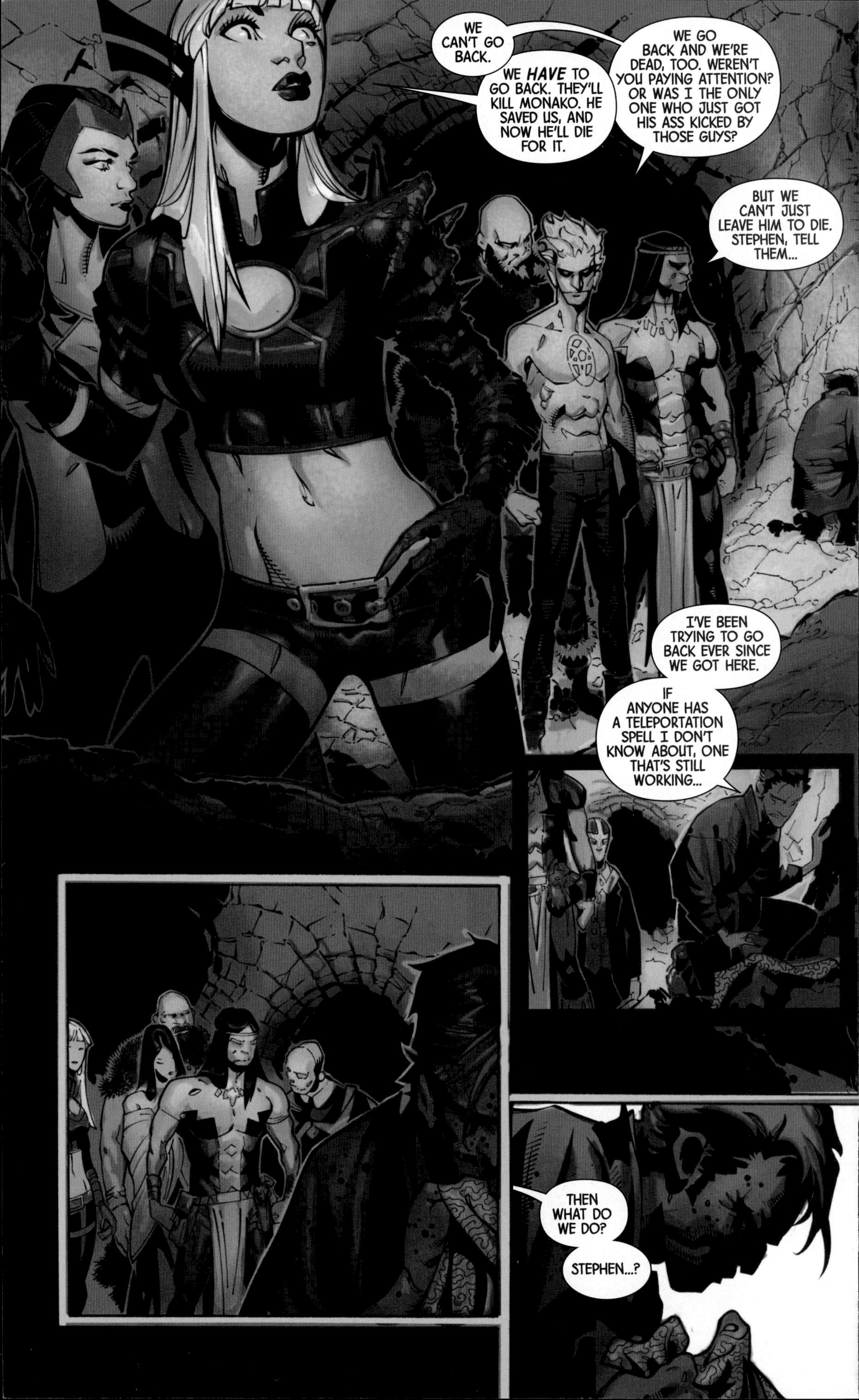
WE CAN'T GO BACK.
WE *HAVE* TO GO BACK. THEY'LL KILL MONAKO. HE SAVED US, AND NOW HE'LL DIE FOR IT.
WE GO BACK AND WE'RE DEAD, TOO. WEREN'T YOU PAYING ATTENTION? OR WAS I THE ONLY ONE WHO JUST GOT HIS ASS KICKED BY THOSE GUYS?
BUT WE CAN'T JUST LEAVE HIM TO DIE. STEPHEN, TELL THEM...
I'VE BEEN TRYING TO GO BACK EVER SINCE WE GOT HERE.
IF ANYONE HAS A TELEPORTATION SPELL I DON'T KNOW ABOUT, ONE THAT'S STILL WORKING...
THEN WHAT DO WE DO?
STEPHEN...?

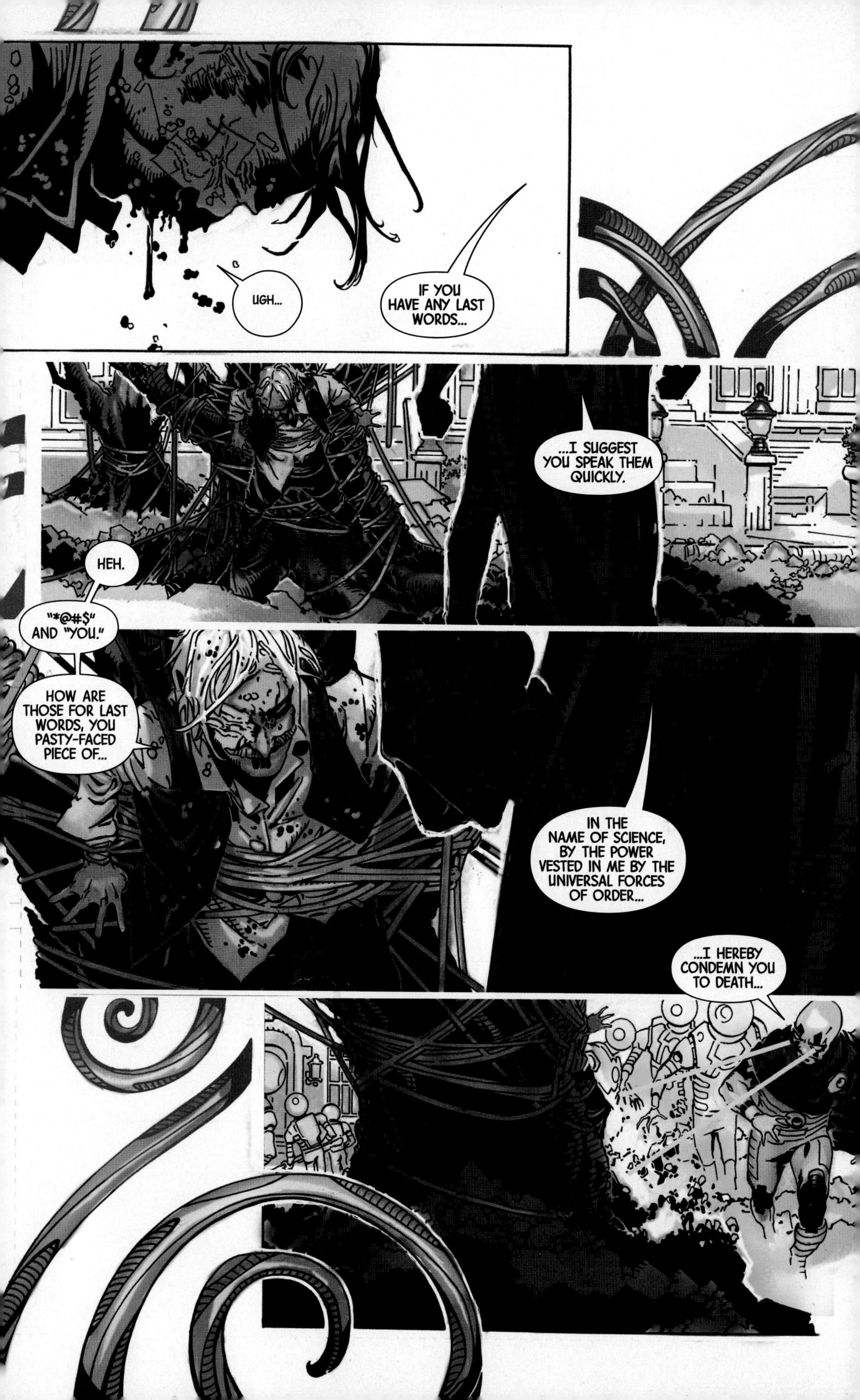
UGH...
IF YOU HAVE ANY LAST WORDS...
...I SUGGEST YOU SPEAK THEM QUICKLY.
HEH.
"*@#$" AND "YOU."
HOW ARE THOSE FOR LAST WORDS, YOU PASTY-FACED PIECE OF...
IN THE NAME OF SCIENCE, BY THE POWER VESTED IN ME BY THE UNIVERSAL FORCES OF ORDER...
...I HEREBY CONDEMN YOU TO DEATH...

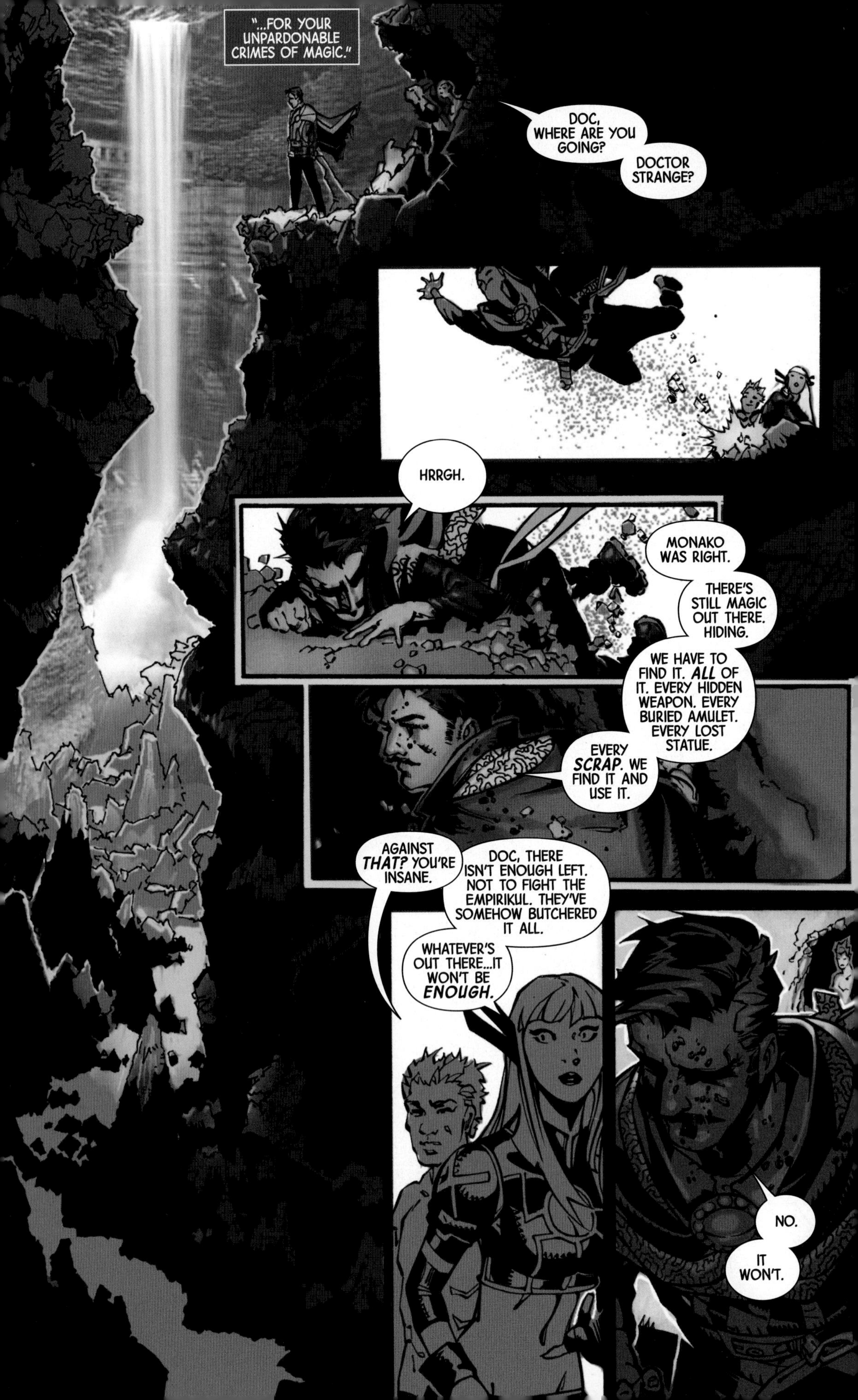
"...FOR YOUR UNPARDONABLE CRIMES OF MAGIC."
DOC, WHERE ARE YOU GOING?
DOCTOR STRANGE?
HRRGH.
MONAKO WAS RIGHT.
THERE'S STILL MAGIC OUT THERE. HIDING.
WE HAVE TO FIND IT. ALL OF IT. EVERY HIDDEN WEAPON. EVERY BURIED AMULET. EVERY LOST STATUE.
EVERY SCRAP. WE FIND IT AND USE IT.
AGAINST THAT? YOU'RE INSANE.
DOC, THERE ISN'T ENOUGH LEFT. NOT TO FIGHT THE EMPIRIKUL. THEY'VE SOMEHOW BUTCHERED IT ALL.
WHATEVER'S OUT THERE...IT WON'T BE ENOUGH.
NO.
IT WON'T.

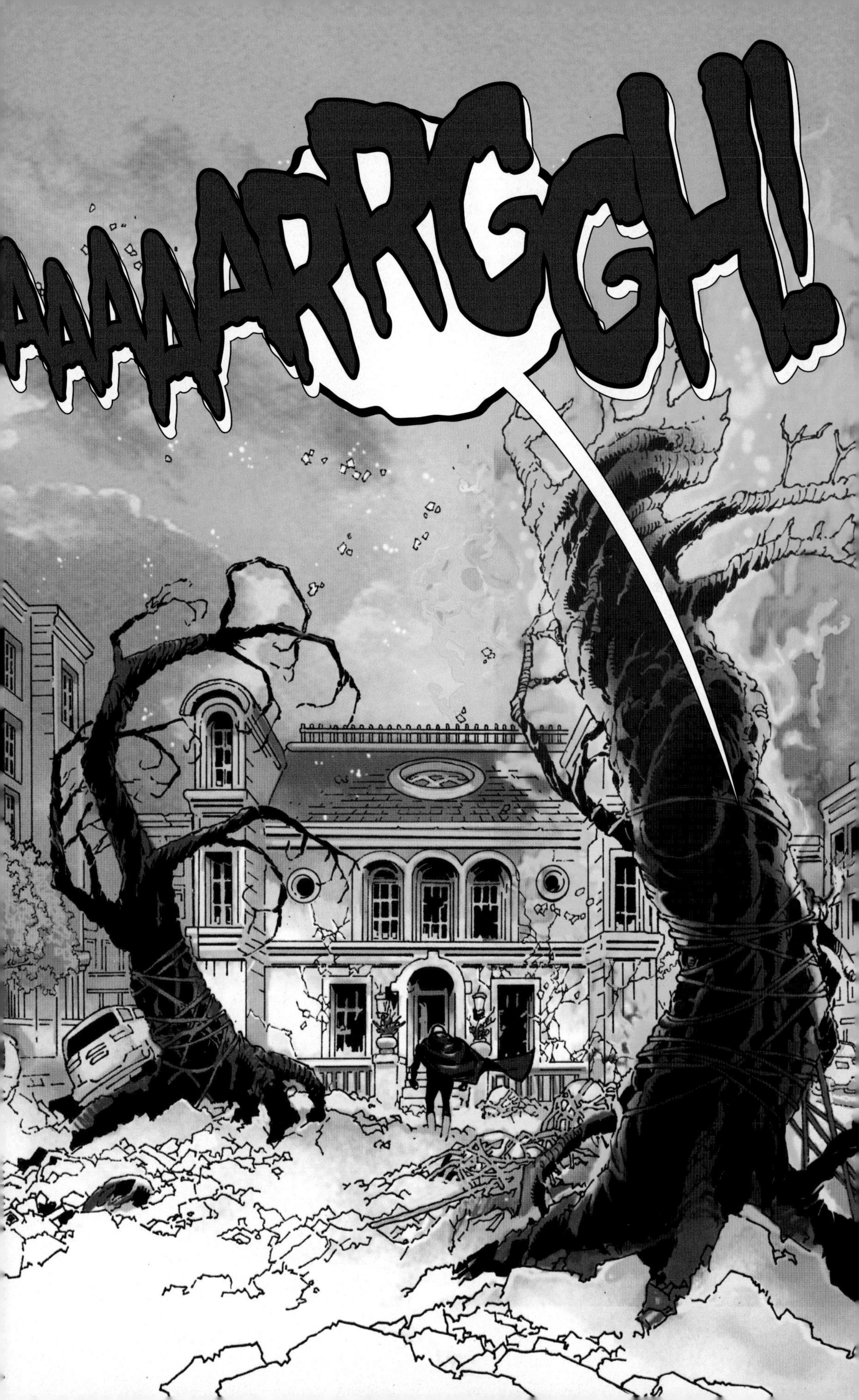
AAAAARRRGGH!

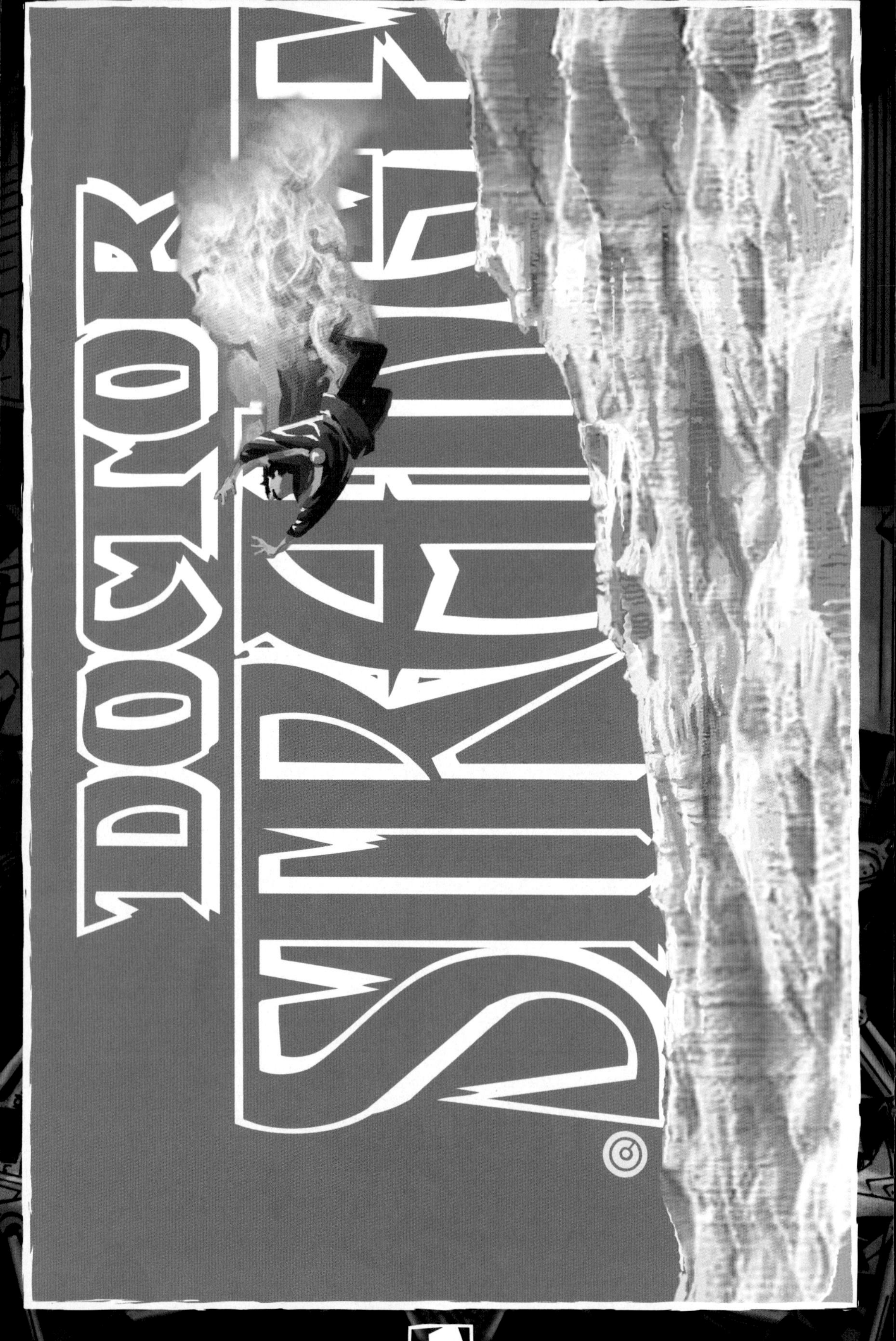
DOCTOR STRANGE

DOCTOR STRANGE

THE LAST DAYS OF MAGIC
CHAPTER THREE

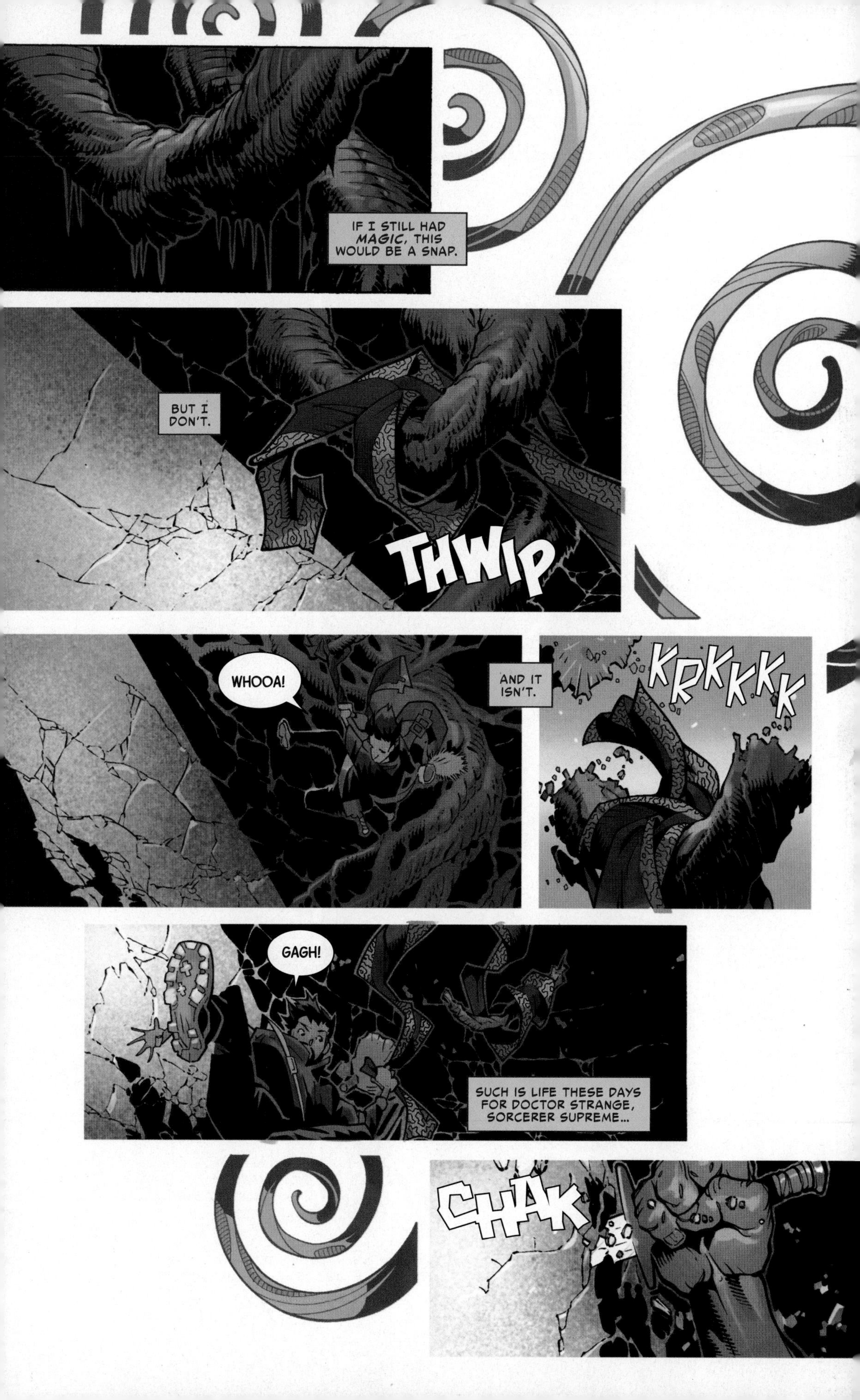

IF I STILL HAD *MAGIC*, THIS WOULD BE A SNAP.
BUT I DON'T.
THWIP
WHOOA!
AND IT ISN'T.
KRKKKK
GAGH!
SUCH IS LIFE THESE DAYS FOR DOCTOR STRANGE, SORCERER SUPREME...
CHAK

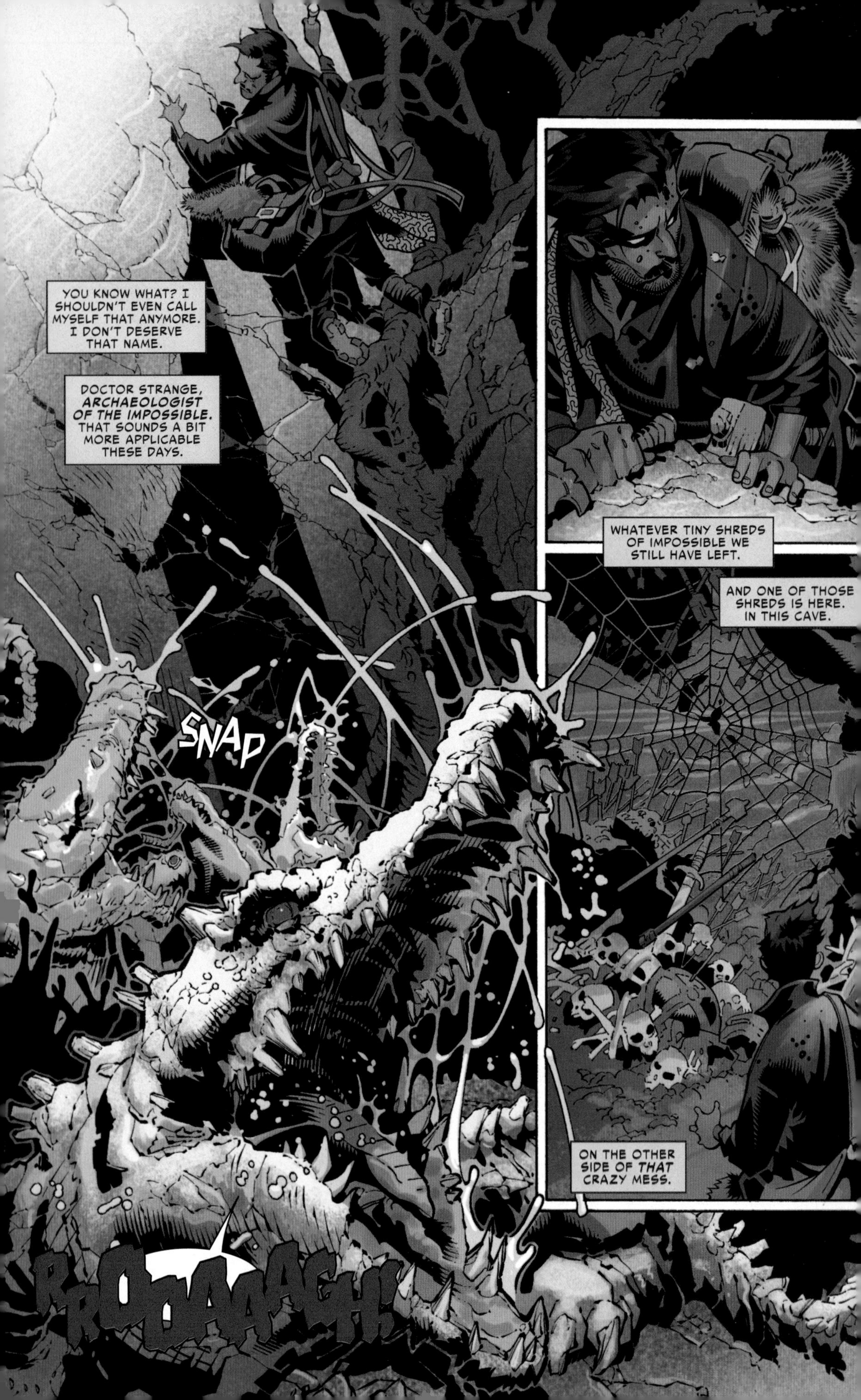
YOU KNOW WHAT? I SHOULDN'T EVEN CALL MYSELF THAT ANYMORE. I DON'T DESERVE THAT NAME.
DOCTOR STRANGE, *ARCHAEOLOGIST OF THE IMPOSSIBLE.* THAT SOUNDS A BIT MORE APPLICABLE THESE DAYS.
WHATEVER TINY SHREDS OF IMPOSSIBLE WE STILL HAVE LEFT.
AND ONE OF THOSE SHREDS IS HERE. IN THIS CAVE.
ON THE OTHER SIDE OF *THAT* CRAZY MESS.
SNAP
RROOAAAGH!

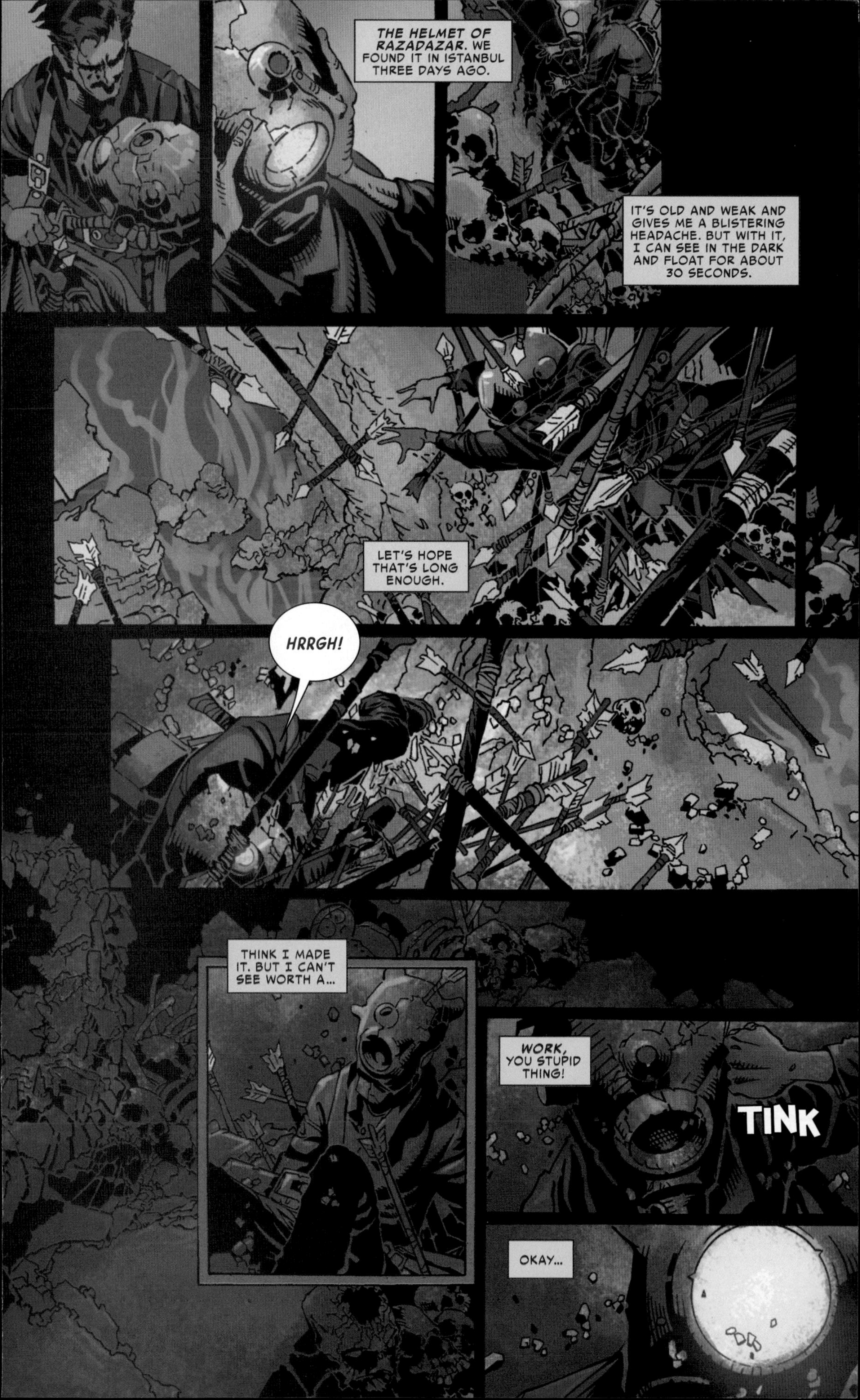
THE HELMET OF RAZADAZAR. WE FOUND IT IN ISTANBUL THREE DAYS AGO.
IT'S OLD AND WEAK AND GIVES ME A BLISTERING HEADACHE. BUT WITH IT, I CAN SEE IN THE DARK AND FLOAT FOR ABOUT 30 SECONDS.
LET'S HOPE THAT'S LONG ENOUGH.
HRRGH!
THINK I MADE IT. BUT I CAN'T SEE WORTH A...
WORK, YOU STUPID THING!
TINK
OKAY...

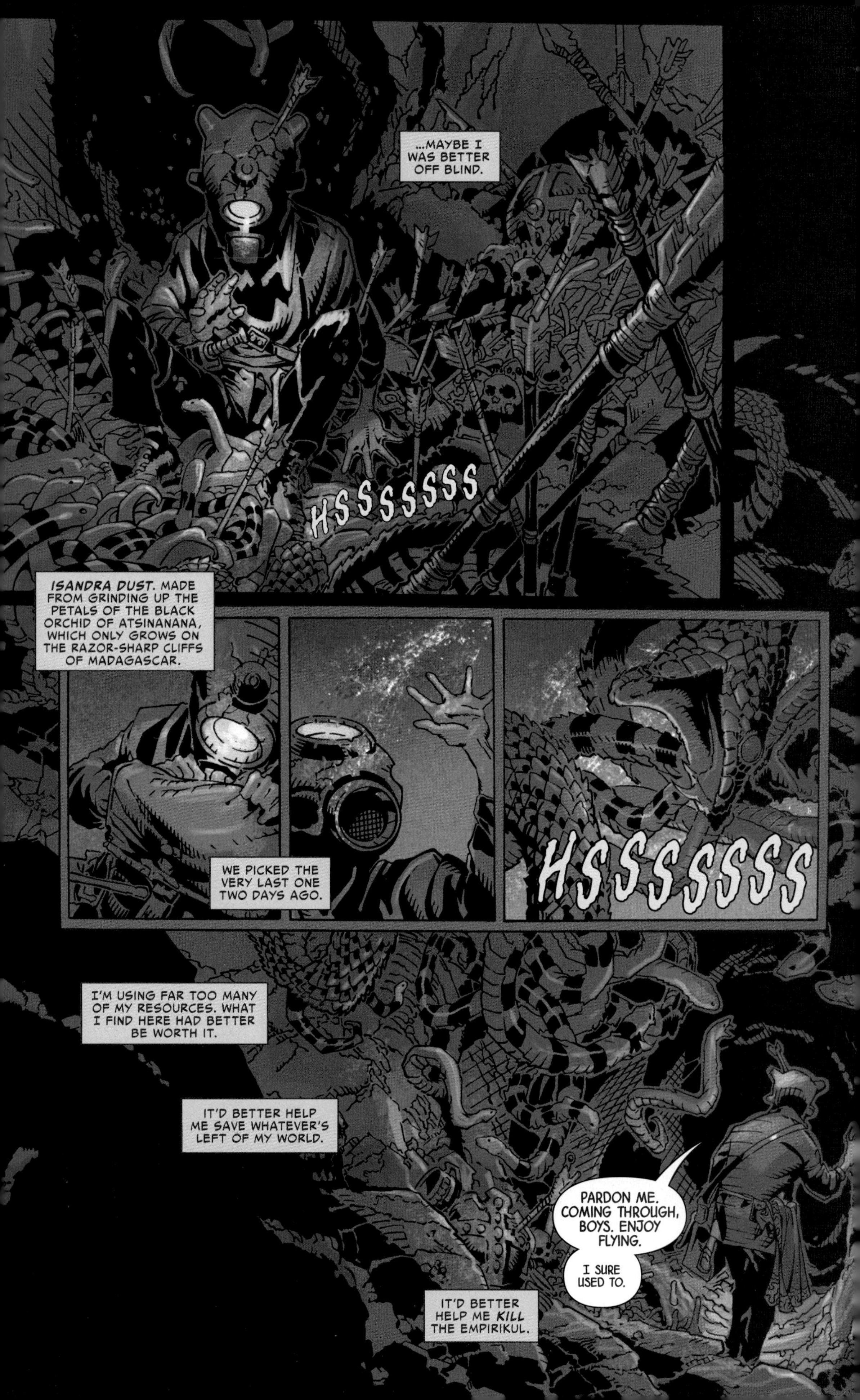
...MAYBE I WAS BETTER OFF BLIND.
HSSSSSSS
ISANDRA DUST. MADE FROM GRINDING UP THE PETALS OF THE BLACK ORCHID OF ATSINANANA, WHICH ONLY GROWS ON THE RAZOR-SHARP CLIFFS OF MADAGASCAR.
WE PICKED THE VERY LAST ONE TWO DAYS AGO.
HSSSSSSS
I'M USING FAR TOO MANY OF MY RESOURCES. WHAT I FIND HERE HAD BETTER BE WORTH IT.
IT'D BETTER HELP ME SAVE WHATEVER'S LEFT OF MY WORLD.
PARDON ME. COMING THROUGH, BOYS. ENJOY FLYING.
I SURE USED TO.
IT'D BETTER HELP ME KILL THE EMPIRIKUL.

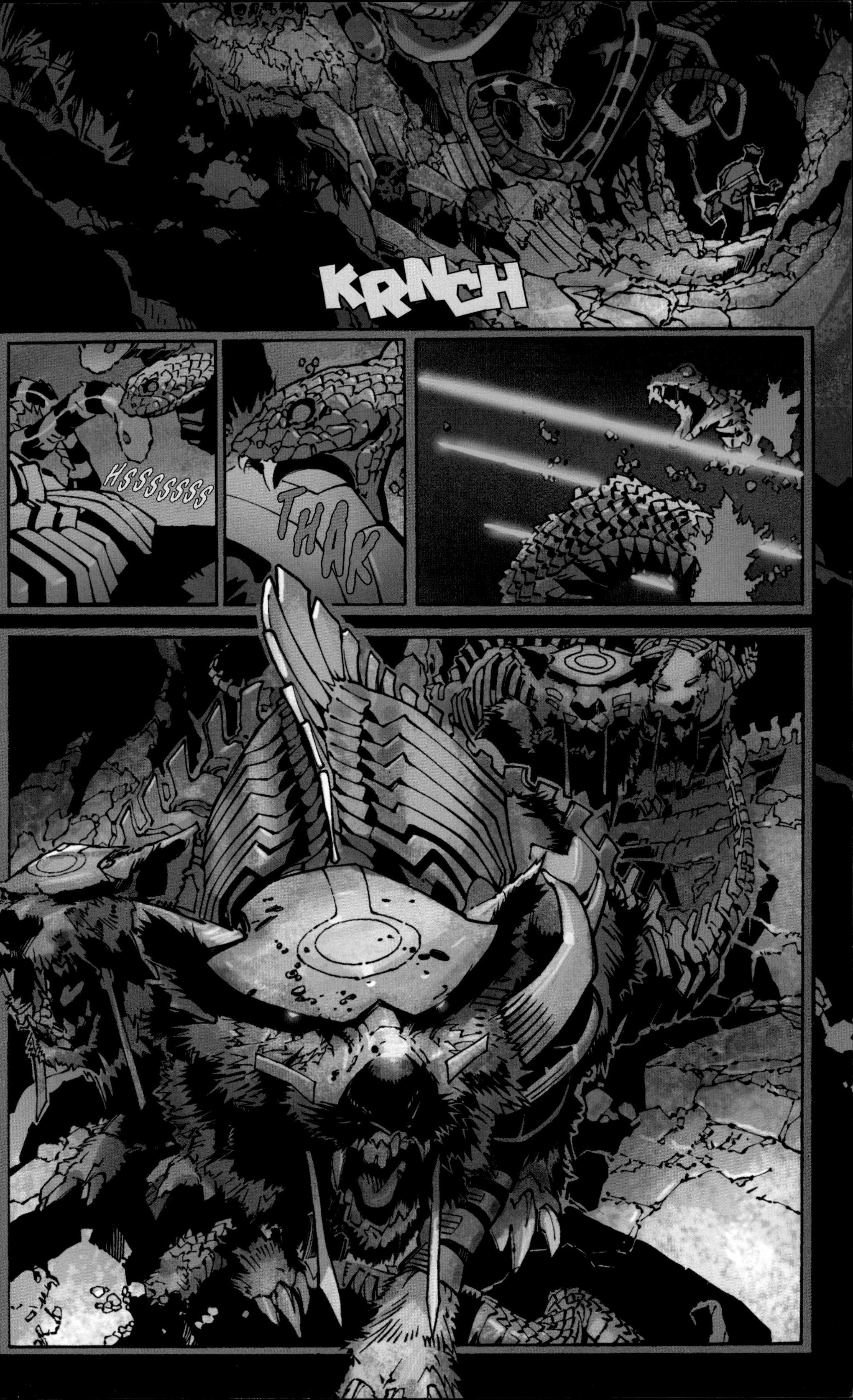
KRNCH
HSSSSSSS
THAK

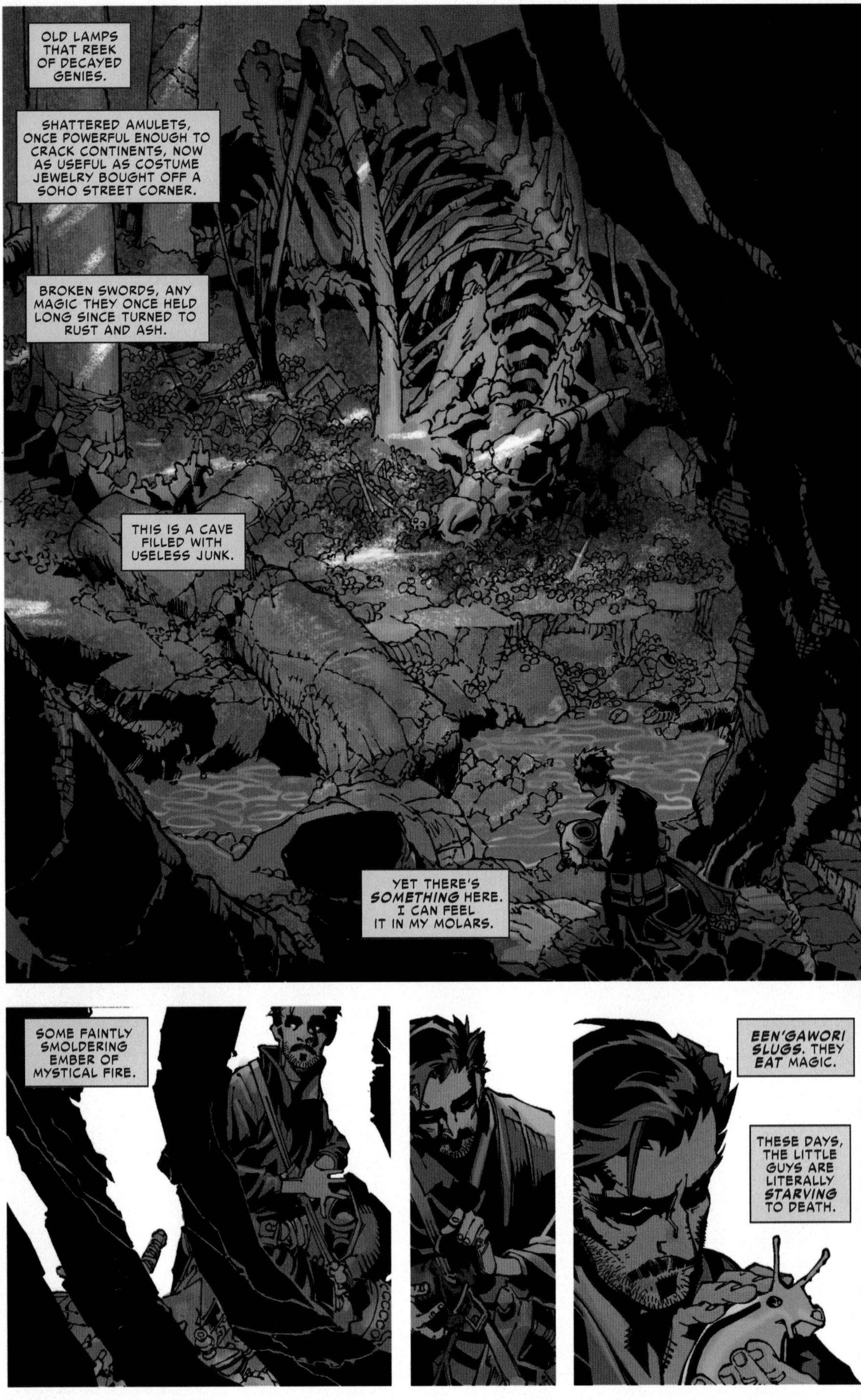
OLD LAMPS THAT REEK OF DECAYED GENIES.
SHATTERED AMULETS, ONCE POWERFUL ENOUGH TO CRACK CONTINENTS, NOW AS USEFUL AS COSTUME JEWELRY BOUGHT OFF A SOHO STREET CORNER.
BROKEN SWORDS, ANY MAGIC THEY ONCE HELD LONG SINCE TURNED TO RUST AND ASH.
THIS IS A CAVE FILLED WITH USELESS JUNK.
YET THERE'S SOMETHING HERE. I CAN FEEL IT IN MY MOLARS.
SOME FAINTLY SMOLDERING EMBER OF MYSTICAL FIRE.
EEN'GAWORI SLUGS. THEY EAT MAGIC.
THESE DAYS, THE LITTLE GUYS ARE LITERALLY STARVING TO DEATH.

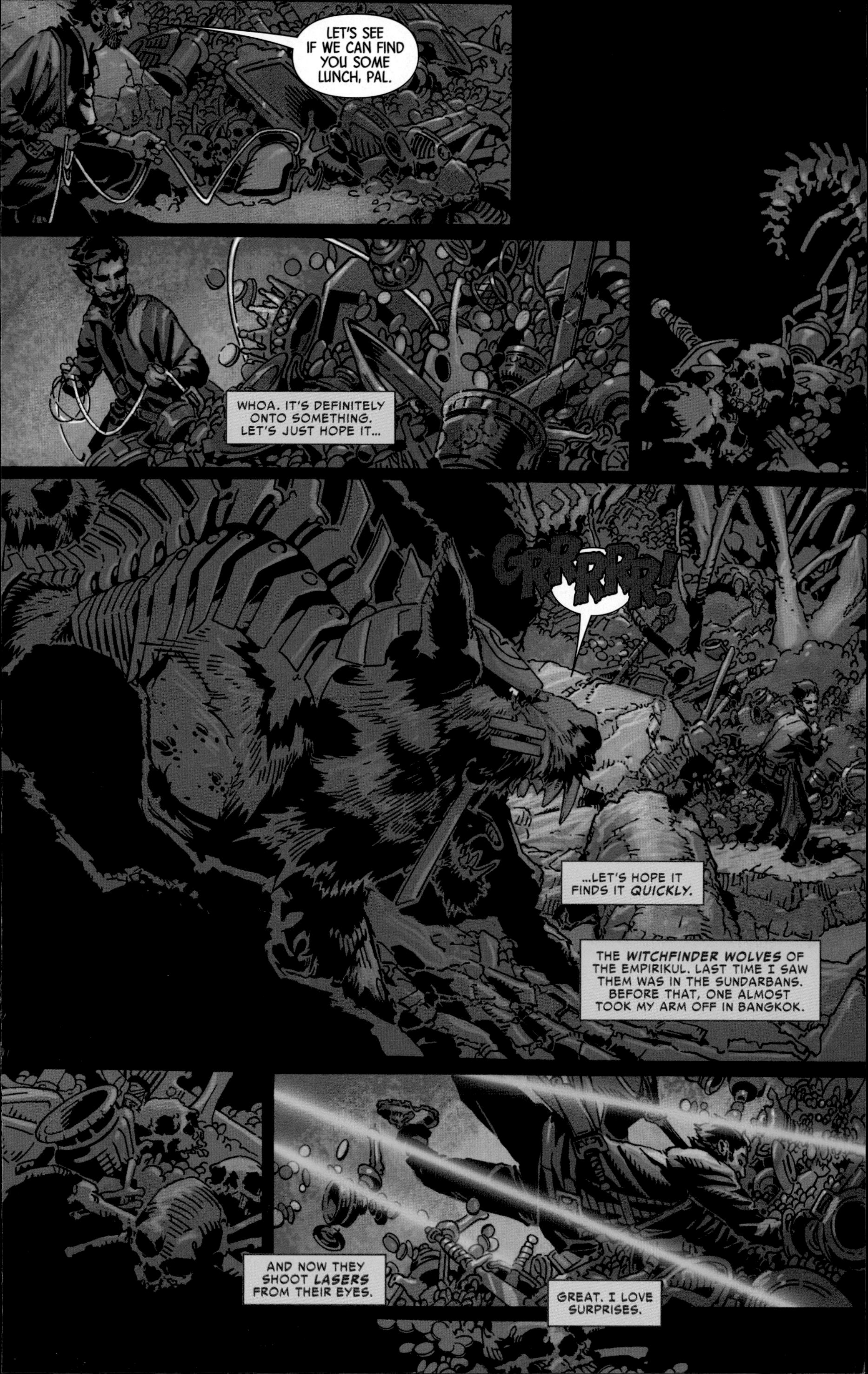

LET'S SEE IF WE CAN FIND YOU SOME LUNCH, PAL.
WHOA. IT'S DEFINITELY ONTO SOMETHING. LET'S JUST HOPE IT...
GRRRRR!
...LET'S HOPE IT FINDS IT QUICKLY.
THE WITCHFINDER WOLVES OF THE EMPIRIKUL. LAST TIME I SAW THEM WAS IN THE SUNDARBANS. BEFORE THAT, ONE ALMOST TOOK MY ARM OFF IN BANGKOK.
AND NOW THEY SHOOT LASERS FROM THEIR EYES.
GREAT. I LOVE SURPRISES.

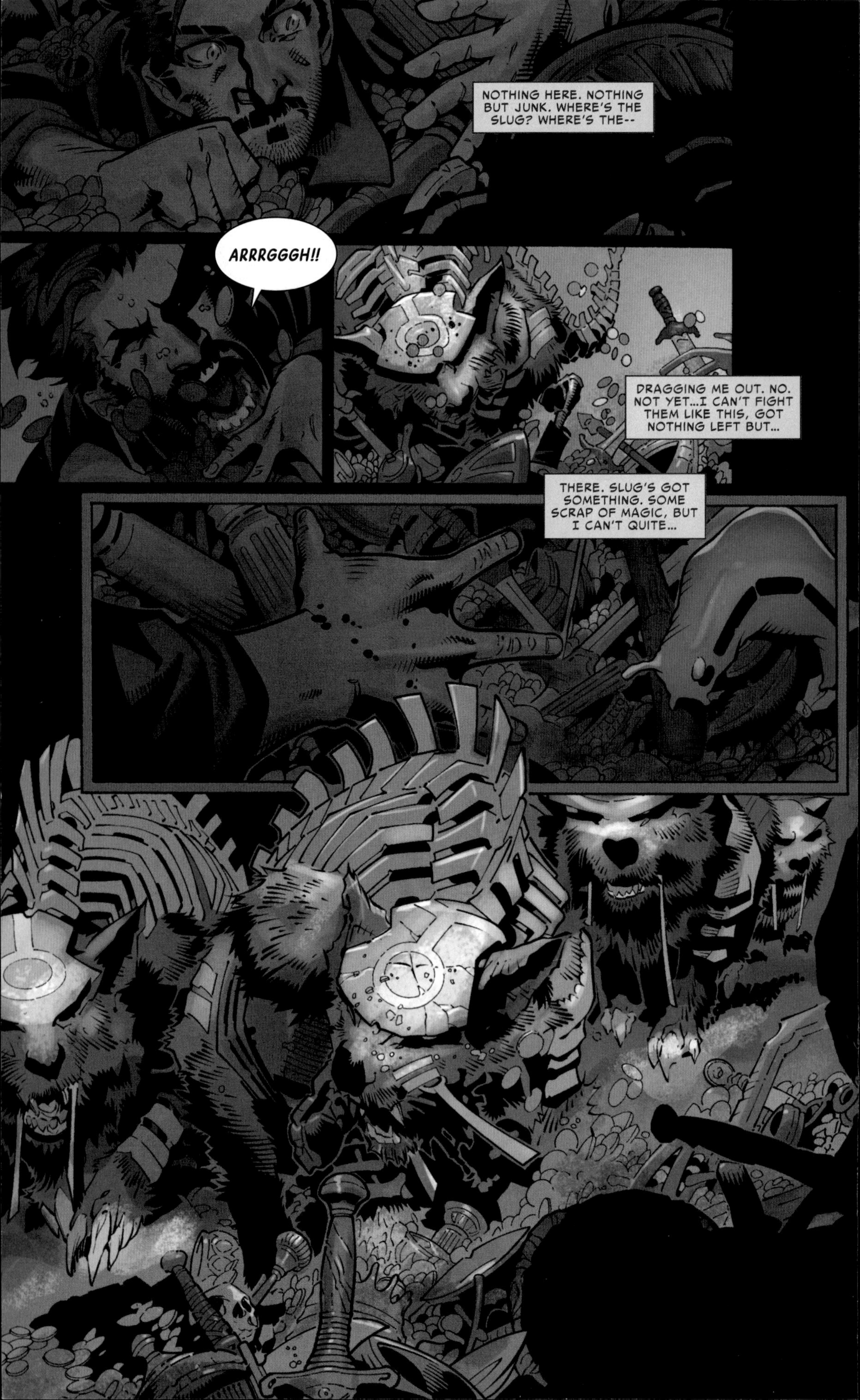
NOTHING HERE. NOTHING BUT JUNK. WHERE'S THE SLUG? WHERE'S THE--
ARRRGGGH!!
DRAGGING ME OUT. NO. NOT YET...I CAN'T FIGHT THEM LIKE THIS, GOT NOTHING LEFT BUT...
THERE. SLUG'S GOT SOMETHING. SOME SCRAP OF MAGIC, BUT I CAN'T QUITE...

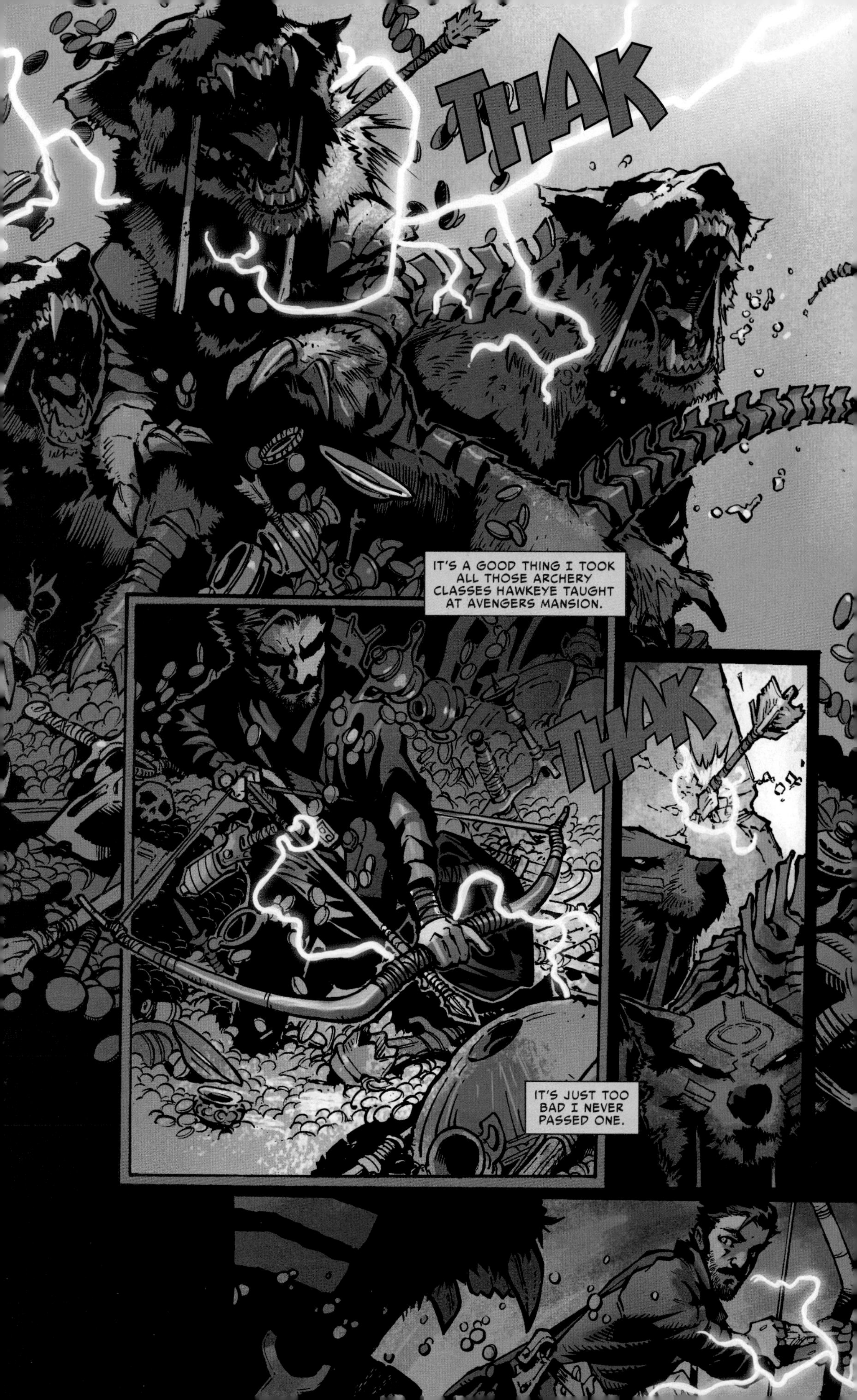
THAK
IT'S A GOOD THING I TOOK ALL THOSE ARCHERY CLASSES HAWKEYE TAUGHT AT AVENGERS MANSION.
THAK
IT'S JUST TOO BAD I NEVER PASSED ONE.

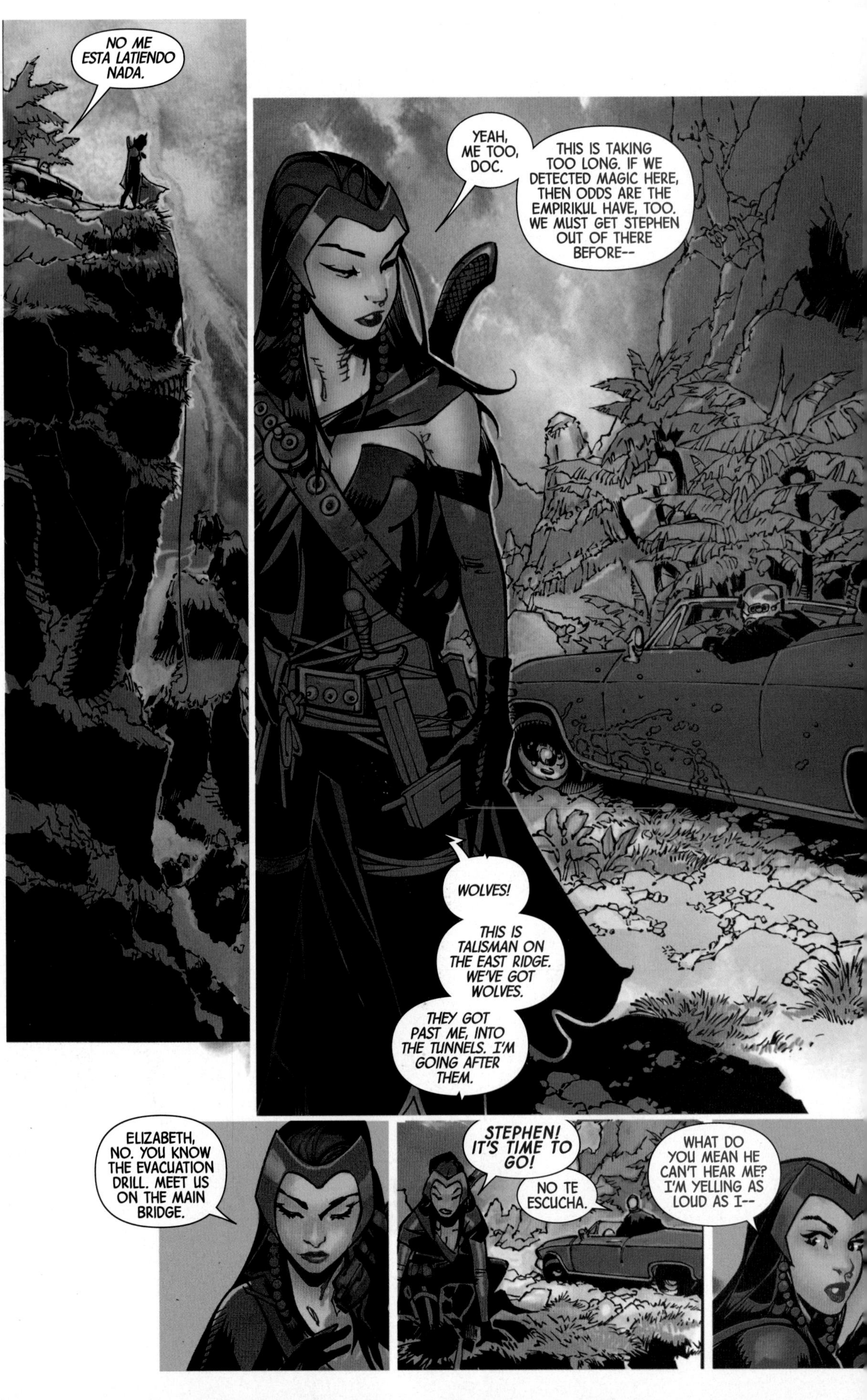
NO ME ESTA LATIENDO NADA.
YEAH, ME TOO, DOC.
THIS IS TAKING TOO LONG. IF WE DETECTED MAGIC HERE, THEN ODDS ARE THE EMPIRIKUL HAVE, TOO. WE MUST GET STEPHEN OUT OF THERE BEFORE--
WOLVES!
THIS IS TALISMAN ON THE EAST RIDGE. WE'VE GOT WOLVES.
THEY GOT PAST ME, INTO THE TUNNELS. I'M GOING AFTER THEM.
ELIZABETH, NO. YOU KNOW THE EVACUATION DRILL. MEET US ON THE MAIN BRIDGE.
STEPHEN! IT'S TIME TO GO!
NO TE ESCUCHA.
WHAT DO YOU MEAN HE CAN'T HEAR ME? I'M YELLING AS LOUD AS I--

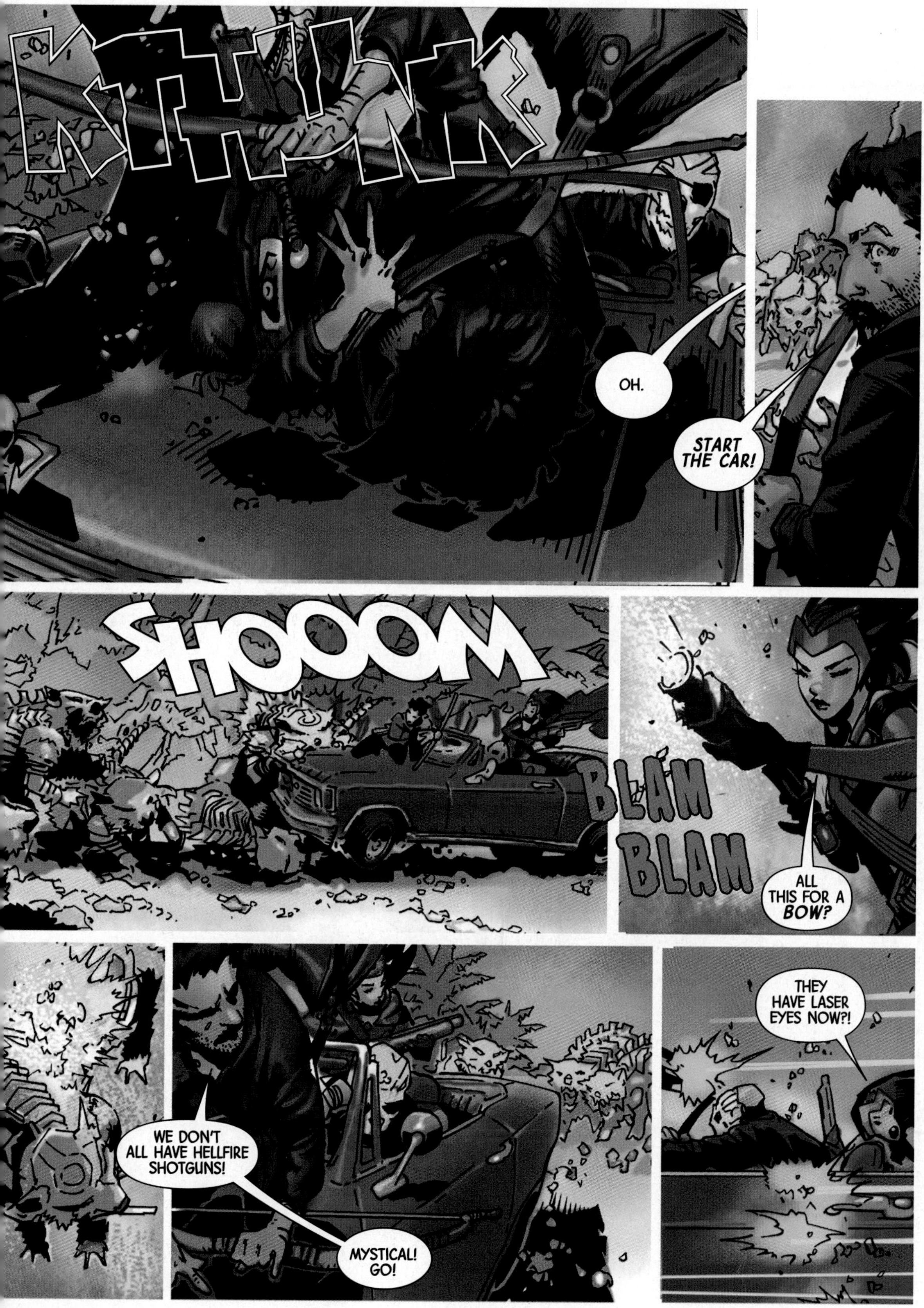
KTHUNK
OH.
START THE CAR!
SHOOOM
BLAM BLAM
ALL THIS FOR A BOW?
WE DON'T ALL HAVE HELLFIRE SHOTGUNS!
MYSTICAL! GO!
THEY HAVE LASER EYES NOW?!

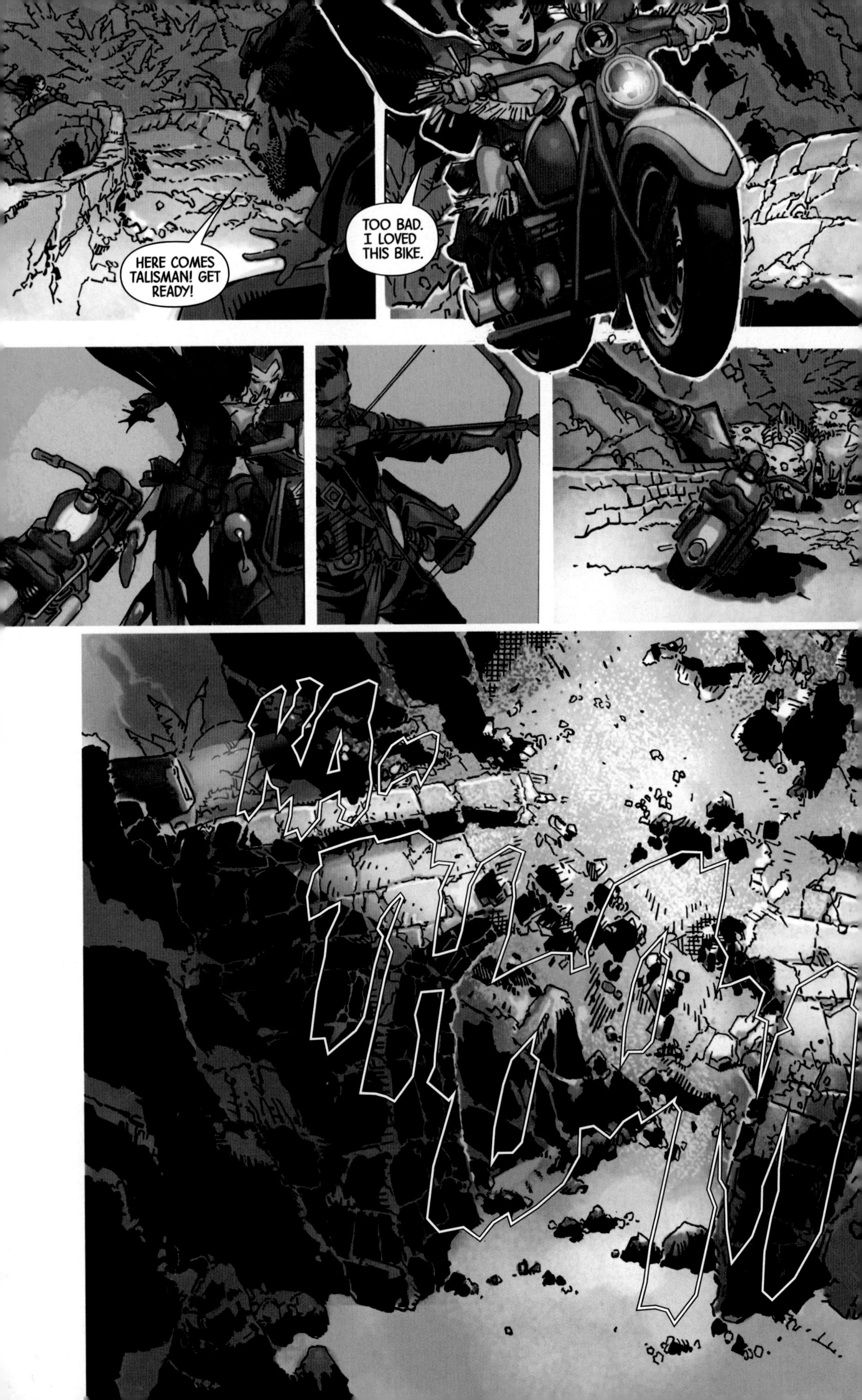
HERE COMES TALISMAN! GET READY!
TOO BAD. I LOVED THIS BIKE.

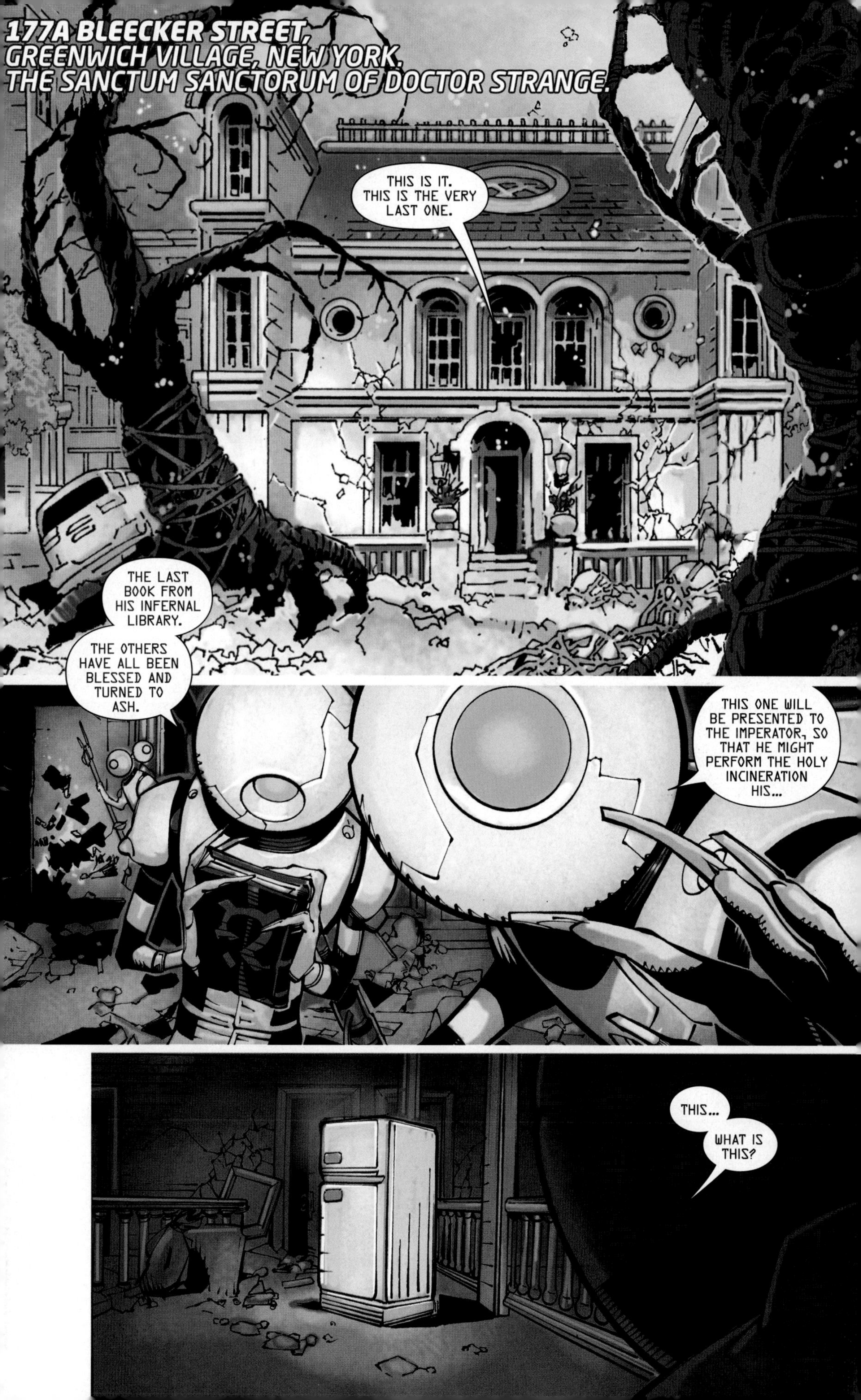
177A BLEECKER STREET,
GREENWICH VILLAGE, NEW YORK.
THE SANCTUM SANCTORUM OF DOCTOR STRANGE.
THIS IS IT. THIS IS THE VERY LAST ONE.
THE LAST BOOK FROM HIS INFERNAL LIBRARY.
THE OTHERS HAVE ALL BEEN BLESSED AND TURNED TO ASH.
THIS ONE WILL BE PRESENTED TO THE IMPERATOR, SO THAT HE MIGHT PERFORM THE HOLY INCINERATION HIS...
THIS...
WHAT IS THIS?

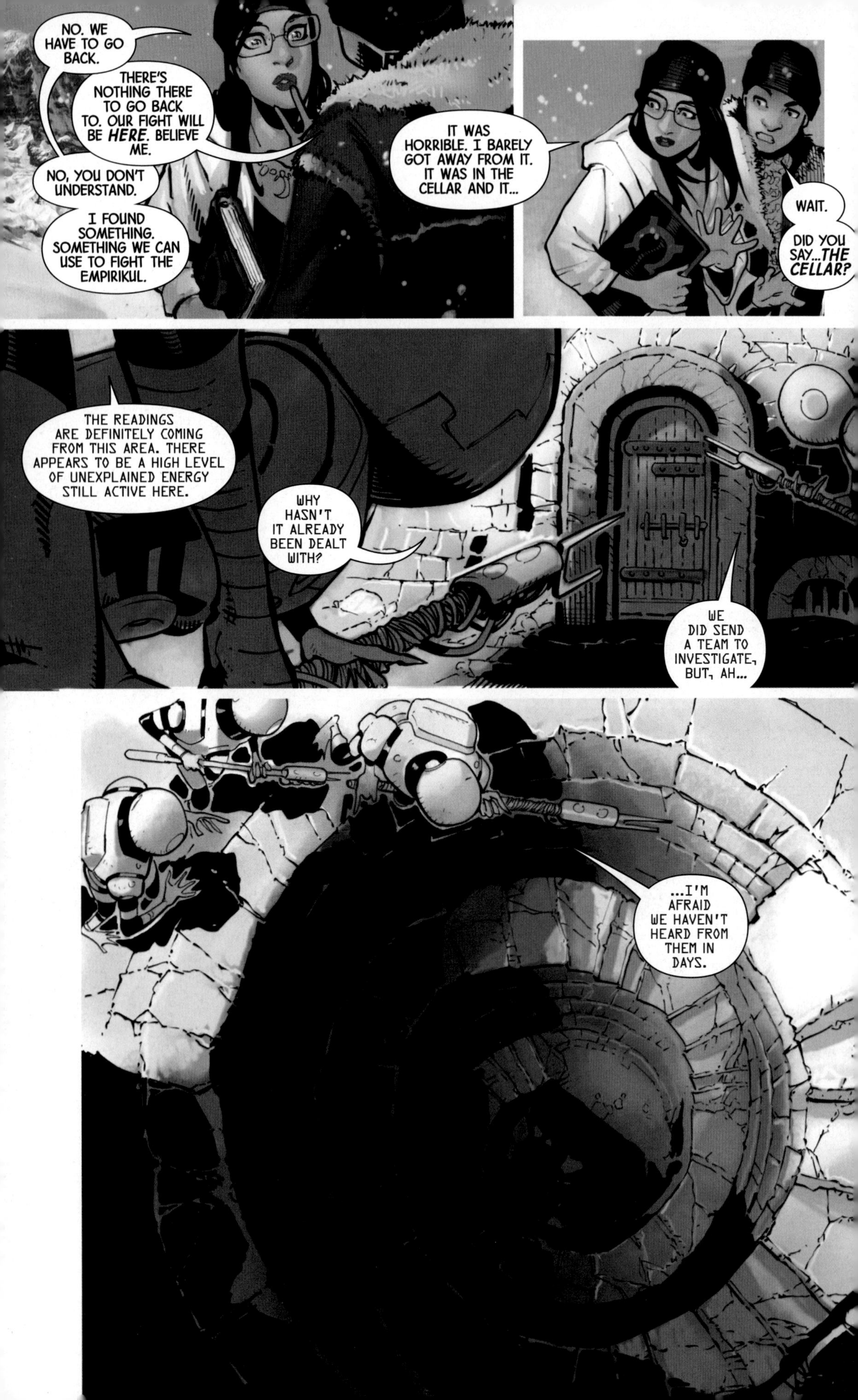
NO. WE HAVE TO GO BACK.
THERE'S NOTHING THERE TO GO BACK TO. OUR FIGHT WILL BE *HERE*. BELIEVE ME.
NO, YOU DON'T UNDERSTAND.
I FOUND SOMETHING. SOMETHING WE CAN USE TO FIGHT THE EMPIRIKUL.
IT WAS HORRIBLE. I BARELY GOT AWAY FROM IT. IT WAS IN THE CELLAR AND IT...
WAIT.
DID YOU SAY...*THE CELLAR?*
THE READINGS ARE DEFINITELY COMING FROM THIS AREA. THERE APPEARS TO BE A HIGH LEVEL OF UNEXPLAINED ENERGY STILL ACTIVE HERE.
WHY HASN'T IT ALREADY BEEN DEALT WITH?
WE DID SEND A TEAM TO INVESTIGATE, BUT, AH...
...I'M AFRAID WE HAVEN'T HEARD FROM THEM IN DAYS.

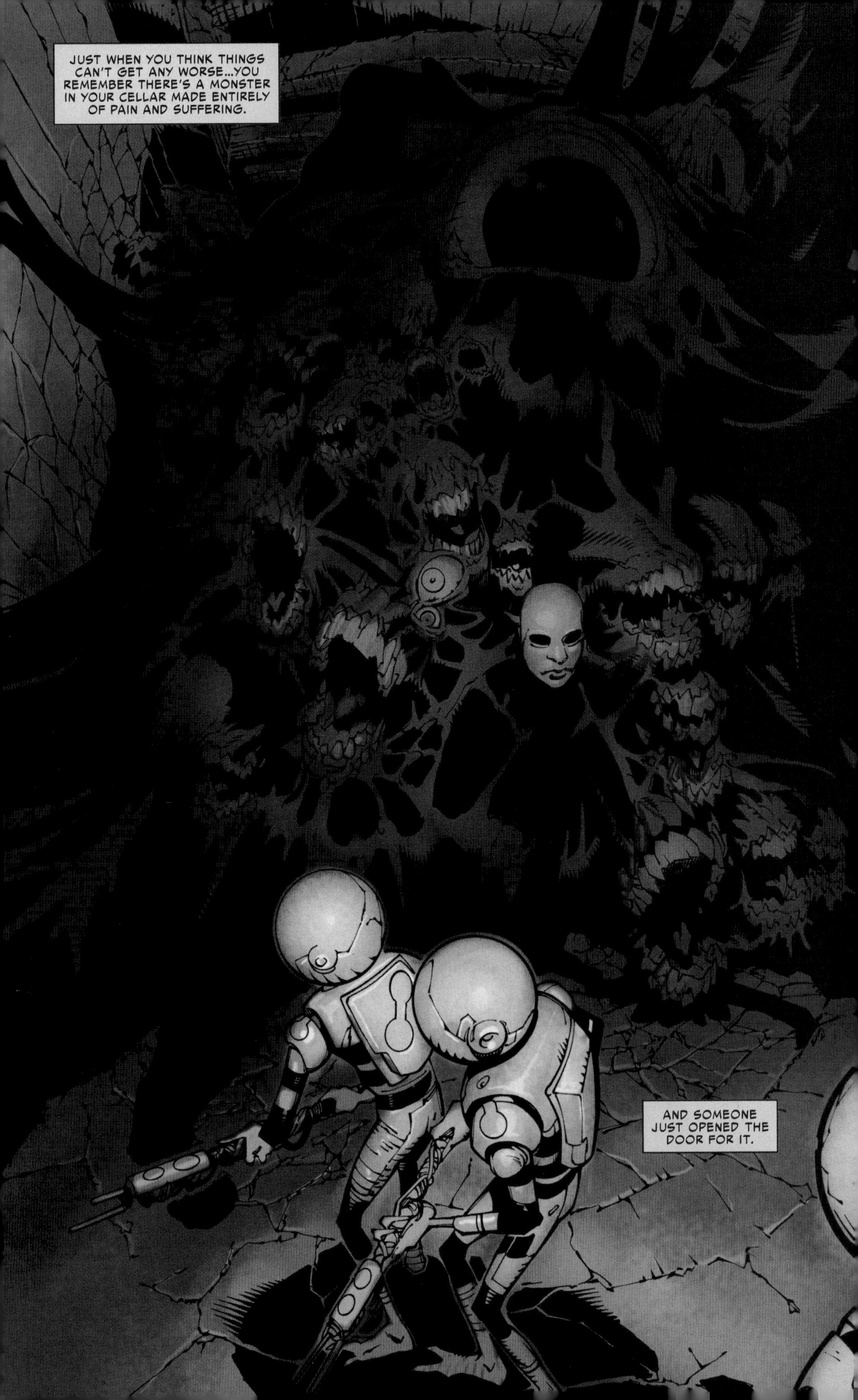
JUST WHEN YOU THINK THINGS CAN'T GET ANY WORSE...YOU REMEMBER THERE'S A MONSTER IN YOUR CELLAR MADE ENTIRELY OF PAIN AND SUFFERING.
AND SOMEONE JUST OPENED THE DOOR FOR IT.

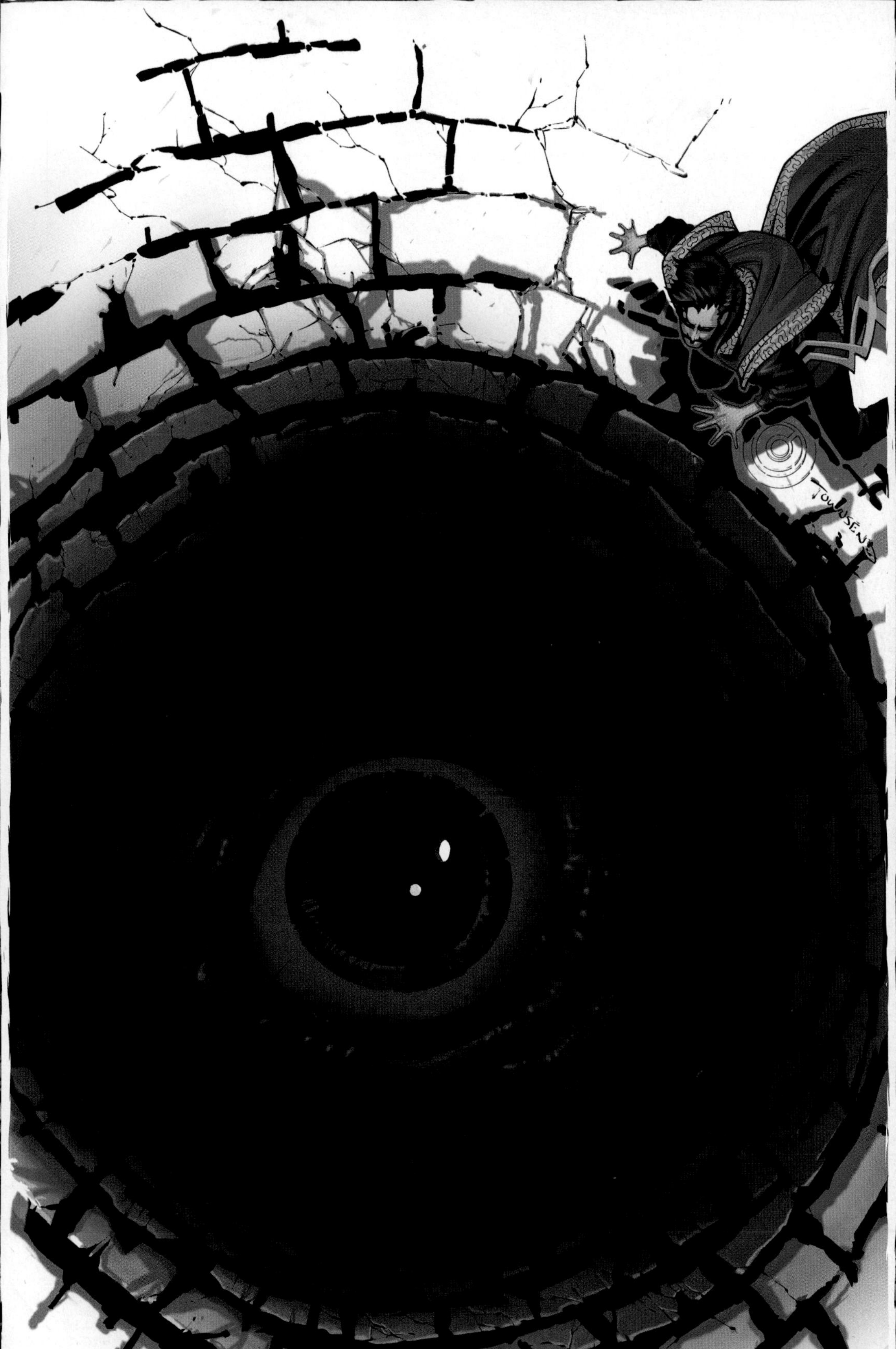

DOCTOR STRANGE

THE LAST DAYS OF MAGIC
CHAPTER FOUR

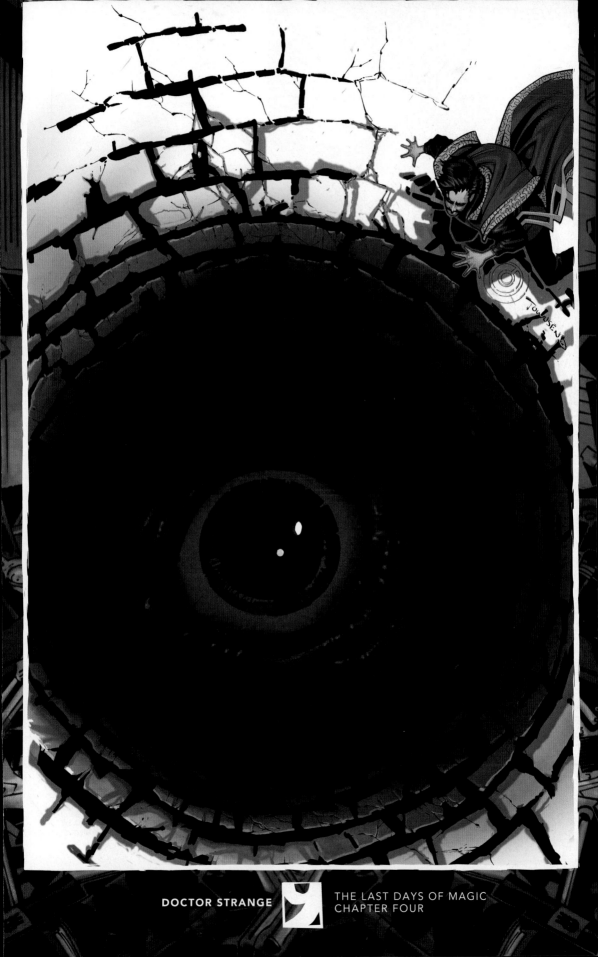

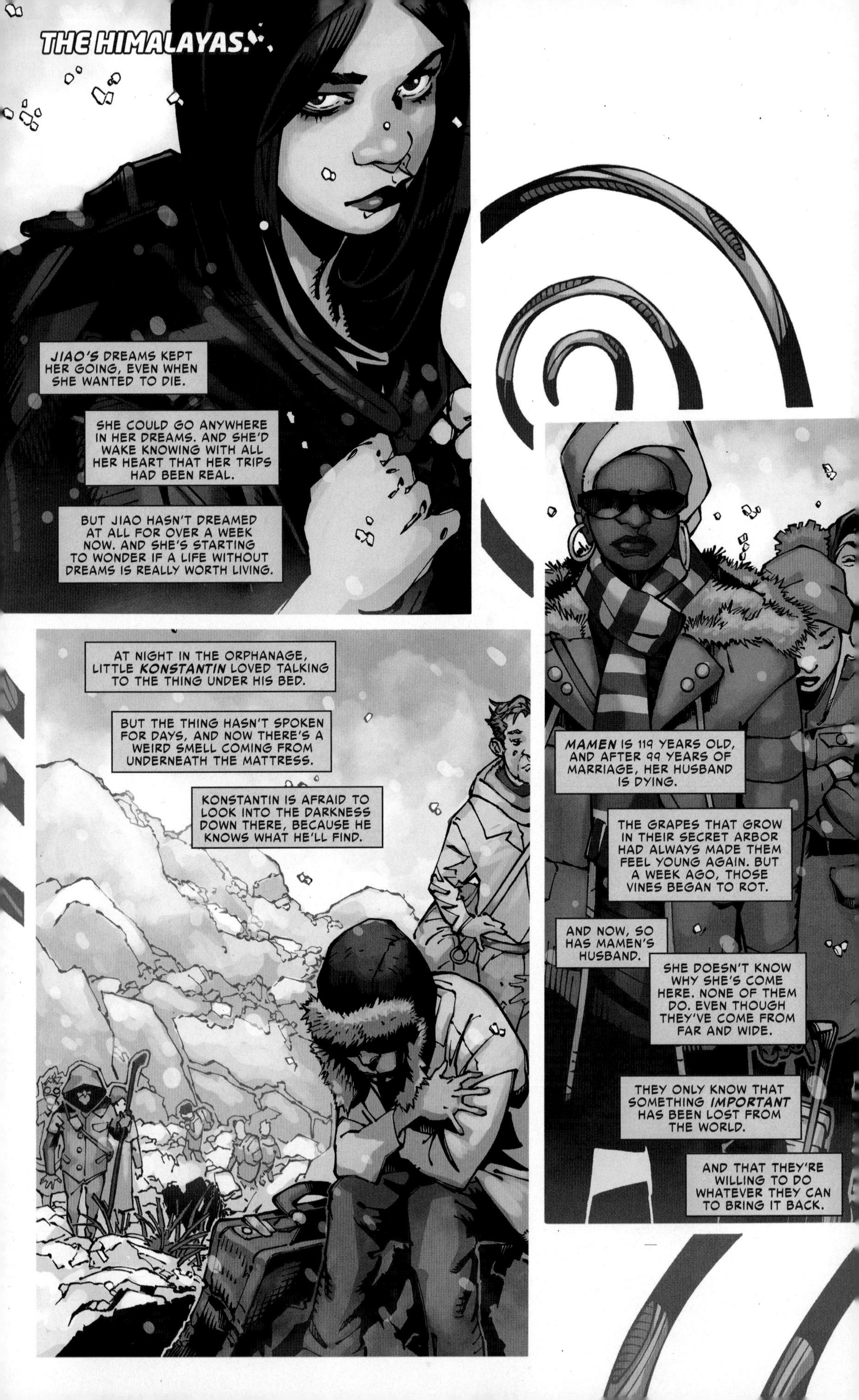
THE HIMALAYAS.
JIAO'S DREAMS KEPT HER GOING, EVEN WHEN SHE WANTED TO DIE.
SHE COULD GO ANYWHERE IN HER DREAMS. AND SHE'D WAKE KNOWING WITH ALL HER HEART THAT HER TRIPS HAD BEEN REAL.
BUT JIAO HASN'T DREAMED AT ALL FOR OVER A WEEK NOW. AND SHE'S STARTING TO WONDER IF A LIFE WITHOUT DREAMS IS REALLY WORTH LIVING.
AT NIGHT IN THE ORPHANAGE, LITTLE KONSTANTIN LOVED TALKING TO THE THING UNDER HIS BED.
BUT THE THING HASN'T SPOKEN FOR DAYS, AND NOW THERE'S A WEIRD SMELL COMING FROM UNDERNEATH THE MATTRESS.
KONSTANTIN IS AFRAID TO LOOK INTO THE DARKNESS DOWN THERE, BECAUSE HE KNOWS WHAT HE'LL FIND.
MAMEN IS 119 YEARS OLD, AND AFTER 99 YEARS OF MARRIAGE, HER HUSBAND IS DYING.
THE GRAPES THAT GROW IN THEIR SECRET ARBOR HAD ALWAYS MADE THEM FEEL YOUNG AGAIN. BUT A WEEK AGO, THOSE VINES BEGAN TO ROT.
AND NOW, SO HAS MAMEN'S HUSBAND.
SHE DOESN'T KNOW WHY SHE'S COME HERE. NONE OF THEM DO. EVEN THOUGH THEY'VE COME FROM FAR AND WIDE.
THEY ONLY KNOW THAT SOMETHING IMPORTANT HAS BEEN LOST FROM THE WORLD.
AND THAT THEY'RE WILLING TO DO WHATEVER THEY CAN TO BRING IT BACK.

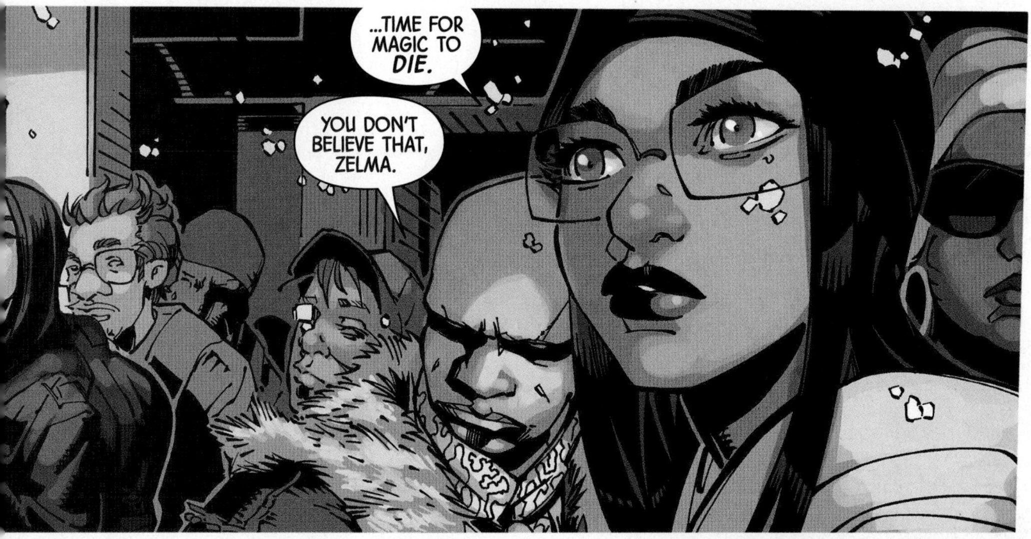
...TIME FOR MAGIC TO DIE.
YOU DON'T BELIEVE THAT, ZELMA.

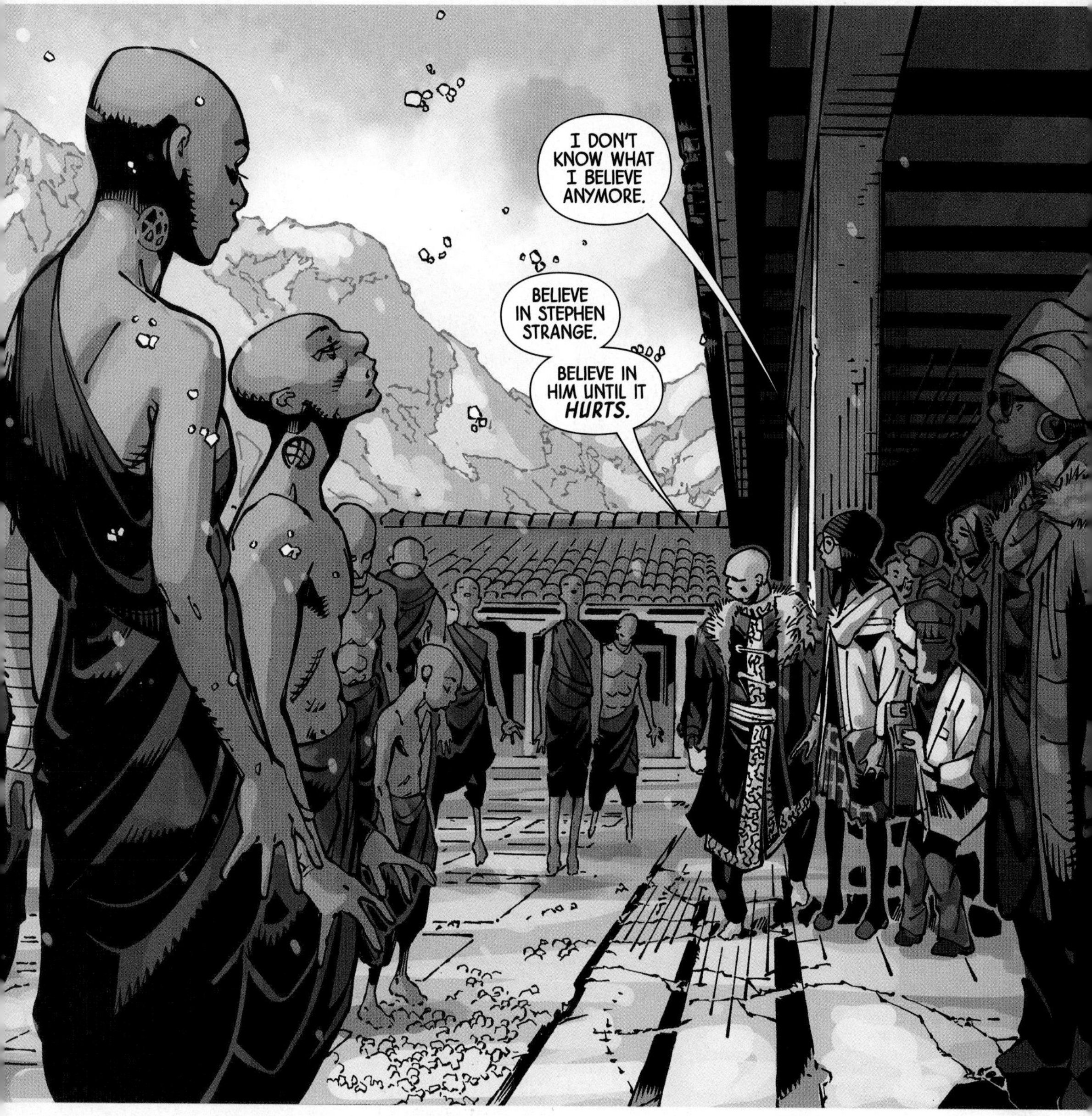
I DON'T KNOW WHAT I BELIEVE ANYMORE.
BELIEVE IN STEPHEN STRANGE.
BELIEVE IN HIM UNTIL IT HURTS.

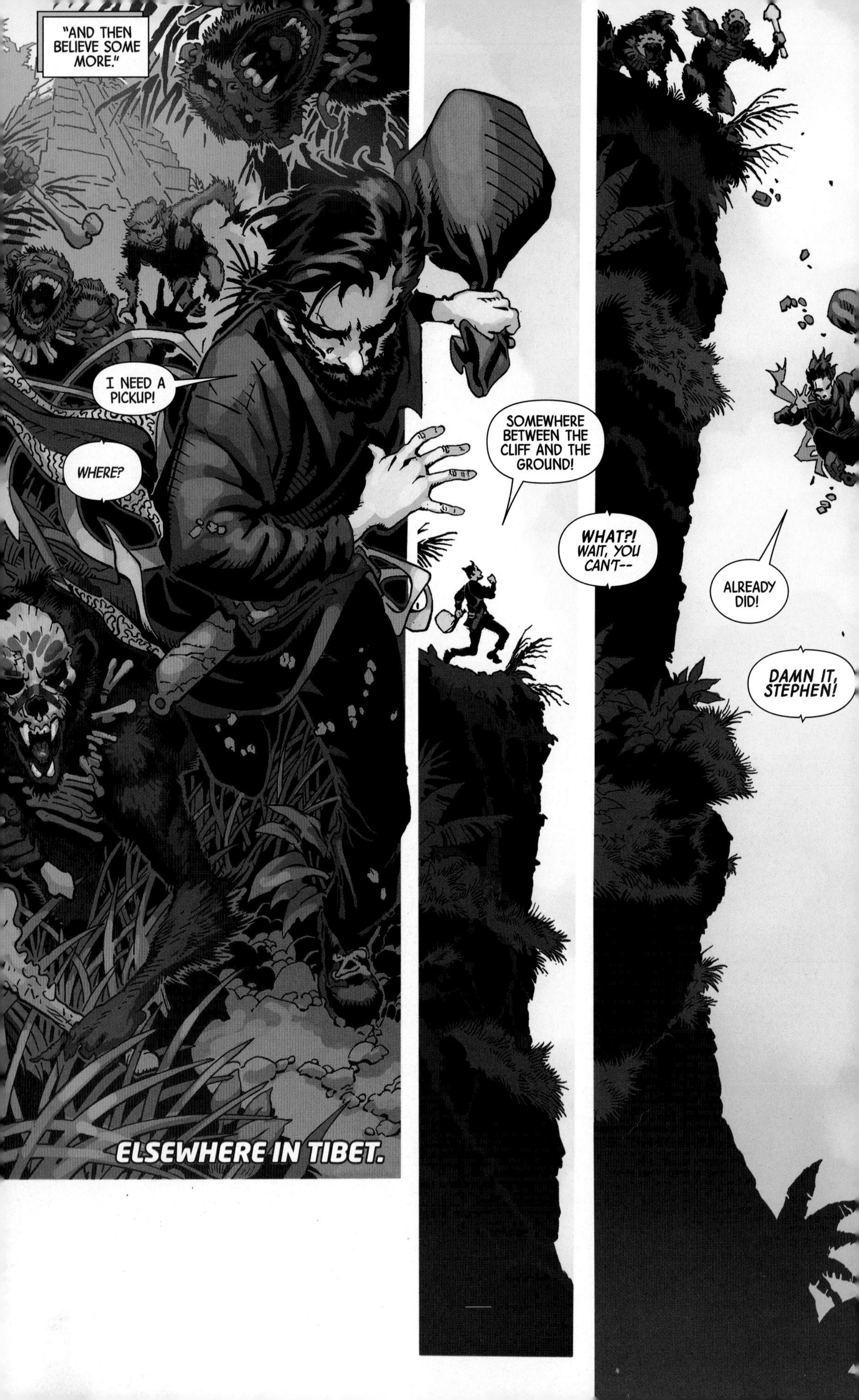
"AND THEN BELIEVE SOME MORE."
I NEED A PICKUP!
WHERE?
SOMEWHERE BETWEEN THE CLIFF AND THE GROUND!
WHAT?! WAIT, YOU CAN'T--
ALREADY DID!
DAMN IT, STEPHEN!
ELSEWHERE IN TIBET.

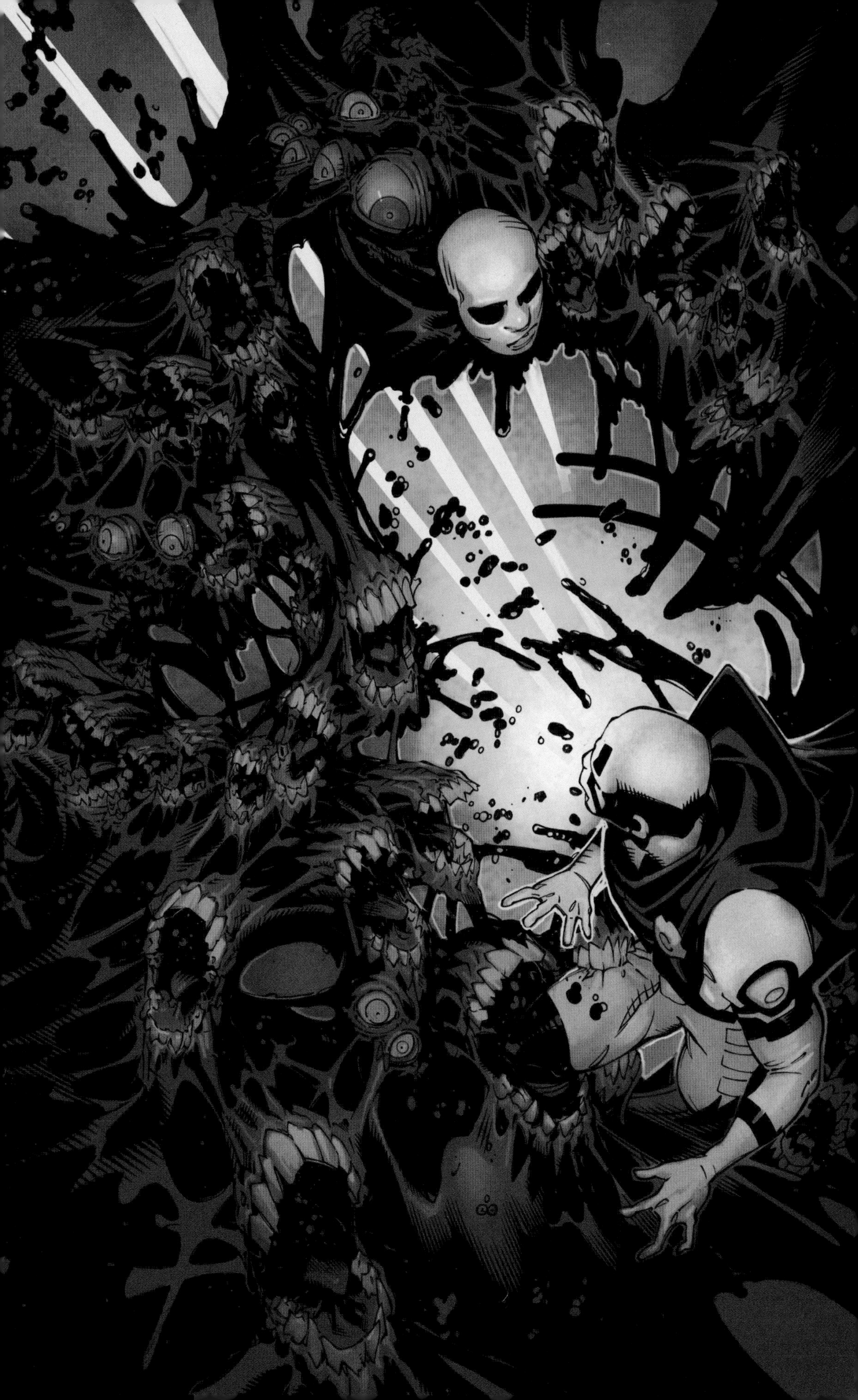

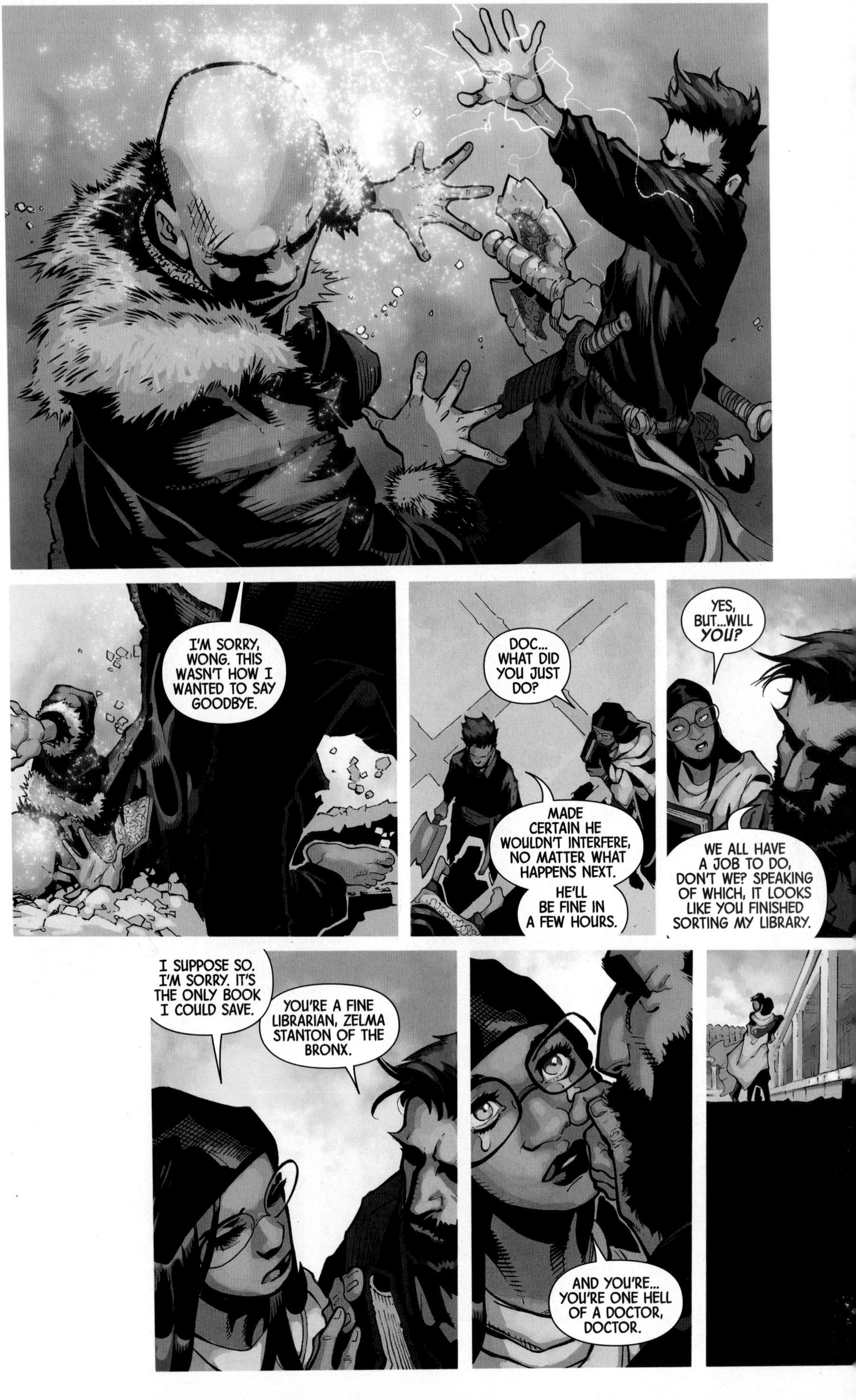
I'M SORRY, WONG. THIS WASN'T HOW I WANTED TO SAY GOODBYE.
DOC... WHAT DID YOU JUST DO?
MADE CERTAIN HE WOULDN'T INTERFERE, NO MATTER WHAT HAPPENS NEXT.
HE'LL BE FINE IN A FEW HOURS.
YES, BUT...WILL YOU?
WE ALL HAVE A JOB TO DO, DON'T WE? SPEAKING OF WHICH, IT LOOKS LIKE YOU FINISHED SORTING MY LIBRARY.
I SUPPOSE SO. I'M SORRY. IT'S THE ONLY BOOK I COULD SAVE.
YOU'RE A FINE LIBRARIAN, ZELMA STANTON OF THE BRONX.
AND YOU'RE... YOU'RE ONE HELL OF A DOCTOR, DOCTOR.

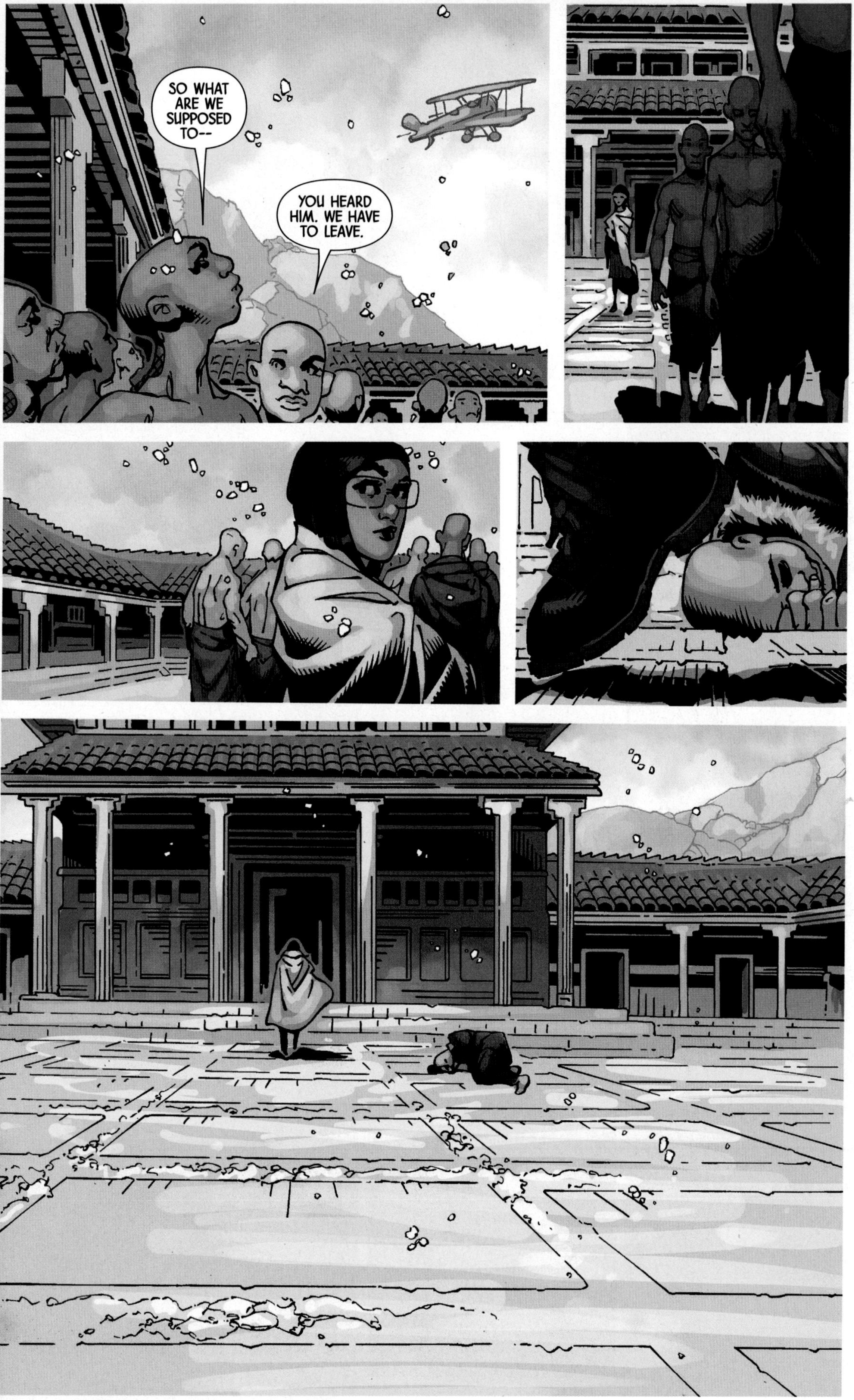
SO WHAT ARE WE SUPPOSED TO--
YOU HEARD HIM. WE HAVE TO LEAVE.

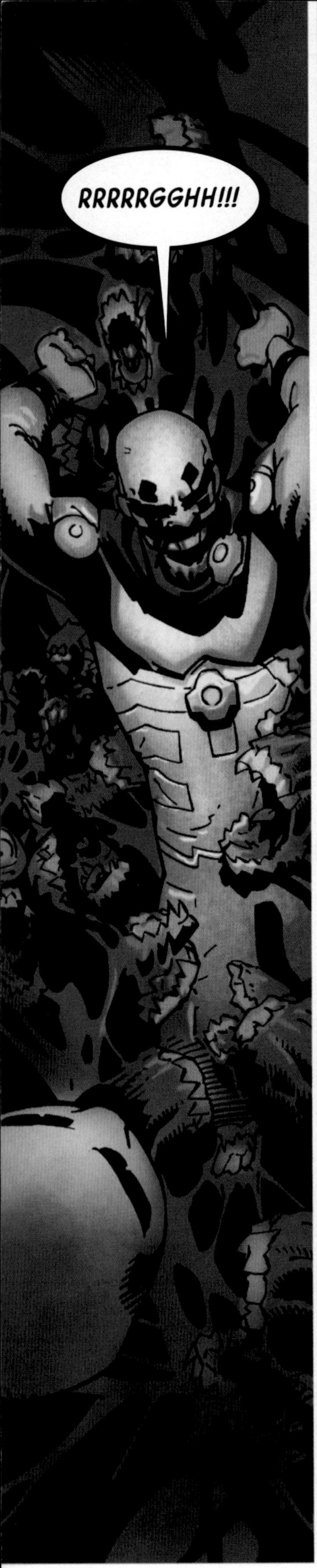
RRRRRGGHH!!!

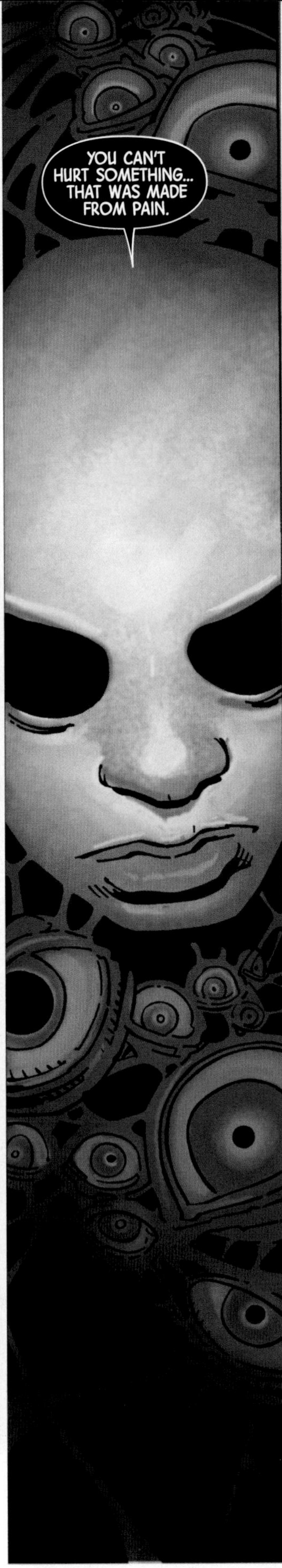
YOU CAN'T HURT SOMETHING... THAT WAS MADE FROM PAIN.

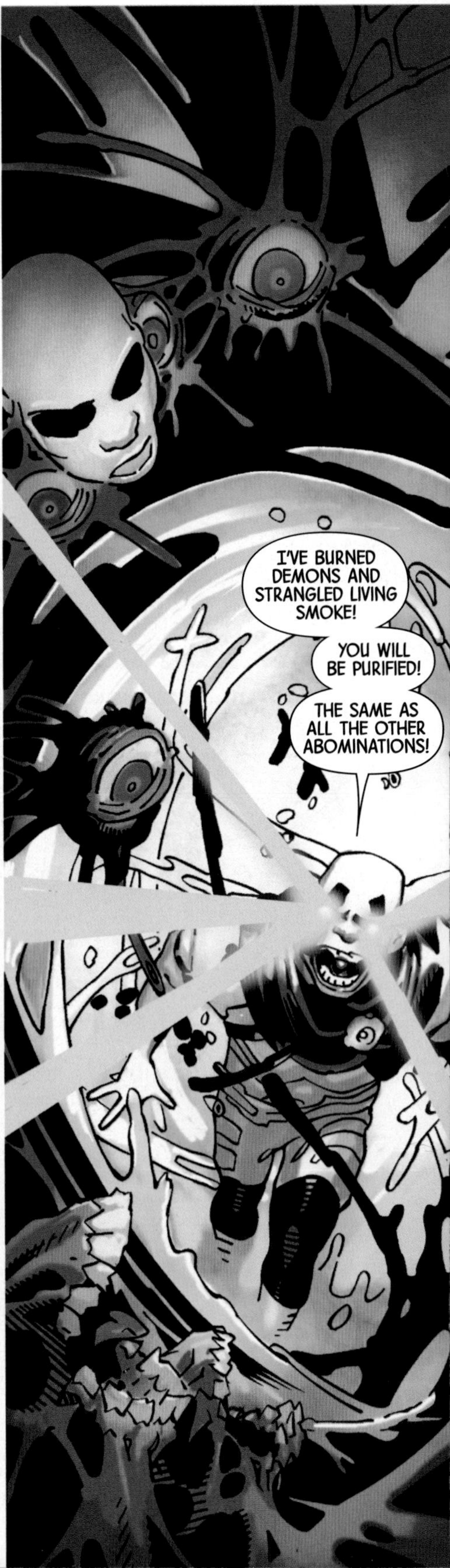
I'VE BURNED DEMONS AND STRANGLED LIVING SMOKE!
YOU WILL BE PURIFIED!
THE SAME AS ALL THE OTHER ABOMINATIONS!

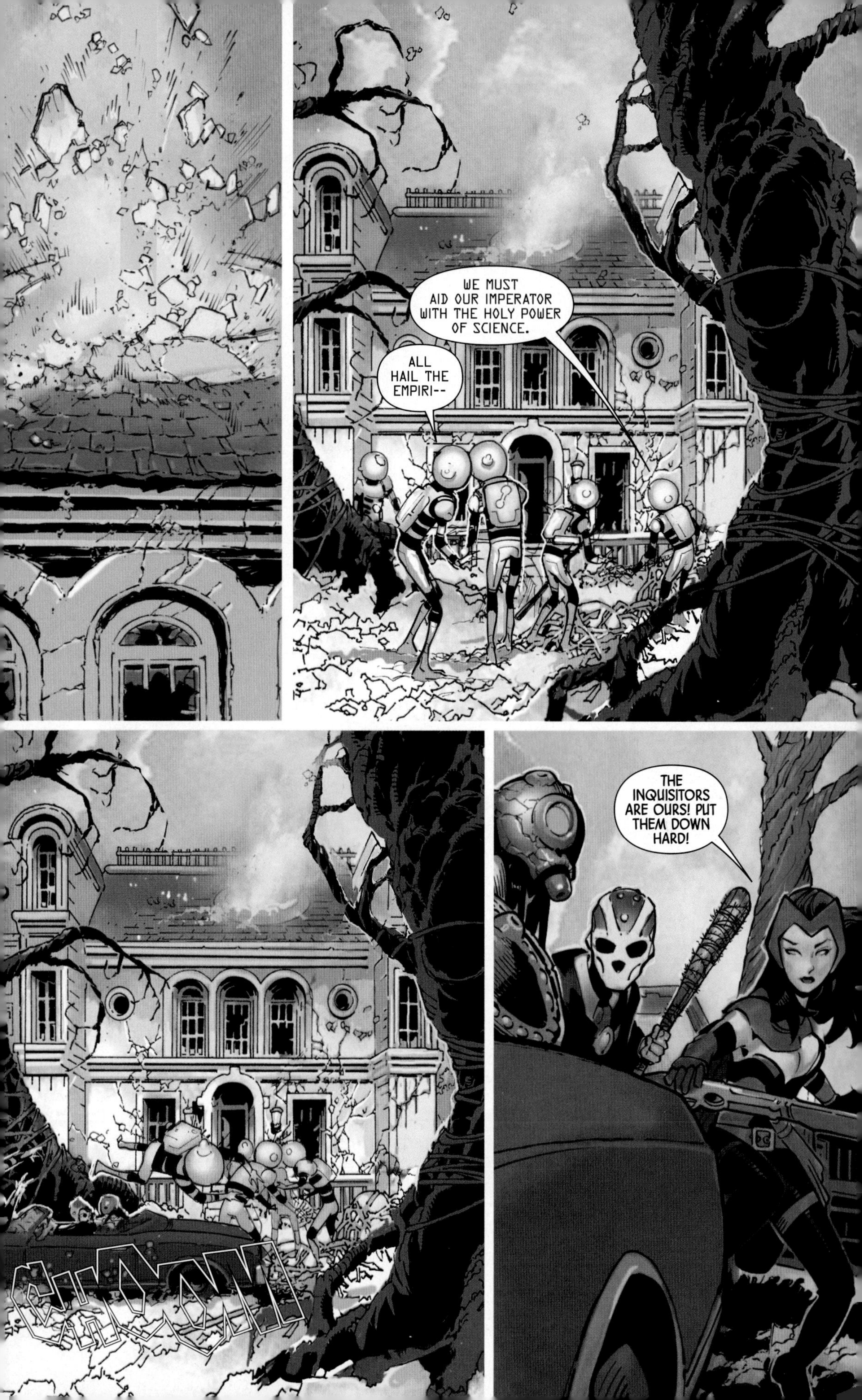
WE MUST AID OUR IMPERATOR WITH THE HOLY POWER OF SCIENCE.
ALL HAIL THE EMPIRI--
THE INQUISITORS ARE OURS! PUT THEM DOWN HARD!

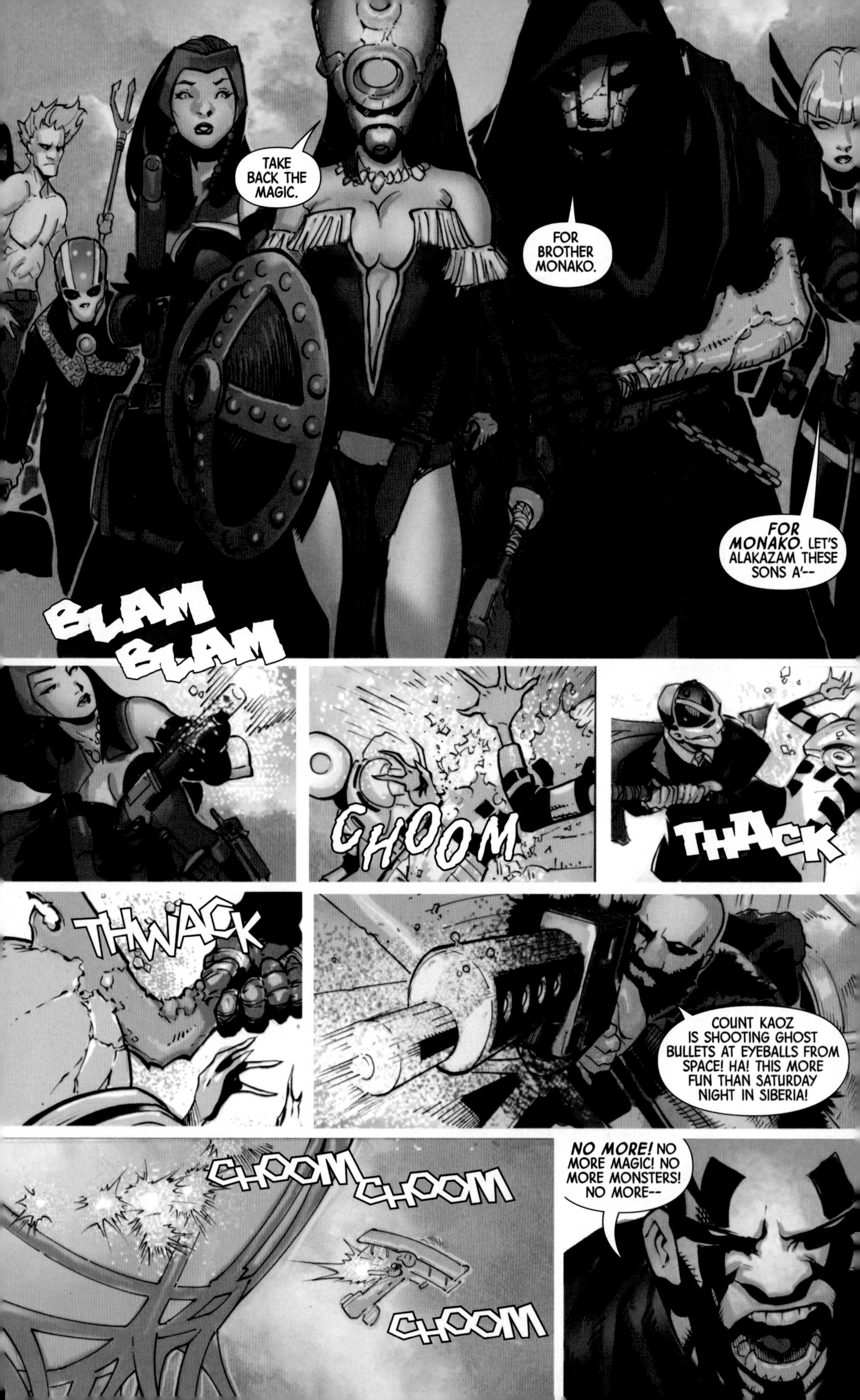
TAKE BACK THE MAGIC.
FOR BROTHER MONAKO.
FOR MONAKO. LET'S ALAKAZAM THESE SONS A'--
BLAM BLAM
CHOOM
THACK
THWACK
COUNT KAOZ IS SHOOTING GHOST BULLETS AT EYEBALLS FROM SPACE! HA! THIS MORE FUN THAN SATURDAY NIGHT IN SIBERIA!
CHOOM CHOOM
CHOOM
NO MORE! NO MORE MAGIC! NO MORE MONSTERS! NO MORE--

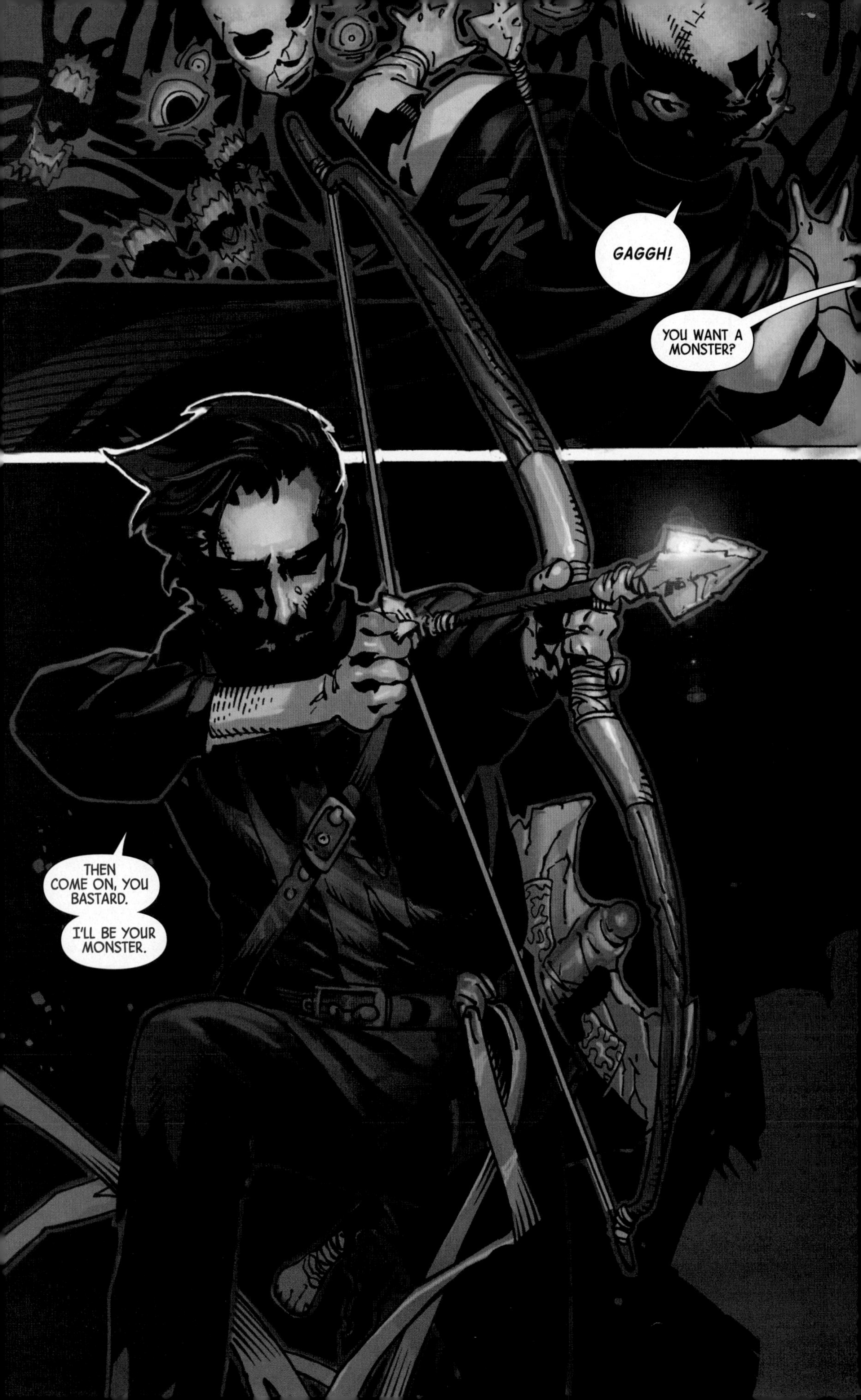
SNK
GAGGH!
YOU WANT A MONSTER?
THEN COME ON, YOU BASTARD.
I'LL BE YOUR MONSTER.

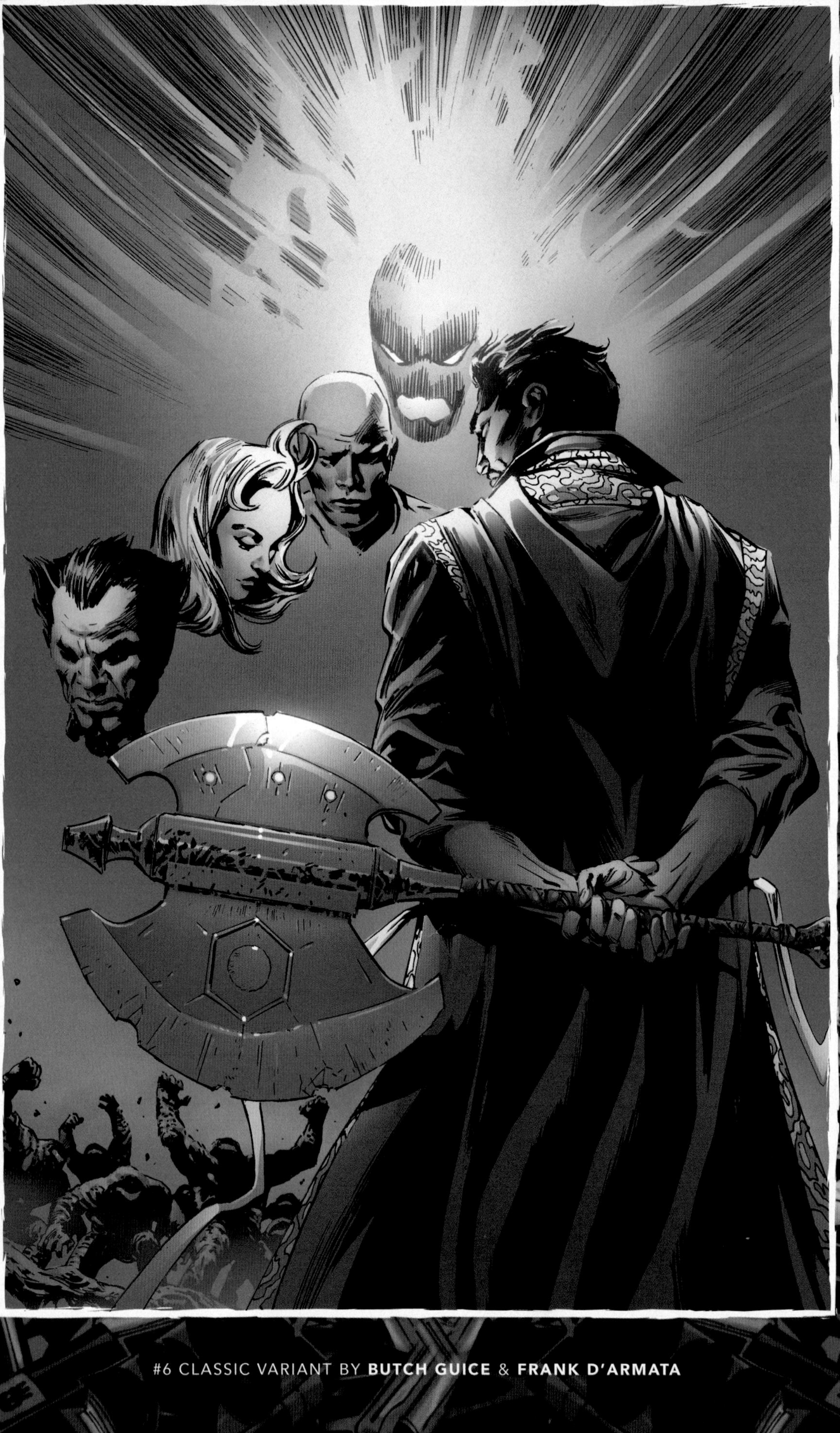

#6 CLASSIC VARIANT BY **BUTCH GUICE** & **FRANK D'ARMATA**

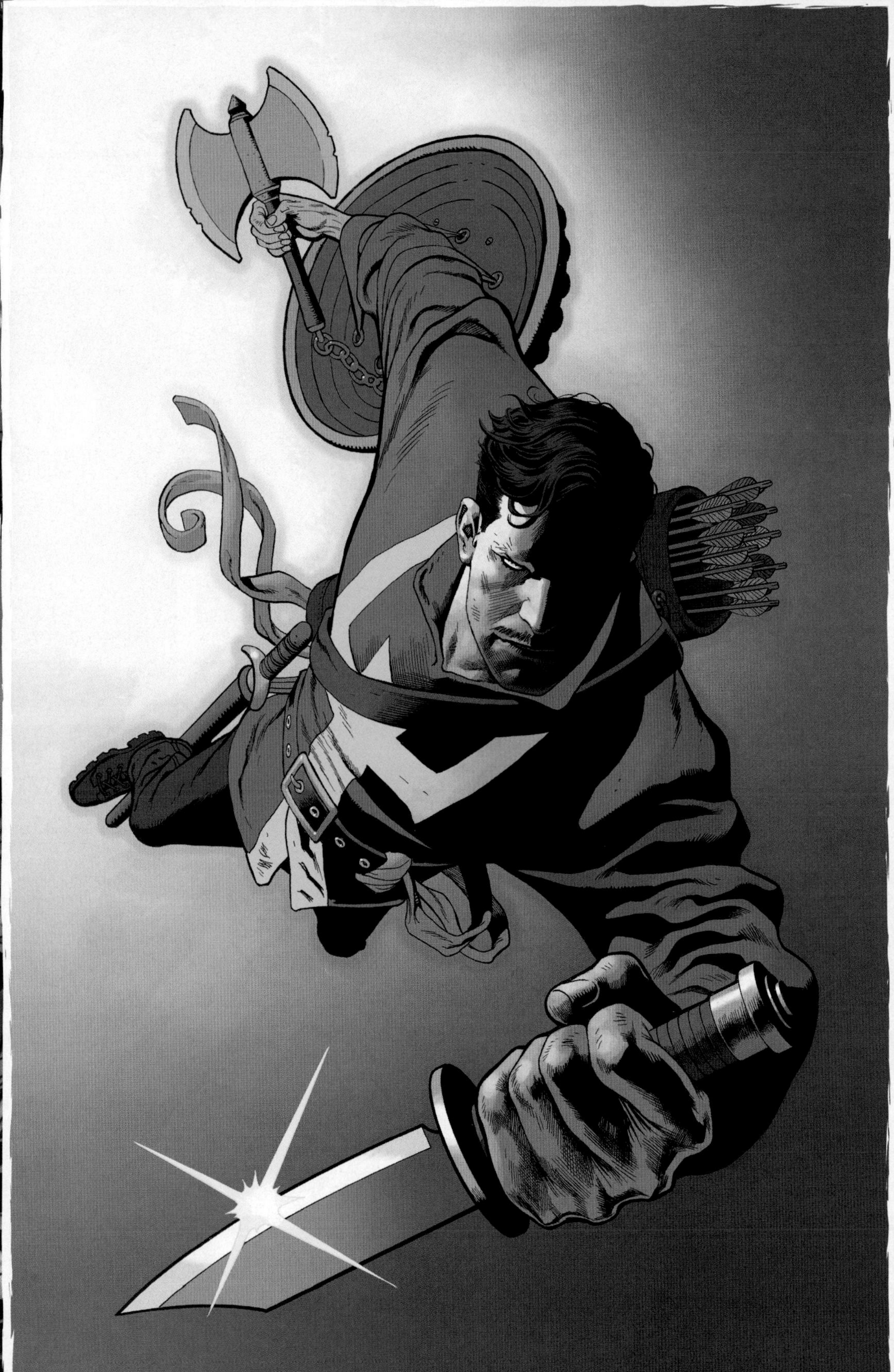

DOCTOR STRANGE 10 THE LAST DAYS OF MAGIC CONCLUSION

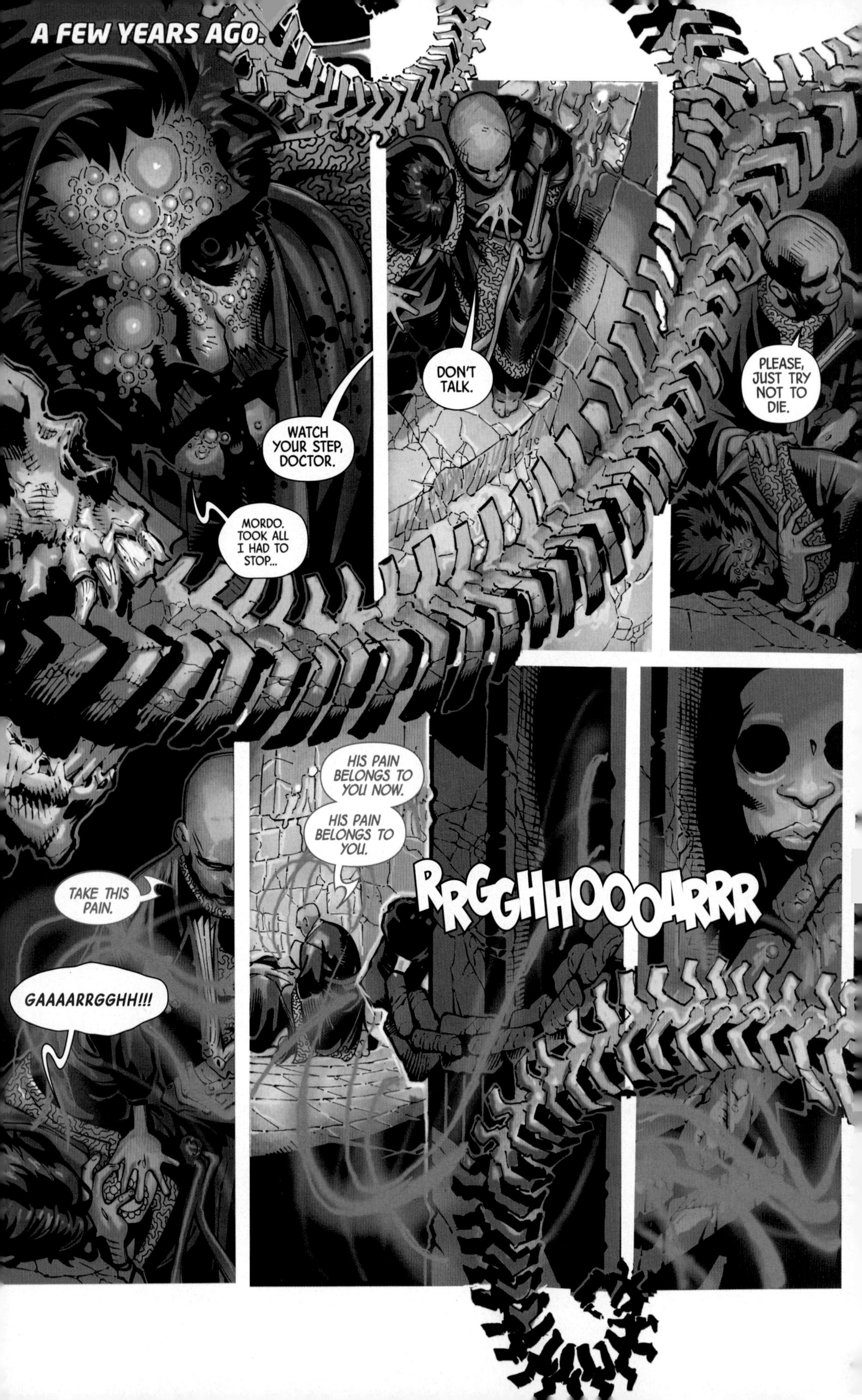
A FEW YEARS AGO.
WATCH YOUR STEP, DOCTOR.
MORDO. TOOK ALL I HAD TO STOP...
DON'T TALK.
PLEASE, JUST TRY NOT TO DIE.
TAKE THIS PAIN.
GAAAARRGGHH!!!
HIS PAIN BELONGS TO YOU NOW.
HIS PAIN BELONGS TO YOU.
RRGGHHOOOOARRR

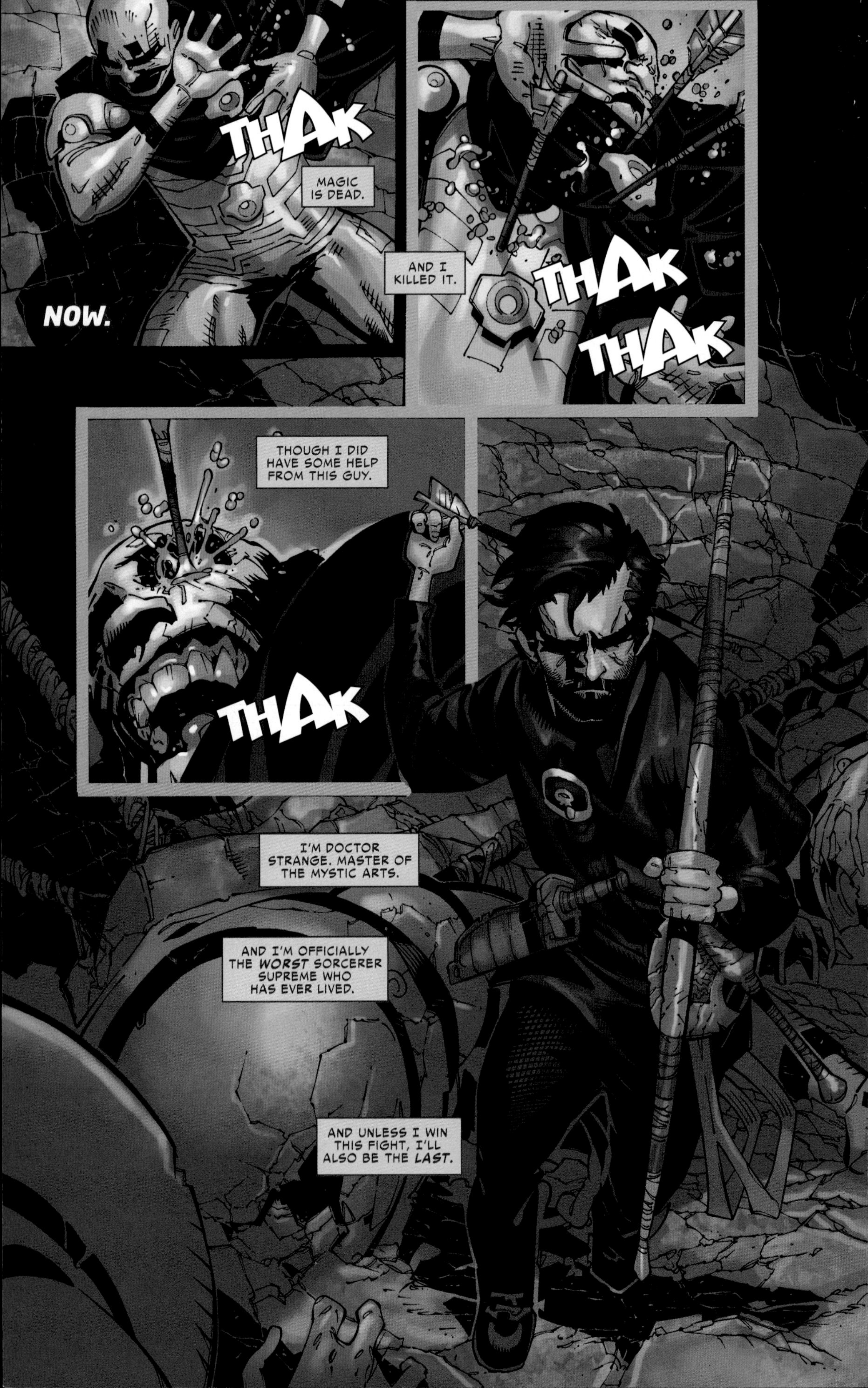
THAK
MAGIC IS DEAD.
NOW.
AND I KILLED IT.
THAK
THAK
THOUGH I DID HAVE SOME HELP FROM THIS GUY.
THAK
I'M DOCTOR STRANGE. MASTER OF THE MYSTIC ARTS.
AND I'M OFFICIALLY THE *WORST* SORCERER SUPREME WHO HAS EVER LIVED.
AND UNLESS I WIN THIS FIGHT, I'LL ALSO BE THE *LAST*.

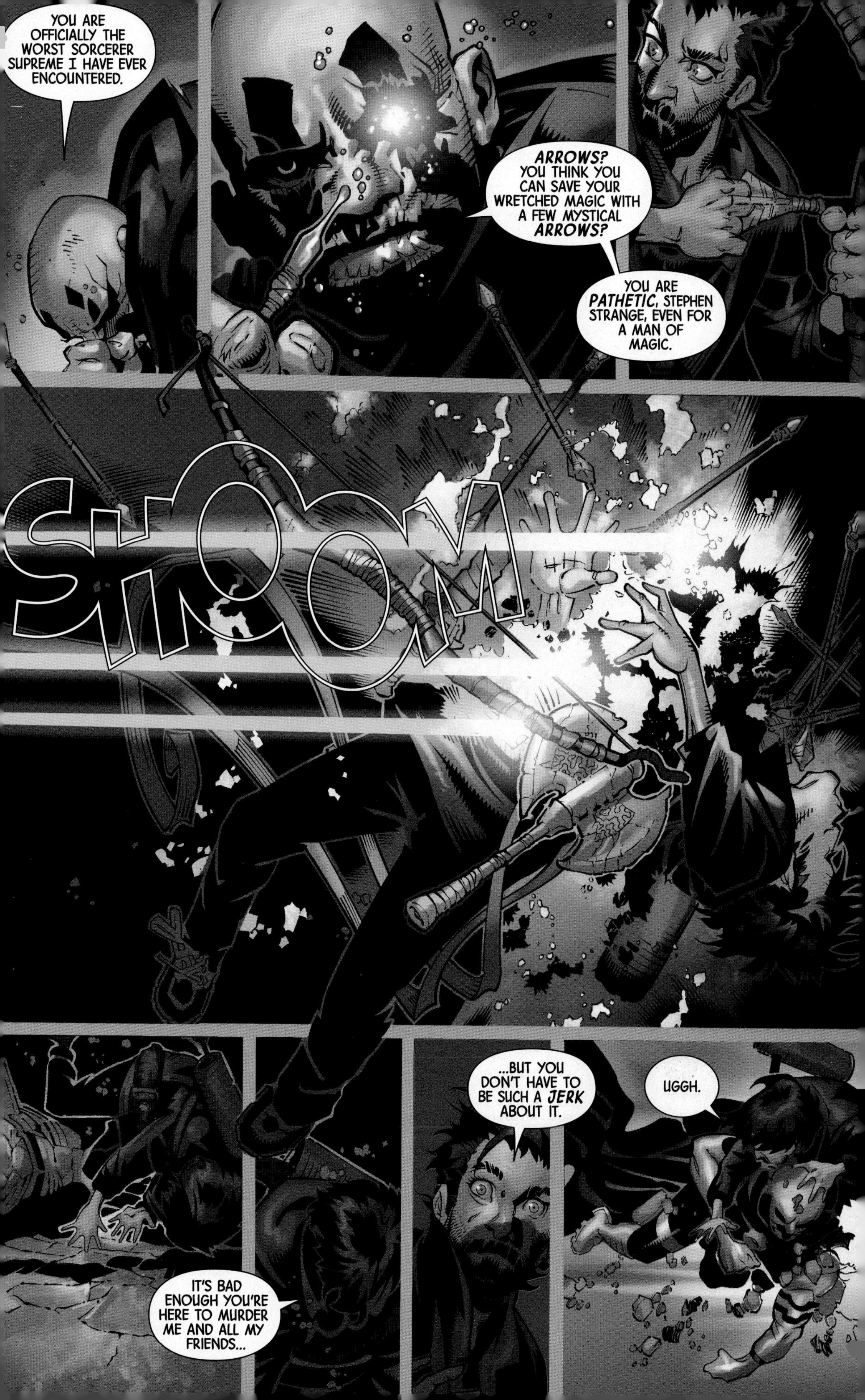

YOU ARE OFFICIALLY THE WORST SORCERER SUPREME I HAVE EVER ENCOUNTERED.
ARROWS? YOU THINK YOU CAN SAVE YOUR WRETCHED MAGIC WITH A FEW MYSTICAL ARROWS?
YOU ARE PATHETIC, STEPHEN STRANGE, EVEN FOR A MAN OF MAGIC.
STROOM
IT'S BAD ENOUGH YOU'RE HERE TO MURDER ME AND ALL MY FRIENDS...
...BUT YOU DON'T HAVE TO BE SUCH A JERK ABOUT IT.
UGGH.

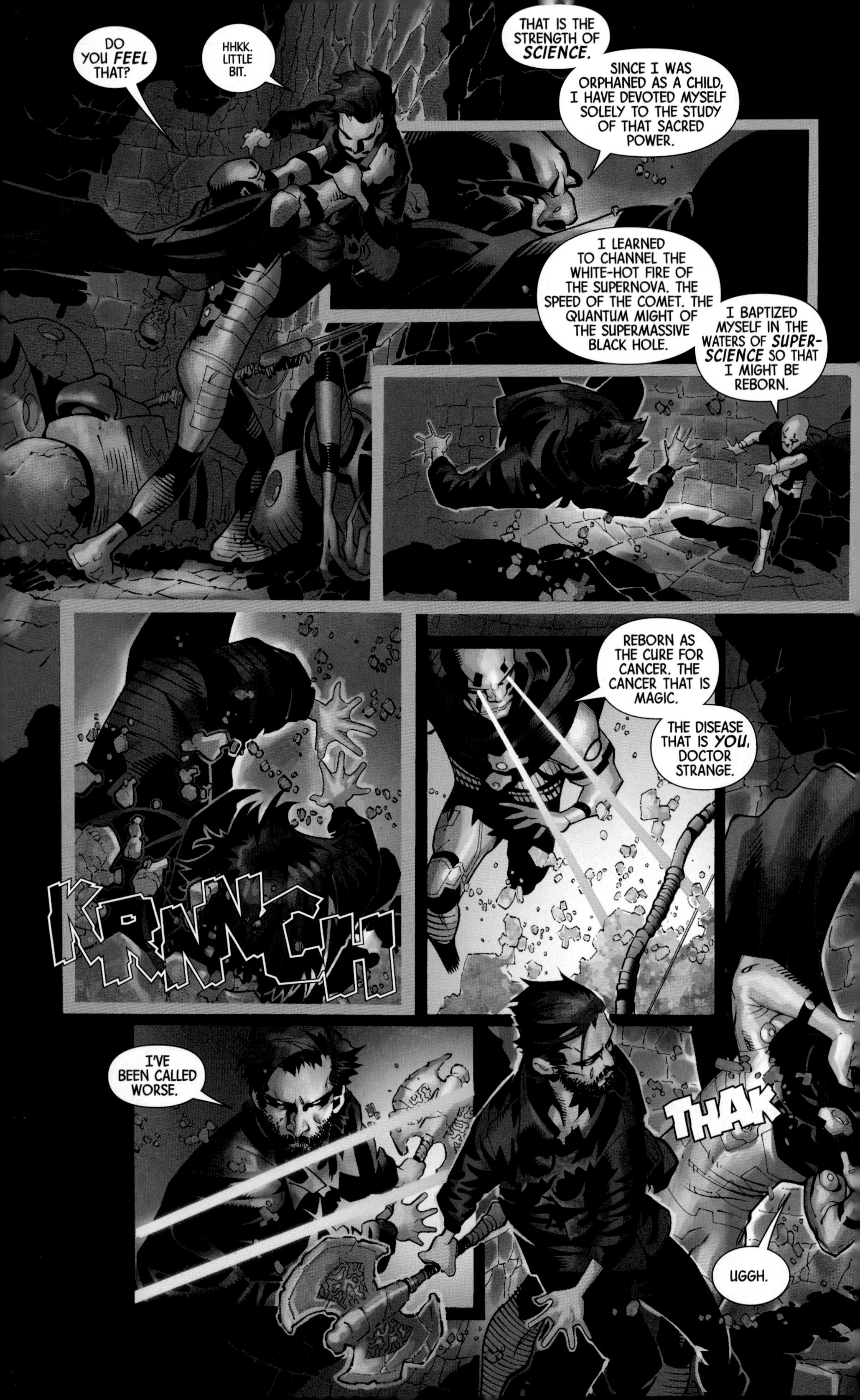

DO YOU *FEEL* THAT?
HHKK. LITTLE BIT.
THAT IS THE STRENGTH OF *SCIENCE.*
SINCE I WAS ORPHANED AS A CHILD, I HAVE DEVOTED MYSELF SOLELY TO THE STUDY OF THAT SACRED POWER.
I LEARNED TO CHANNEL THE WHITE-HOT FIRE OF THE SUPERNOVA. THE SPEED OF THE COMET. THE QUANTUM MIGHT OF THE SUPERMASSIVE BLACK HOLE.
I BAPTIZED MYSELF IN THE WATERS OF *SUPER-SCIENCE* SO THAT I MIGHT BE REBORN.
KRNNCH
REBORN AS THE CURE FOR CANCER. THE CANCER THAT IS MAGIC.
THE DISEASE THAT IS *YOU,* DOCTOR STRANGE.
I'VE BEEN CALLED WORSE.
THAK
UGGH.

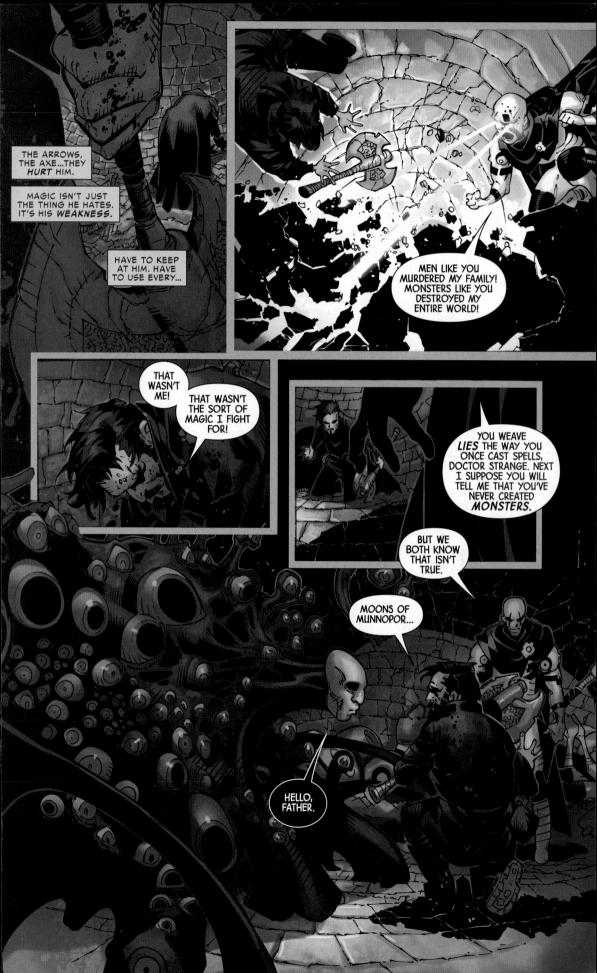

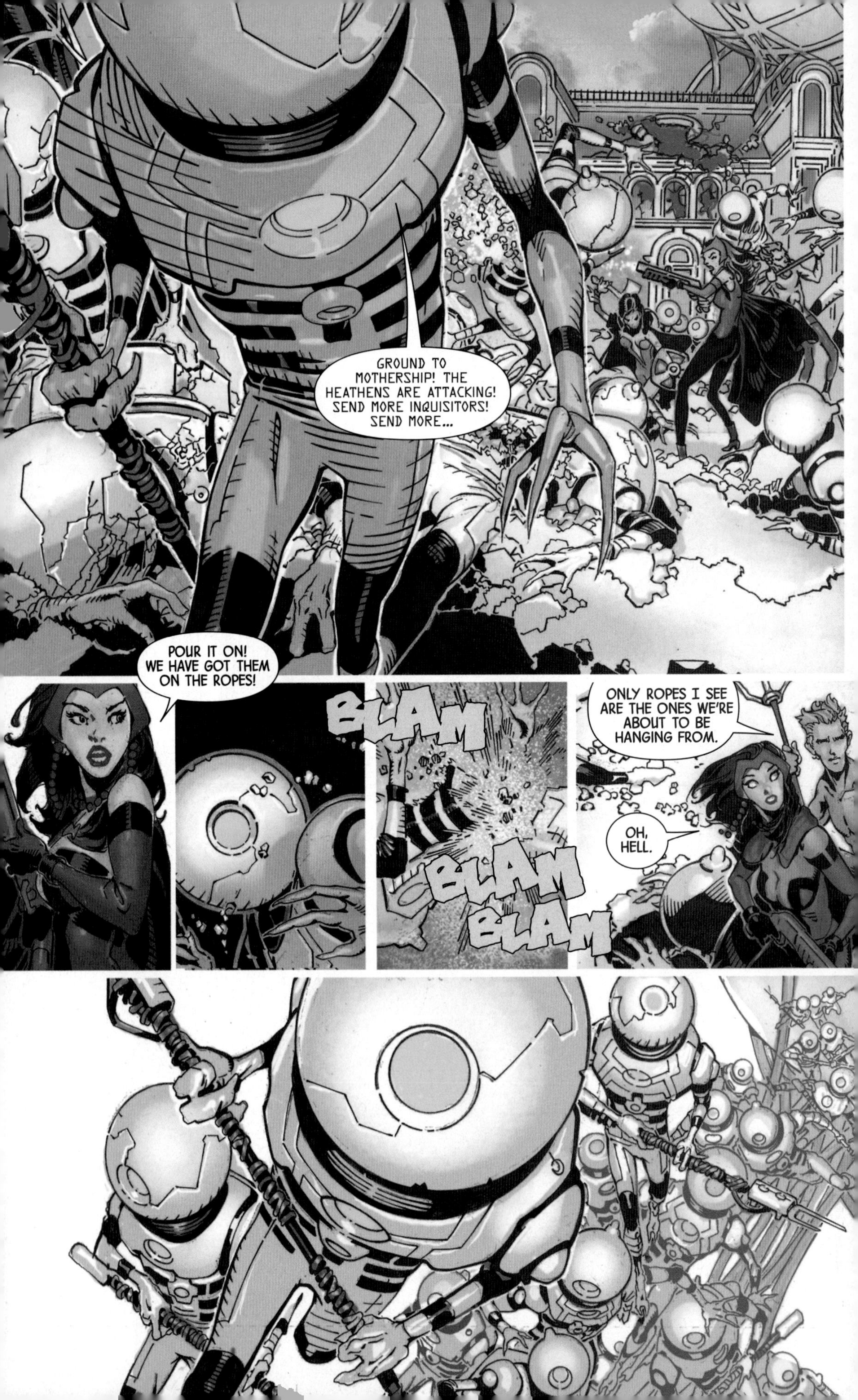
GROUND TO MOTHERSHIP! THE HEATHENS ARE ATTACKING! SEND MORE INQUISITORS! SEND MORE...
POUR IT ON! WE HAVE GOT THEM ON THE ROPES!
BLAM
BLAM
BLAM
ONLY ROPES I SEE ARE THE ONES WE'RE ABOUT TO BE HANGING FROM.
OH, HELL.

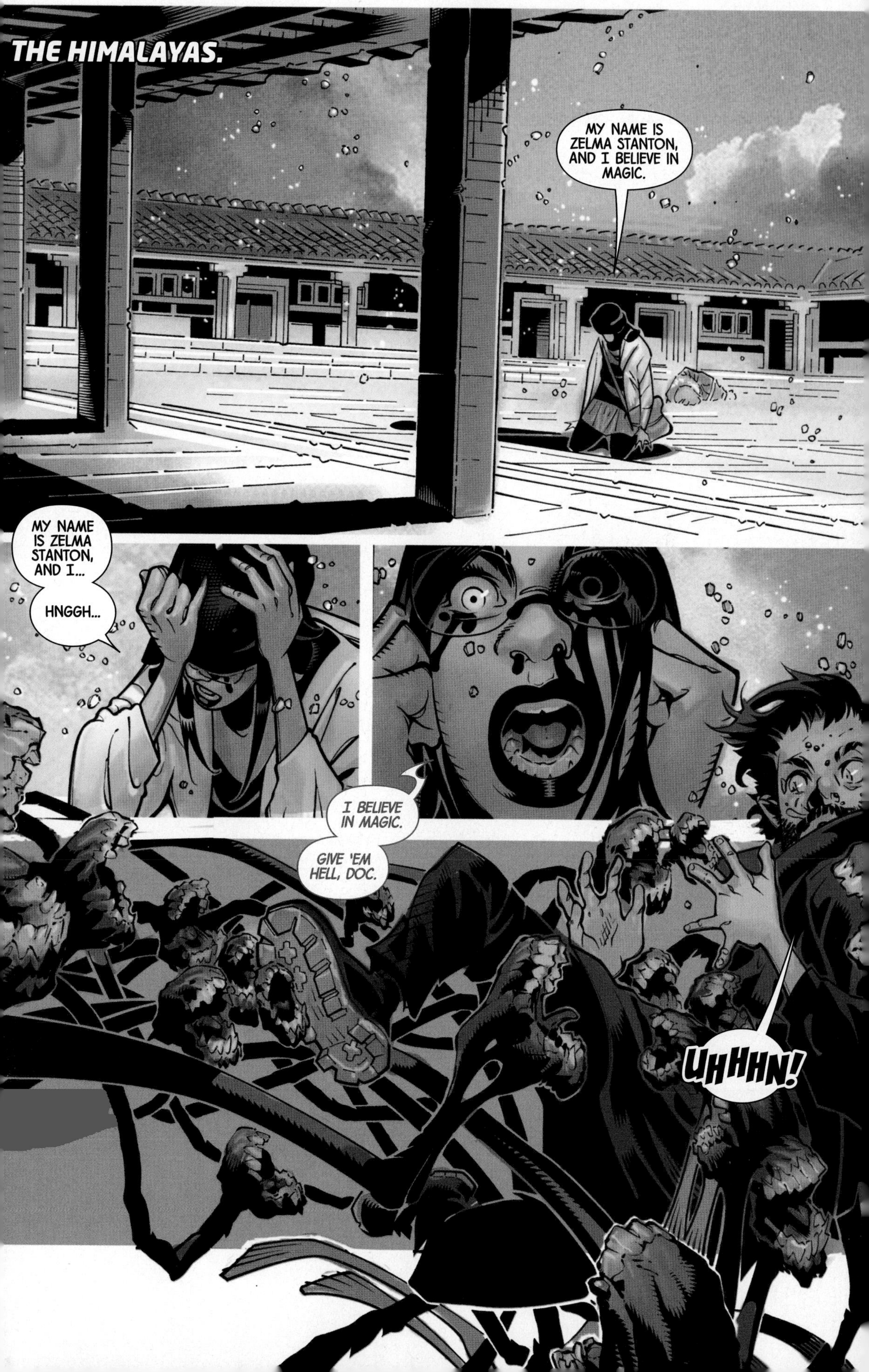
THE HIMALAYAS.
MY NAME IS ZELMA STANTON, AND I BELIEVE IN MAGIC.
MY NAME IS ZELMA STANTON, AND I...
HNGGH...
I BELIEVE IN MAGIC.
GIVE 'EM HELL, DOC.
UHHHN!

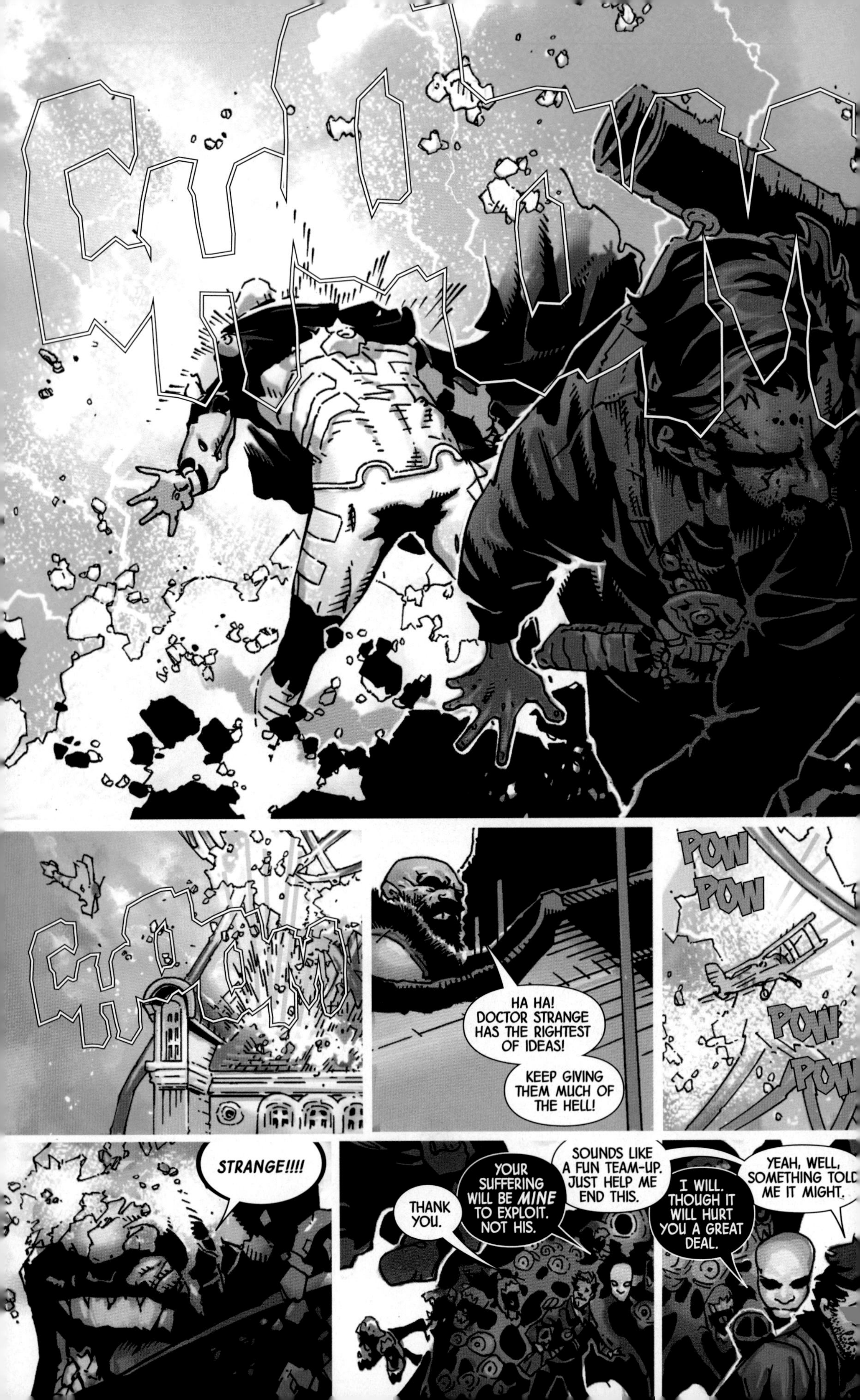
HA HA! DOCTOR STRANGE HAS THE RIGHTEST OF IDEAS!
KEEP GIVING THEM MUCH OF THE HELL!
POW
POW
POW
POW
STRANGE!!!!
THANK YOU.
YOUR SUFFERING WILL BE *MINE* TO EXPLOIT. NOT HIS.
SOUNDS LIKE A FUN TEAM-UP. JUST HELP ME END THIS.
I WILL. THOUGH IT WILL HURT YOU A GREAT DEAL.
YEAH, WELL, SOMETHING TOLD ME IT MIGHT.

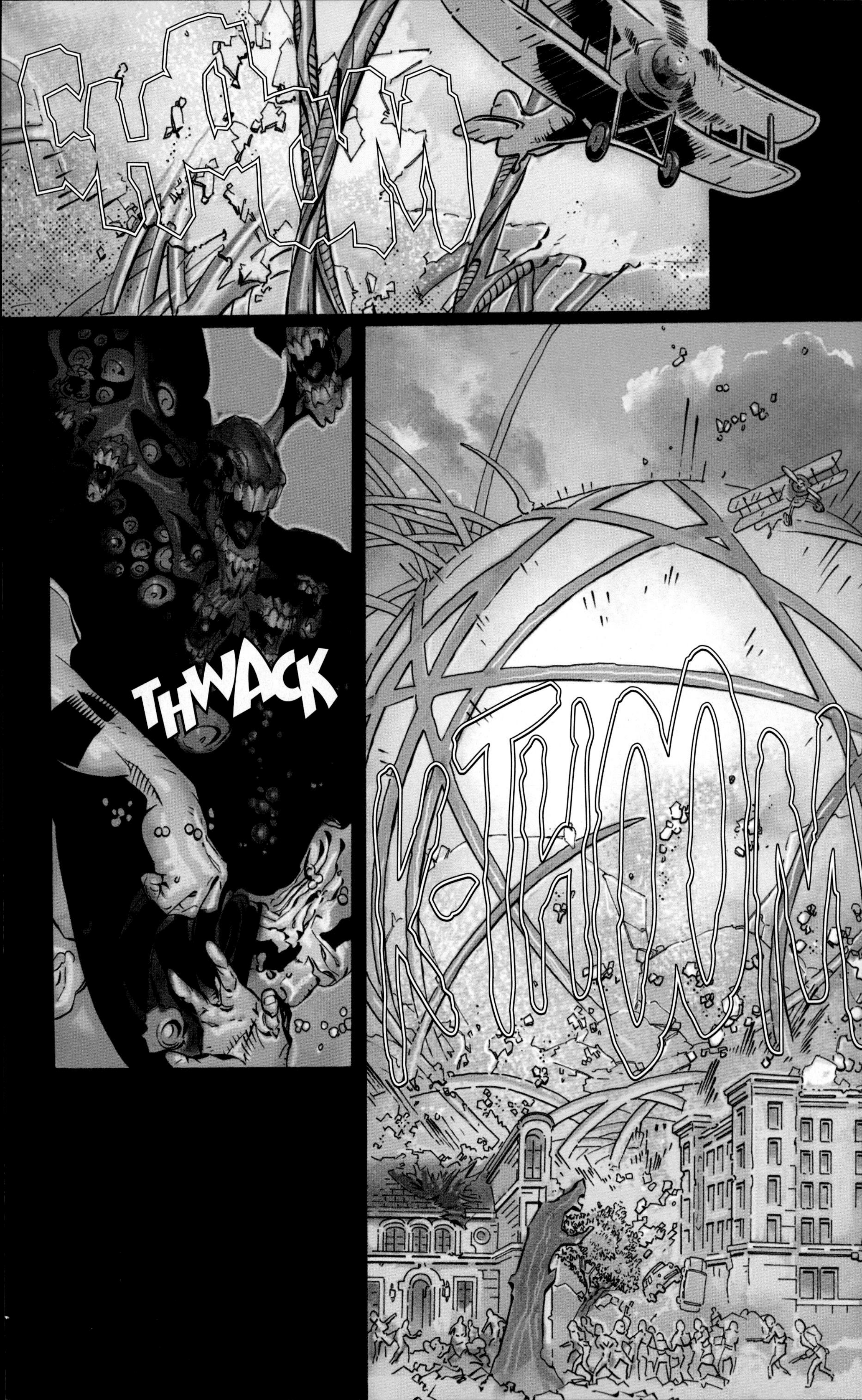
THWACK
K-THOOM

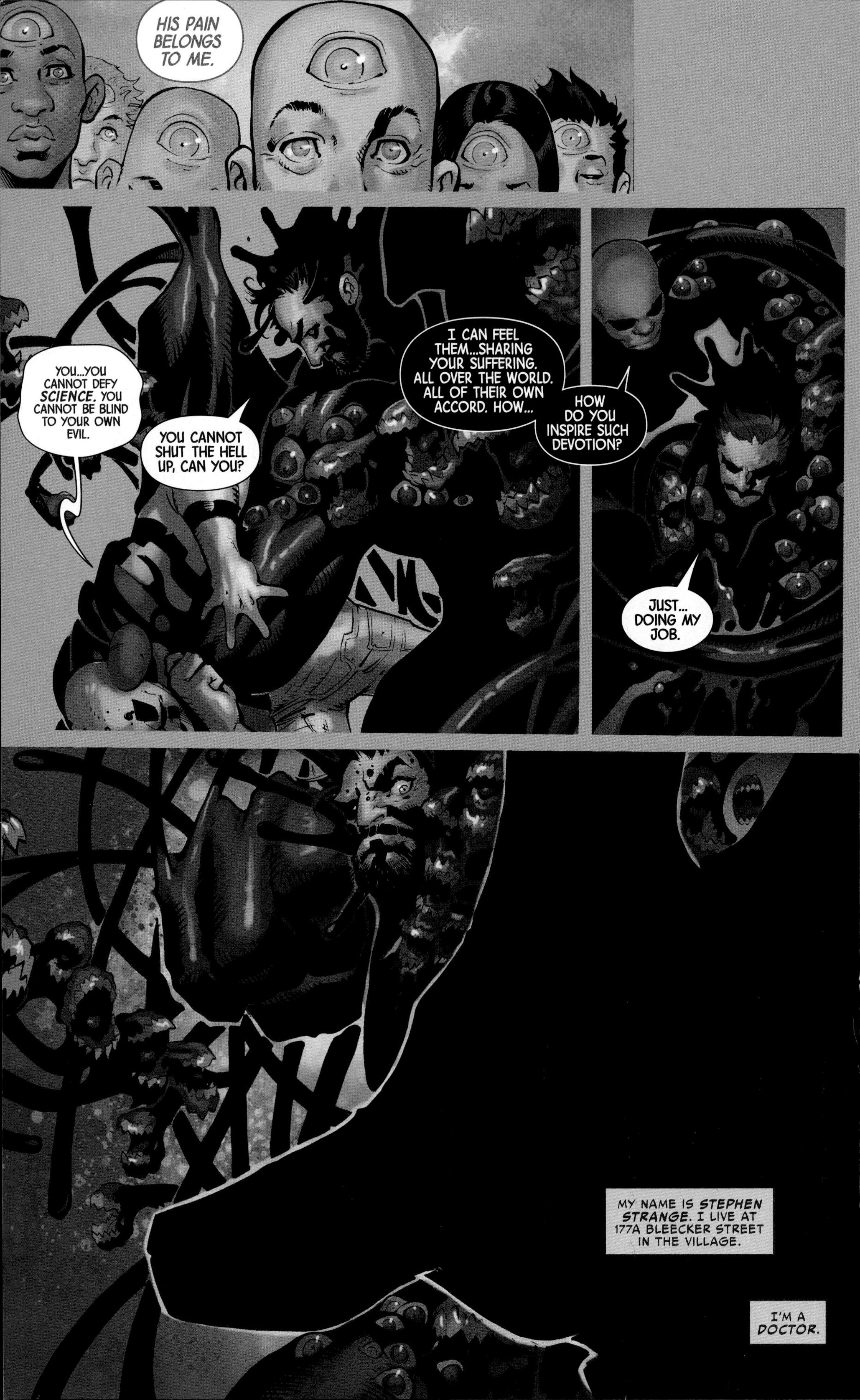
HIS PAIN BELONGS TO ME.
YOU...YOU CANNOT DEFY SCIENCE. YOU CANNOT BE BLIND TO YOUR OWN EVIL.
YOU CANNOT SHUT THE HELL UP, CAN YOU?
I CAN FEEL THEM...SHARING YOUR SUFFERING. ALL OVER THE WORLD. ALL OF THEIR OWN ACCORD. HOW...
HOW DO YOU INSPIRE SUCH DEVOTION?
JUST... DOING MY JOB.
MY NAME IS STEPHEN STRANGE. I LIVE AT 177A BLEECKER STREET IN THE VILLAGE.
I'M A DOCTOR.

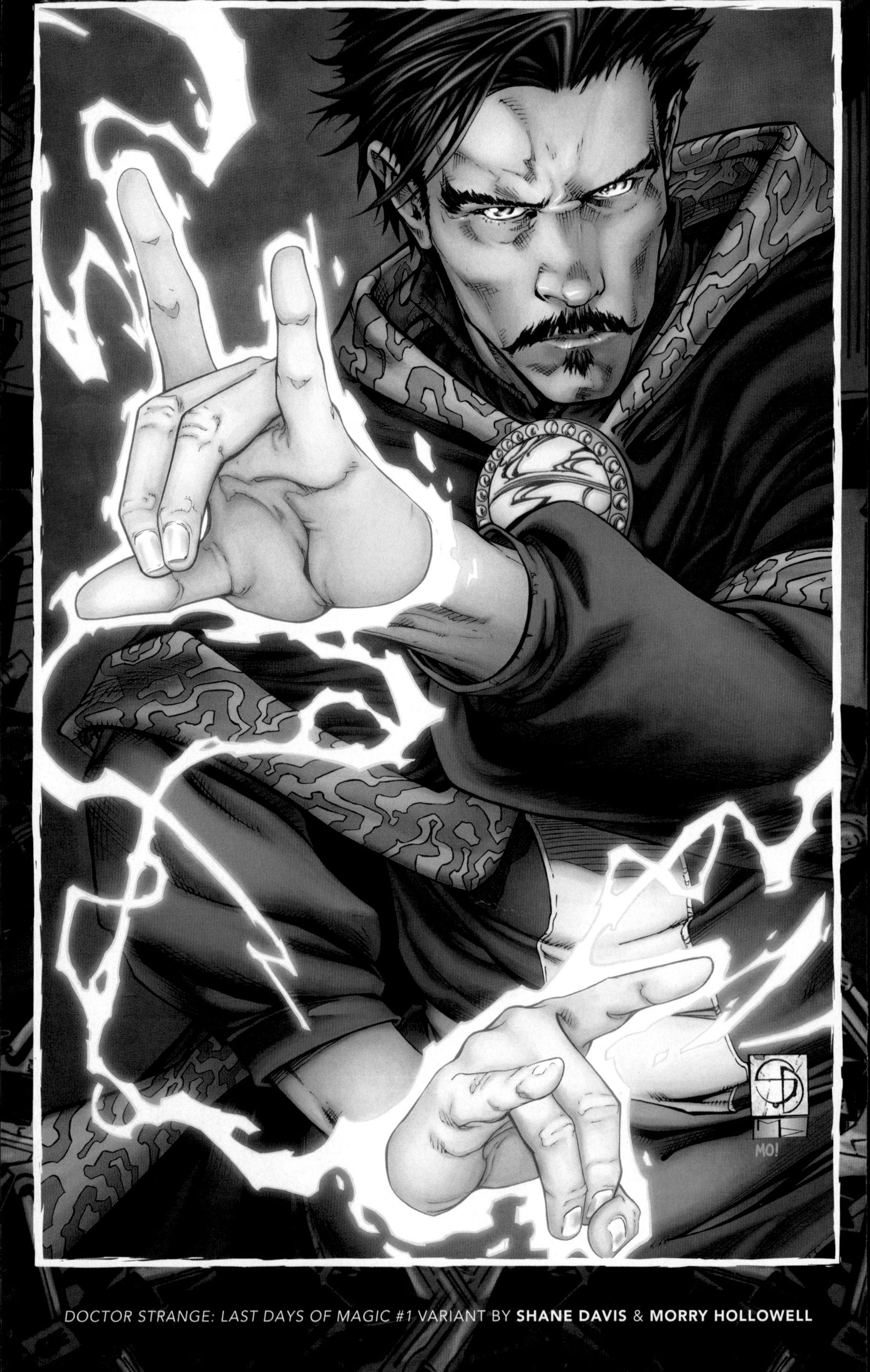
MO!

DOCTOR STRANGE: LAST DAYS OF MAGIC #1 VARIANT BY **SHANE DAVIS** & **MORRY HOLLOWELL**

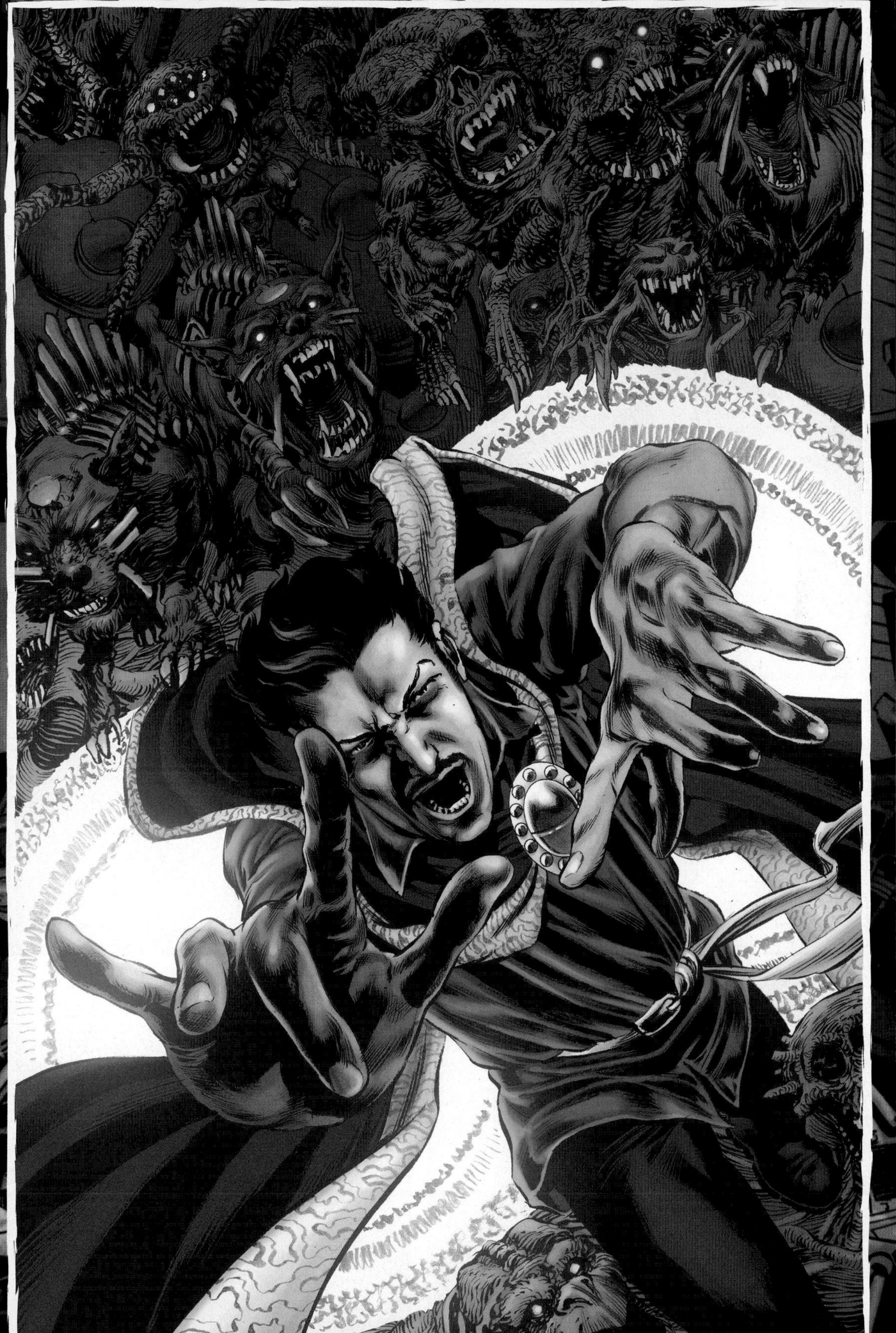

DOCTOR STRANGE: LAST DAYS OF MAGIC #1

(THIS STORY TAKES PLACE BETWEEN ISSUES #6 & #7.)

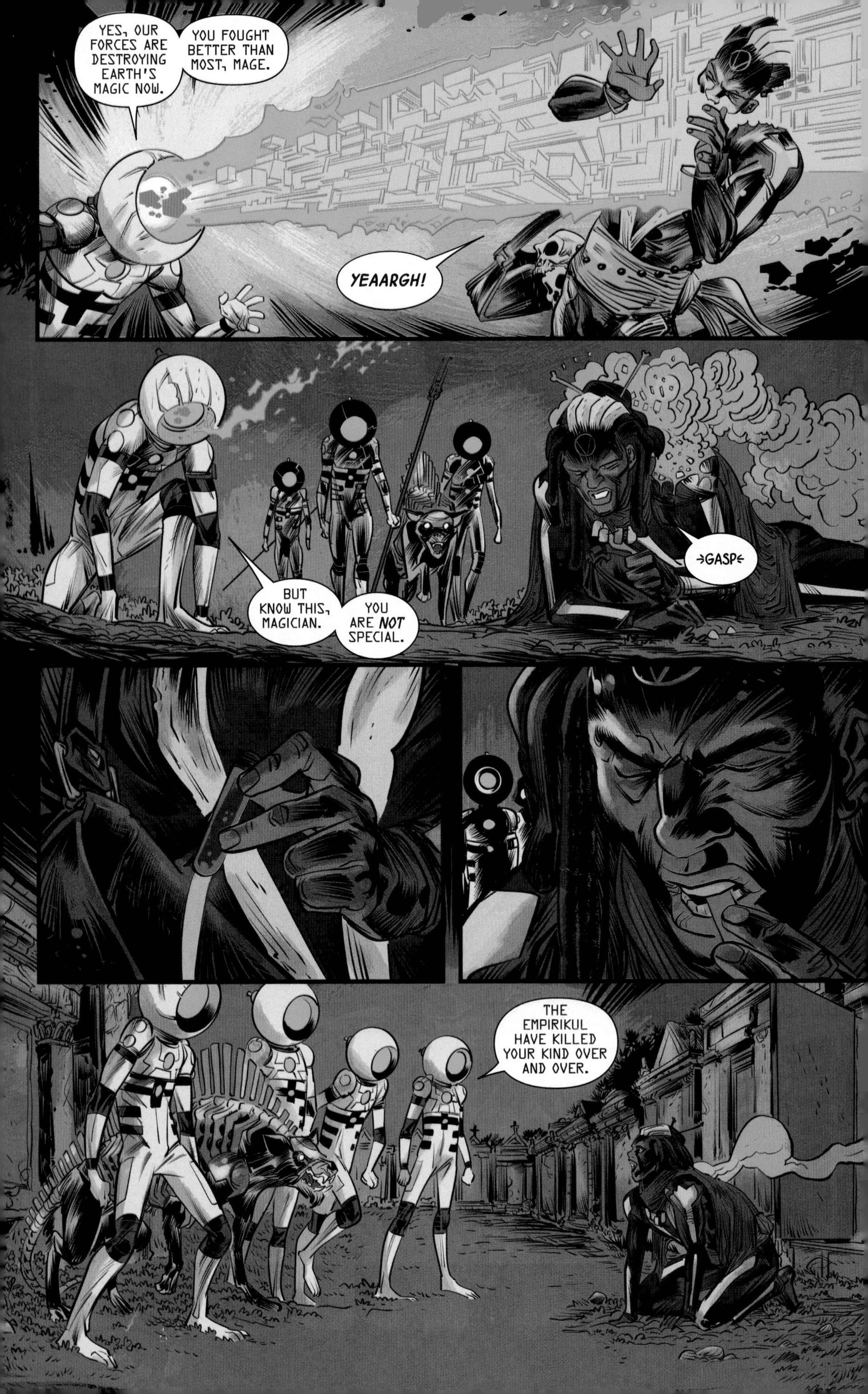
YES, OUR FORCES ARE DESTROYING EARTH'S MAGIC NOW.
YOU FOUGHT BETTER THAN MOST, MAGE.
YEAARGH!
GASP
BUT KNOW THIS, MAGICIAN.
YOU ARE NOT SPECIAL.
THE EMPIRIKUL HAVE KILLED YOUR KIND OVER AND OVER.

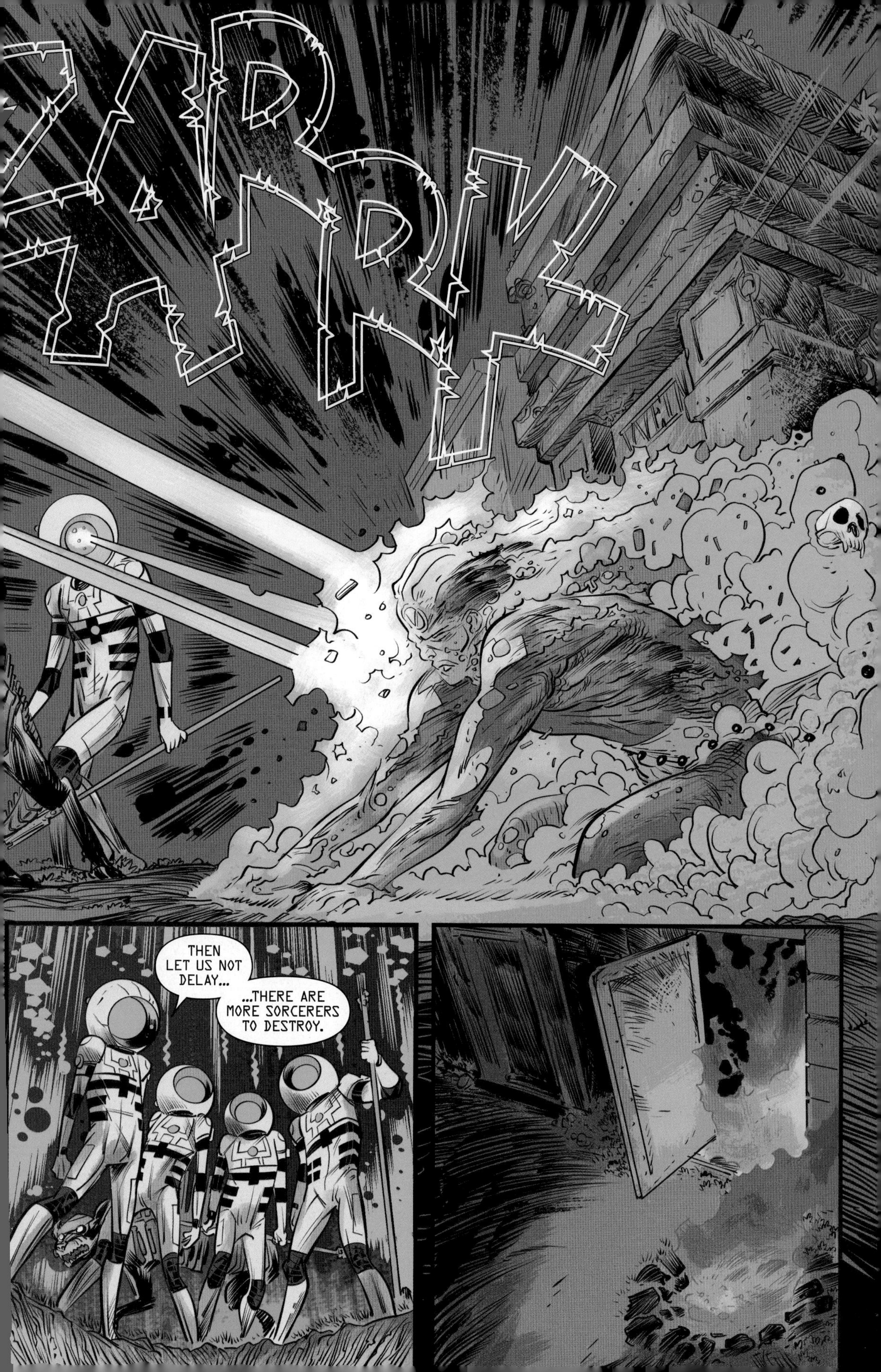
THEN LET US NOT DELAY...
...THERE ARE MORE SORCERERS TO DESTROY.

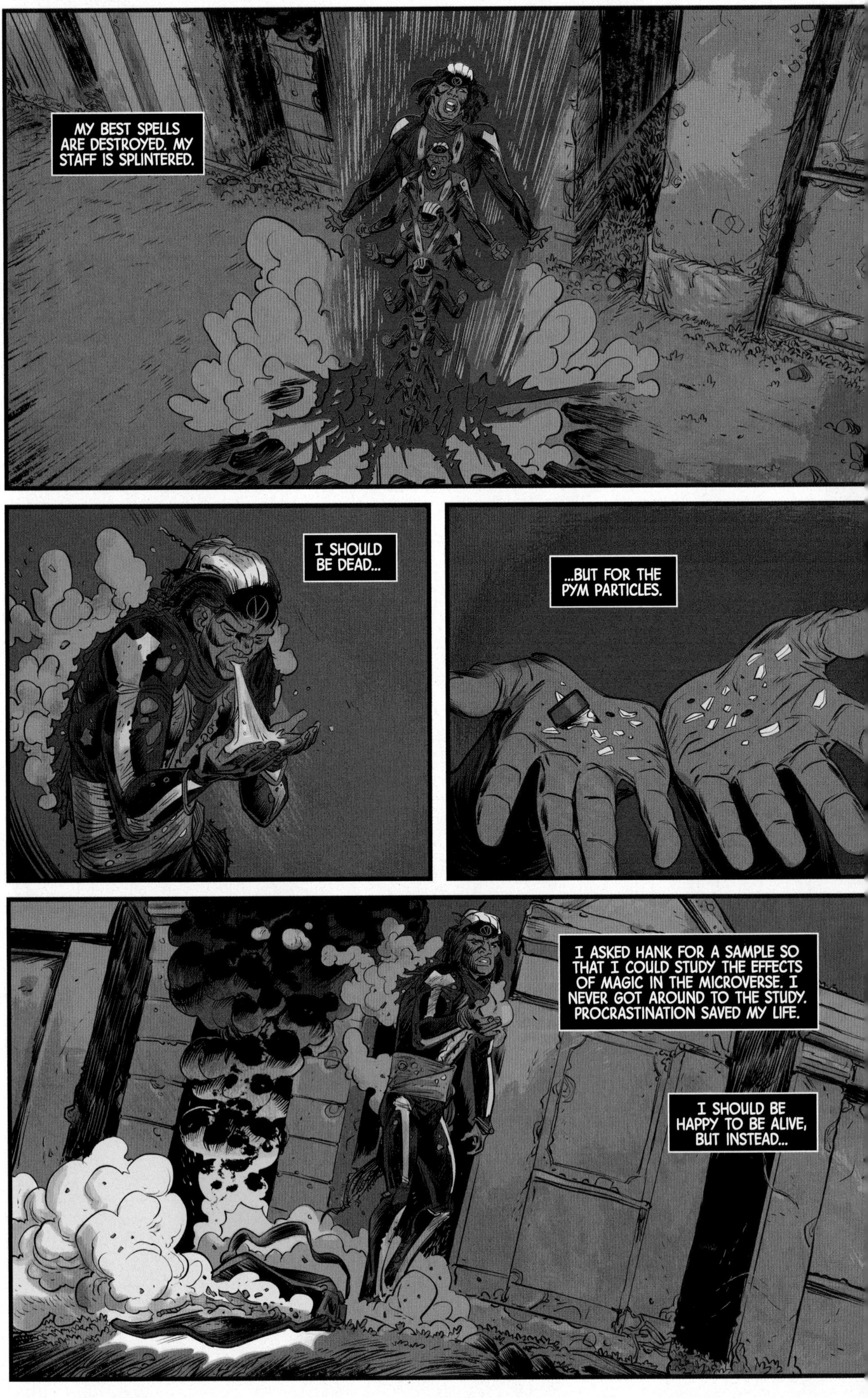
MY BEST SPELLS ARE DESTROYED. MY STAFF IS SPLINTERED.
I SHOULD BE DEAD...
...BUT FOR THE PYM PARTICLES.
I ASKED HANK FOR A SAMPLE SO THAT I COULD STUDY THE EFFECTS OF MAGIC IN THE MICROVERSE. I NEVER GOT AROUND TO THE STUDY. PROCRASTINATION SAVED MY LIFE.
I SHOULD BE HAPPY TO BE ALIVE, BUT INSTEAD...

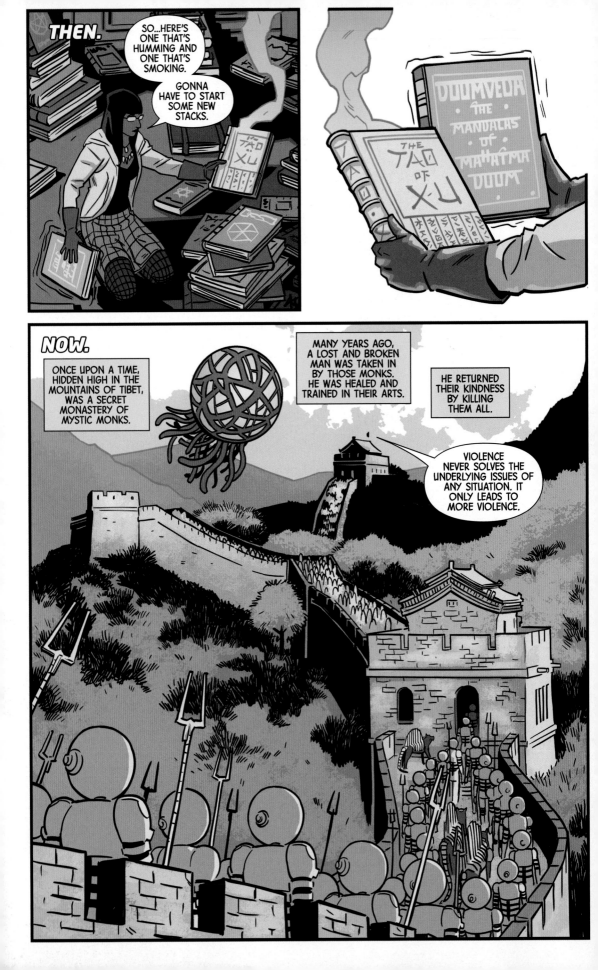

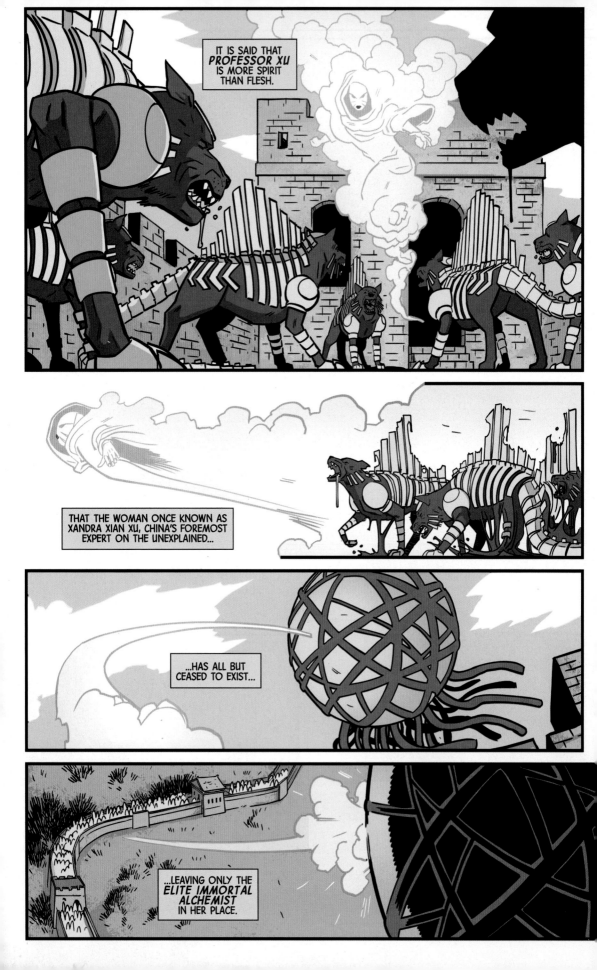

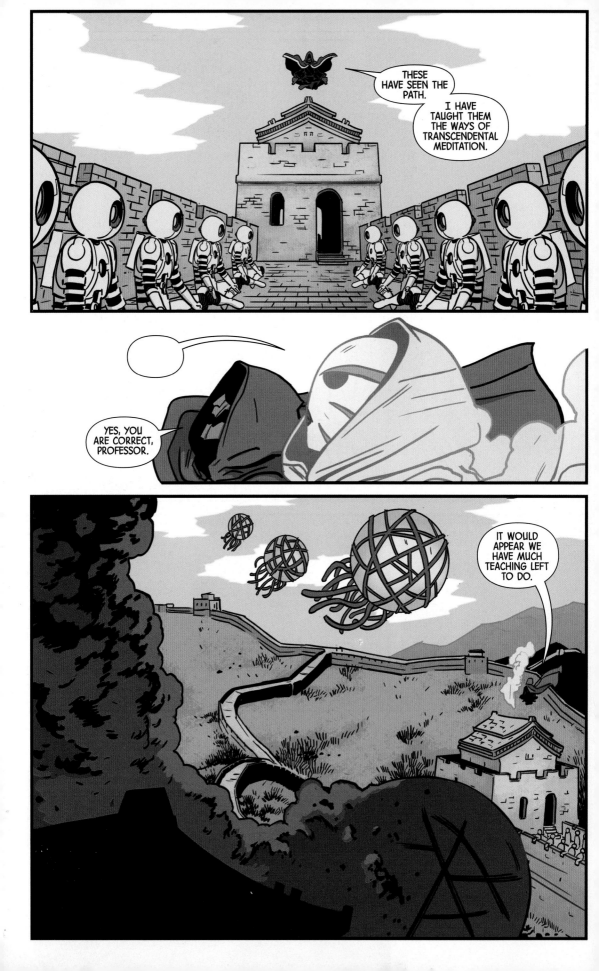

THEN.

ARE YOU ALL RIGHT, ZELMA?...

...YOU LOOK LIKE YOU HAVE A HEADACHE.

AH, THE *MÉDICO MÍSTICO.*

THIS "CATALOGUE" OF MAGES AND WIZARDS GOES ON AND ON.

WITCHES, TOO--

MY HEAD'S A WHIRL, WONG, BUT I'M OKAY, NO NEED FOR ASPIRIN...YET.

I'M JUST BLOWN AWAY BY EVERYTHING I'M READING HERE.

--ONE WITCH WHO I'M READING ABOUT NOW IS RELATIVELY NEW TO THE GAME OF MAGIC.

HER NAME IS *ALICE GULLIVER.*

AND, INTERESTINGLY, HER ORIGIN IS LINKED TO STEPHEN...TO SOME DEGREE, ANYWAY.

BACK WHEN SHE WAS YOUNGER, OF COURSE...

...AND HER HAIR WAS STILL THE COLOR OF *NIGHT.*

NOW.

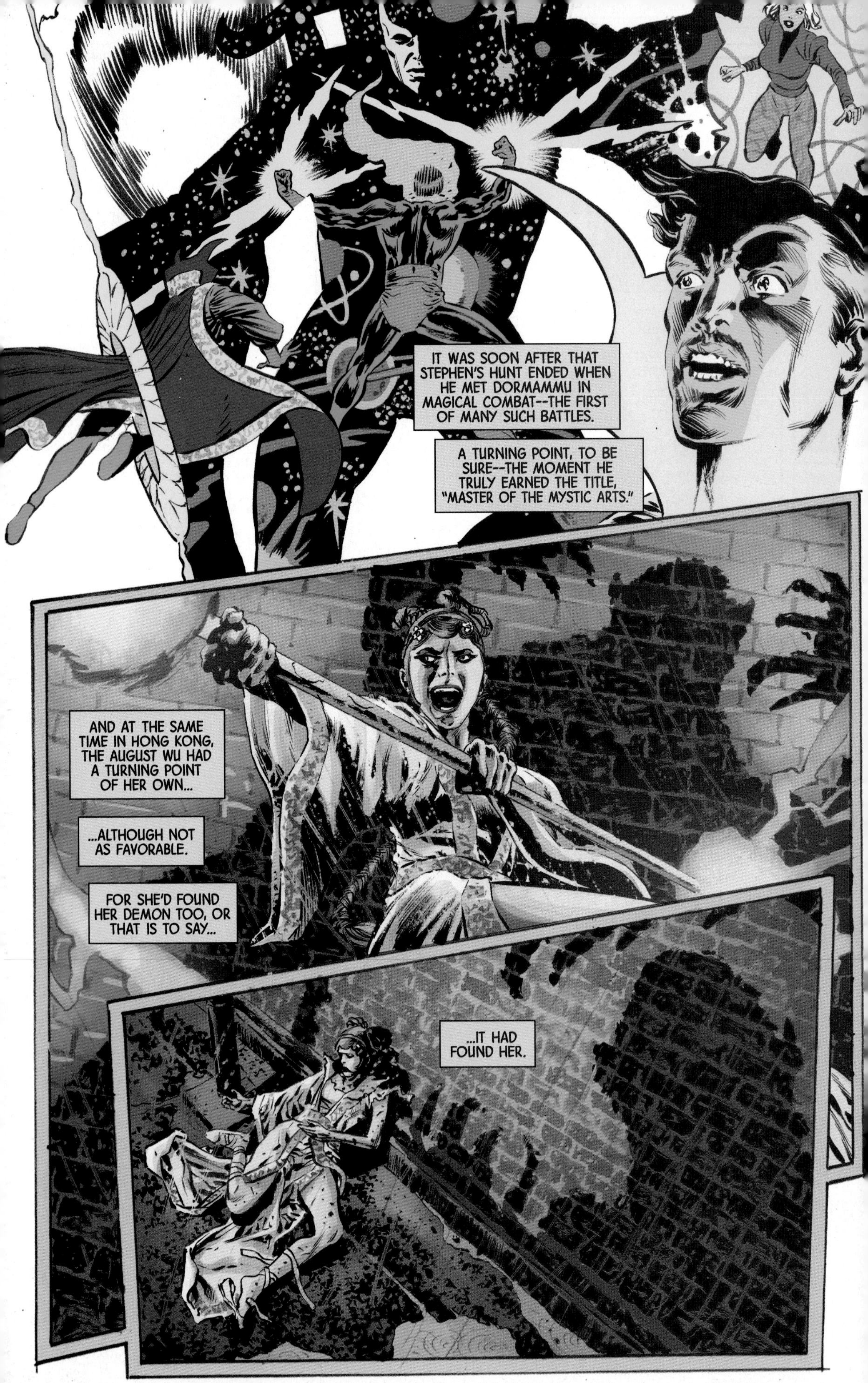
IT WAS SOON AFTER THAT STEPHEN'S HUNT ENDED WHEN HE MET DORMAMMU IN MAGICAL COMBAT--THE FIRST OF MANY SUCH BATTLES.
A TURNING POINT, TO BE SURE--THE MOMENT HE TRULY EARNED THE TITLE, "MASTER OF THE MYSTIC ARTS."
AND AT THE SAME TIME IN HONG KONG, THE AUGUST WU HAD A TURNING POINT OF HER OWN...
...ALTHOUGH NOT AS FAVORABLE.
FOR SHE'D FOUND HER DEMON TOO, OR THAT IS TO SAY...
...IT HAD FOUND HER.

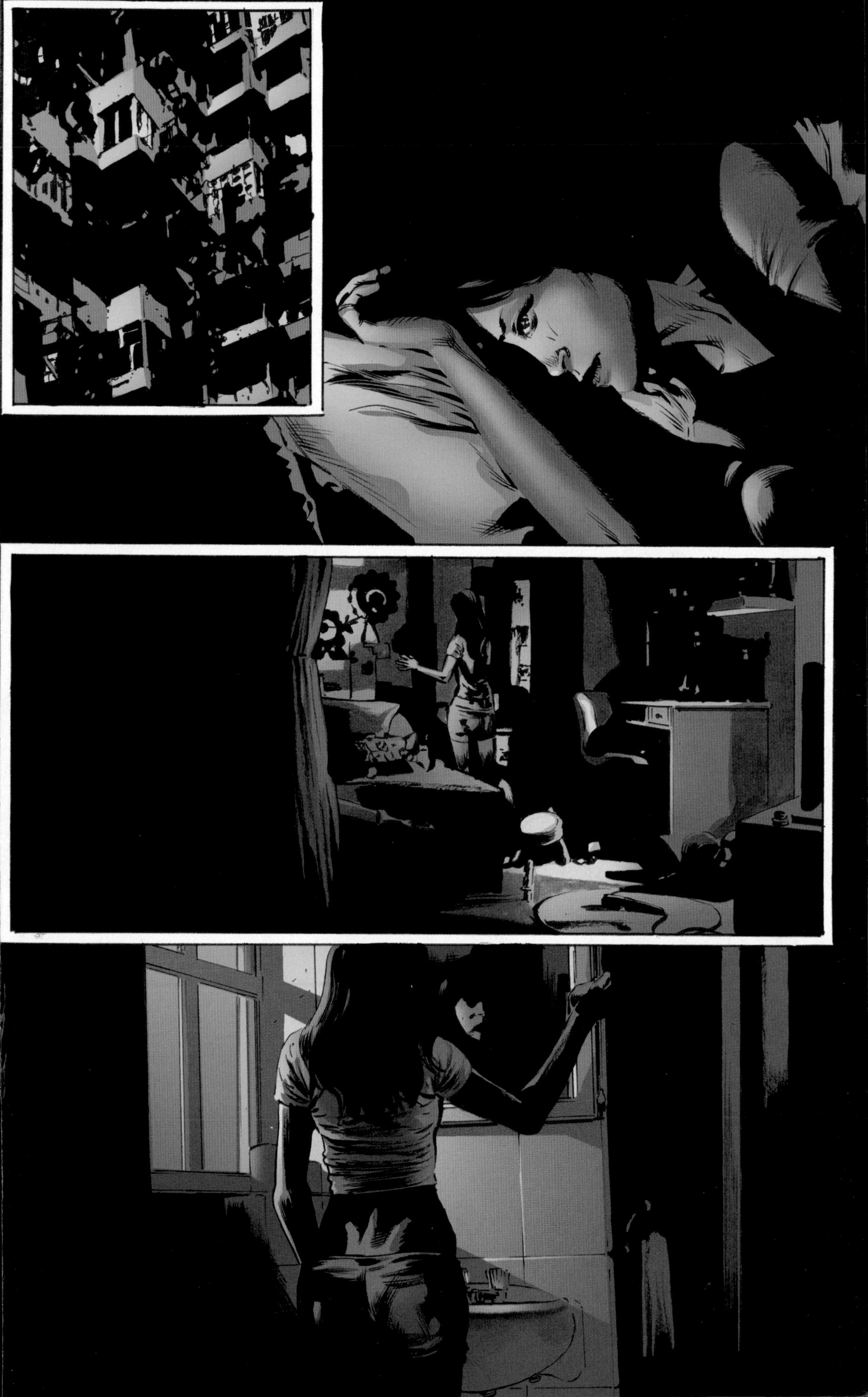

THEN.

GAGH. THIS BOOK SMELLS SO MUCH LIKE *VODKA*, I'D GET DRUNK JUST READING IT.

WE'LL SHELVE THIS IN THE 640s WITH THE REST OF THE COOKBOOKS.

A.K.A. THE *"DO NOT OPEN UNDER ANY CIRCUMSTANCES"* PILE.

NOW.

YOU HAVE LOST. YOUR MAGIC IS DYING. CAN YOU NOT FEEL IT?

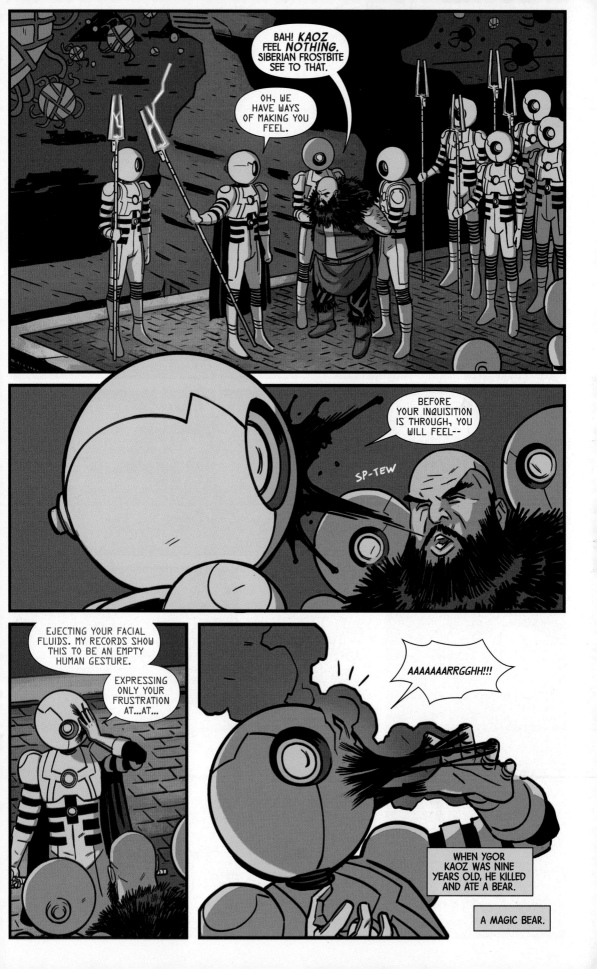

DOCTOR STRANGE
A MARVEL COMICS EVENT

CIVIL WAR

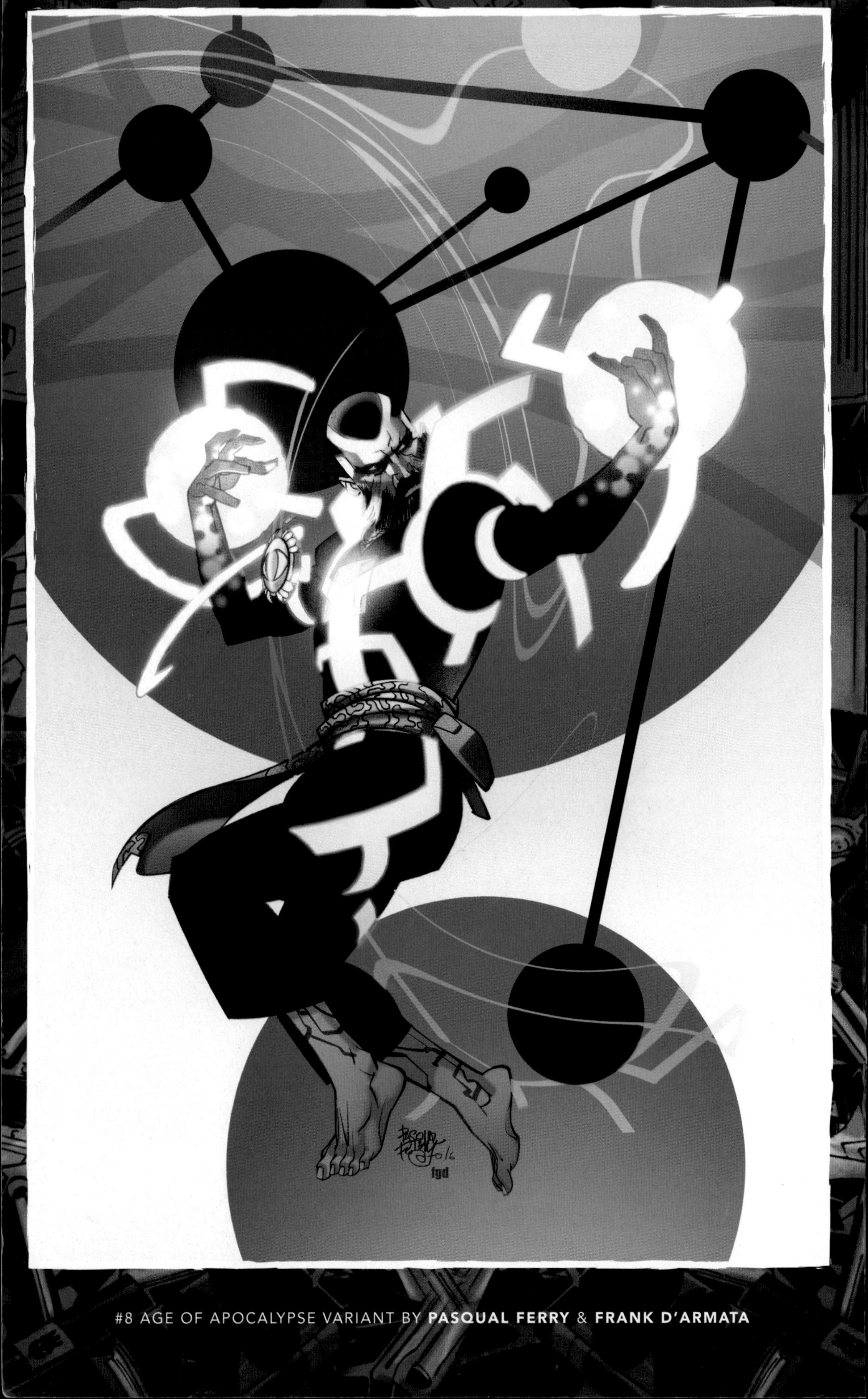

#8 AGE OF APOCALYPSE VARIANT BY **PASQUAL FERRY** & **FRANK D'ARMATA**

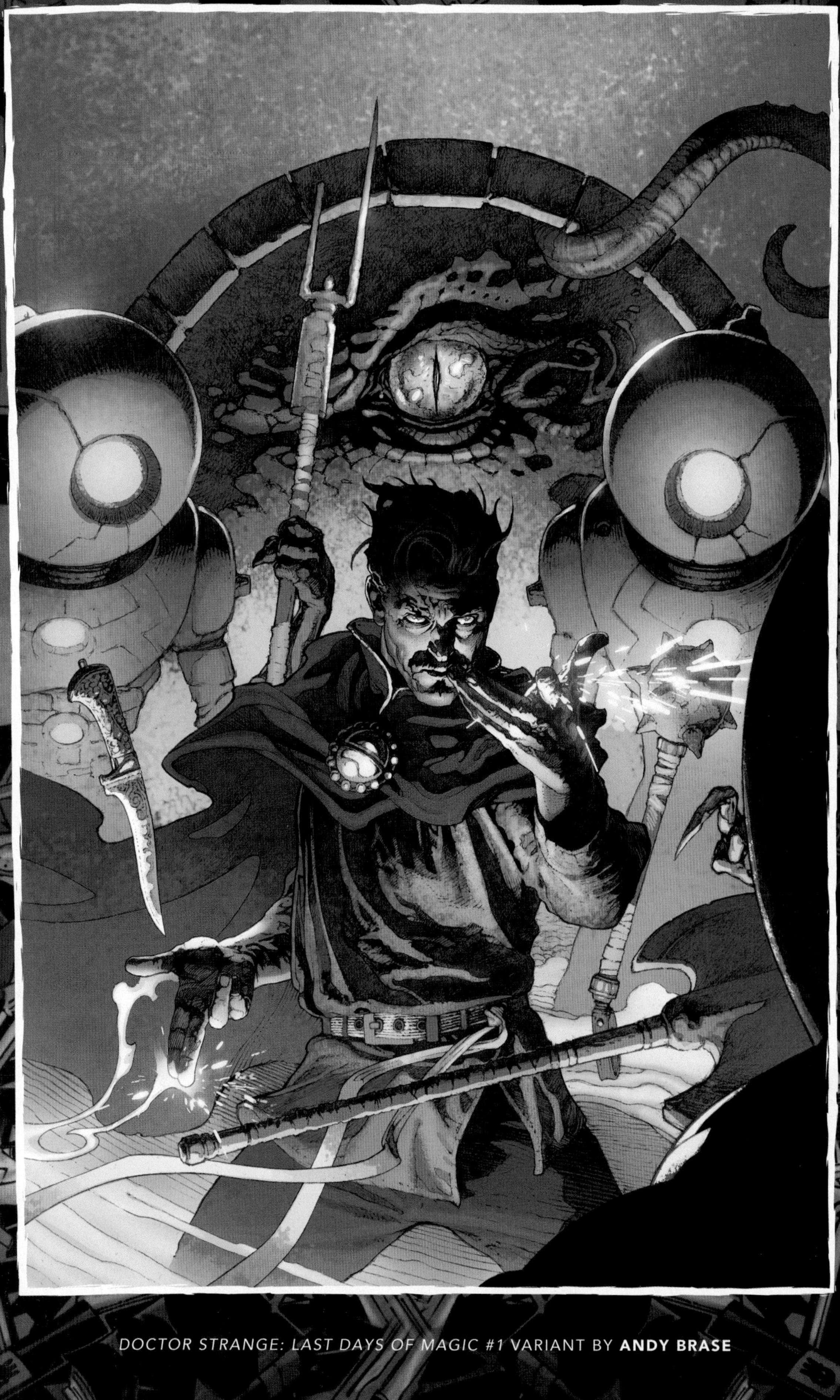

DOCTOR STRANGE: LAST DAYS OF MAGIC #1 VARIANT BY **ANDY BRASE**

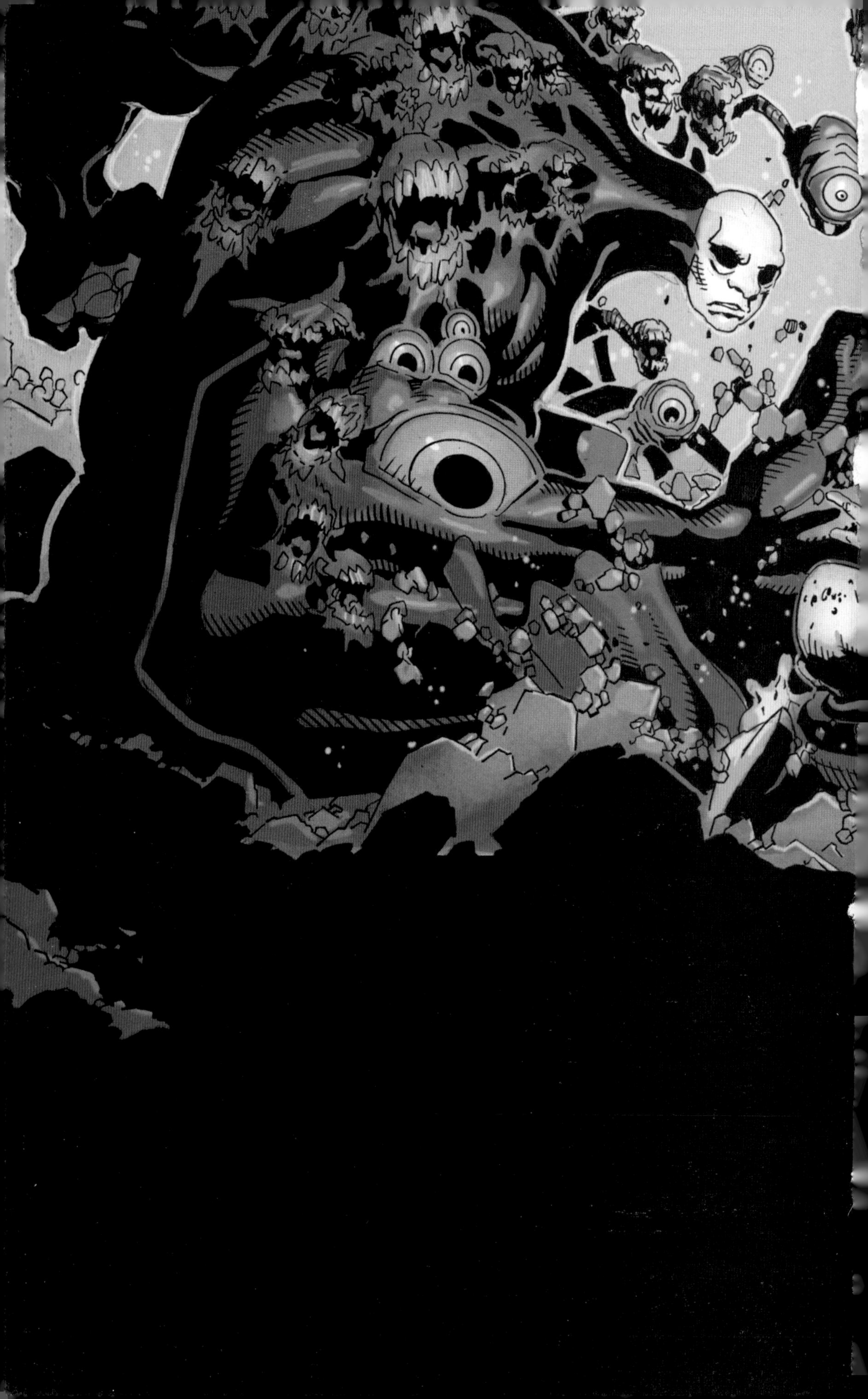